Cosmopolitan

A BARTENDER'S LIFE

Toby Cecchini

Broadway Books
New York

PRINTED IN THE UNITED STATES OF AMERICA

BROADWAY BOOKS and its logo, a letter B bisected on the diagonal, are trademarks of Random House, Inc.

Visit our website at www.broadwaybooks.com

First edition published 2003.

Portions of this book previously appeared in a somewhat different form in the online magazine *Slate.*

Book design by Donna Sinisgalli

Library of Congress Cataloging-in-Publication Data
Cecchini, Toby, 1963–
Cosmopolitan : a bartender's life / Toby Cecchini.—1st ed.
        p.   cm.
1. Cecchini, Toby, 1963—Biography. 2. Bartending.
      3. Bartenders—Miscellanea. I. Title.

TX950.5.C43C43 2003
614.8'74—dc21
2003051883

ISBN 0-7679-1209-8

1   3   5   7   9   10   8   6   4   2

Acknowledgments

The author would like to gratefully acknowledge the insight and forbearance of the following people crucial to this book's gestation: Jodi Kantor, Gavin Brown, Bill Clegg, Gerry Howard, and Jessica Lustig.

For Nancy Ellen Fitzgibbon

Contents

In the little hours of the night every move from place to place was an enormous human jump, an increase in paying for the privilege of slower and slower motion.

—F. Scott Fitzgerald, "Babylon Revisited"

Cosmopolitan

Housing the Drunk

In the town of Eau Claire in northern Wisconsin, where my father lives, there is an old wooden saloon called the Joynt on Water Street, just a short block off the Chippewa River. The Joynt functions to this day as all things to all people in that city. It's an egalitarian space by necessity. There is a satellite college of the University of Wisconsin there, cheek by jowl with the old Uniroyal tire factory and myriad paper processing plants. The Joynt has been by turns, and sometimes all at once, a student hangout, a faculty bar, a cop coop, the town's only gay bar, the beer hall for all the sweaty workers getting off their shifts at the factories nearby, a makeshift canteen for the elderly of the area, the only place in town to see live music, a pickup bar, and a quiet place in the afternoon or early evening to sit in the dentist's chair up front by the plate-glass window and read the paper. Beer has gone up to seventy-five cents a tap, from the quarter it was when I was growing up. That will buy you a choice of Leinenkugel's (locally known as Leinie's), Point Special, Berghoff Dark, and Grain Belt Premium Lager, the outsider from Minnesota. There is a neon sign above the bar that reads frankly NO LIGHT BEER.

For most of my life I would visit Eau Claire for one week or so a year, and for the past twenty years, since I could drink in a bar, the trip meant dragging Dad to the Joynt for his annual visit. He's not someone who likes to go to bars in general, but he will indulge me and walk downtown to take a stool, so that we might have a chat and a drink out of the house. I think, in fact, he has grown fond of this outing. He is an artist and so while we talk and sip and watch the goings-on, he surreptitiously sketches people in a little book he carries with him, as easily as someone else might peel beer labels or smoke. The walls are covered with photos of all the musicians who have performed there, most of them jazz players from the 1960s and '70s, when the Joynt was the only jumping-off point between the larger venues of Madison and Minneapolis. There, unbelievably enough, are the smiles and signatures of Duke Ellington, Charles Mingus, John Lee Hooker, McCoy Tyner, Woody Herman, Taj Mahal, Dizzy Gillespie, and other luminaries who, looking about, you cannot conceive of even walking in here, much less performing. This is coasting of a sort; there hasn't been music at the Joynt for many years. A hard-ridden pool table now squats in the back where the stage was. Above the men's room door is my stepmother's photo, from the time she played a piano recital, along with the tenor Richard Drews, for the Joynt's esteemed patrons. A diminutive woman, she appears in the photo, my dad loves to joke over and over, actual size.

The Joynt was my first real taste of what a bar could be to people, that it is in fact an important catalyst in creating the bonds of a community at its simplest: a place where people meet to talk to those they like and learn to live with those they don't. It is probably still the most hermetically perfect example of that social necessity I know of. The Joynt is like a microcosm of all human needs. Even with no other game in town, it is reassuring to think that, at some end of the spectrum, people still have to go out and meet other people. It remains for me not only a fond memory of learning to drink and hanging with my father, but the ideal of what I would like my bar, any bar, to be.

o   o   o

There is precious little to suggest to even the most intrepidly curious Manhattan pedestrian a worthwhile detour down the cheerless, industrial block of West 15th Street from Ninth Avenue to Tenth. The north side consists entirely of the ass-end of the Chelsea Market, composed of one long, continuous brick rampart, inaccessible save for a couple of loading docks, creating an unpleasant funnel down the street that ushers in grit-filled waves of convection in warmer months and stinging blasts in winter. On the south side there's a lumberyard and hardware store manned by surly, overfed men who drive their pickups in from New Jersey, plastered with Devils and Nets stickers. Beyond that a few low, anonymous buildings house a wholesale bakery and some young designers' studios. There's a parking garage and a taxi garage shoulder to shoulder whose shiftless employees litter the sidewalk night and day, vying in multilingual competition for the most salacious wolfcalls toward any women hapless enough to pass down the street. The block ends on a comparative high note with a sparkling new Mobil station—an improbable winner of recent design awards for its sprawling glass and stainless steel walls and mod signage—tucked underneath the rusting girders of a slice of the long-abandoned Tenth Avenue El tracks. From that end the block opens out onto the West Side Highway and is only an eight-iron from the mighty Hudson herself. In winter, when the days are short, I see on my trek to work the most surprisingly glorious sunsets wash across this busy vista, painting the Palisades across the river in gaudy tones. Those who complain of seasonal affective disorder and consider it melancholic upon leaving work to find the day's light already ebbing should try encountering that same ineffable longing on their way to work. It puts things in a whole different light, so to speak.

Wedged in among this low company is my bar, whose anonymous, single-story gray facade is dwarfed by the buildings shouldering it. There is no sign to announce its existence, nor even an address number. Its single window and door giving out onto the street are glazed with deeply smoked glass, creating yet further opacity to inquisitive eyes. The bar is attached to an art gallery, owned by my business partner, and shares with it an entrance hallway. On weekends and Mondays, when the gallery is closed, the shutters are drawn forbiddingly over the whole enterprise. Unshackling the blocky American locks and shooting up the louvered steel gates makes an unholy roar that still makes me wince every day. There are three of these graffiti-spattered brutes to deal with, one over the hallway to the gallery, one over the window of the bar, and the third over the bar's door. It is this last one into which the porter has jammed the prior night's bagged trash, to keep it off the street during daylight hours when city inspectors cruise for infractions to fatten the municipal coffers. Grabbing each bag by the throat, I drag them from the entryway to the street with each one bleeding a thin trail of the mixture of beer, citrus, and ash that has pooled noxiously where they lay. I palm what we call the shepherd's crook, a long, hooked metal rod used for pulling the gates down, tucked inside the final gate by the bartender who closed last night, and bring it in so that tonight's screwballs don't make off with it. It's happened several times, though we've always gotten it back. They lose interest in it down the block somewhere, and I'll spot it poking out of the hardware store's Dumpster or, if the thief's attention span is particularly long, some-

times as far as the wire trash can on the corner, with one of my pint
glasses on the ground next to it.

Inside the hallway, the universal odor of smoke and beer applied
nightly for years in varying coats licks at me comfortingly, like an
old, flatulent dog. I unlock the inner doors and wind up the opaque
shade that separates the bar from the gallery in daytime. Mixed now
with the stale smell of cigarettes and beer is the tang of Mr. Clean and
bleach from Polo, the porter, having turned back the nightly tide of
filth. He has left for me on the bartop, stuffed between the upside-
down stools lined up like dead trees, a crumpled black windbreaker
and a Palm Pilot, last night's leavings. On the cash register is a note in
his childlike scrawl, with helpful sketches in the margin: "Hi Tobe:
plese we need/its to old the mop/1 mop mop/1 brud vrom/1 pepier
hans/1 beach/also is brok the hammel/only no work for one/Polo."
The paper hand towels, mops, and bleach I get, the broom takes me
a moment. The third part will have to be sent to the linguistics lab for
translation by Polo-ologists. Apparently something's broken.

I notice the light blinking on the answering machine and try to
punch the play button. It is gummed over yet again from someone
carelessly rimming margarita glasses in the salt next to it and won't
budge. I turn on the fans and the underbar lights, startling the resi-
dent fruit fly population vacationing in the drains and setting a cloud
of them flitting about me for a moment. After moving down the line
of the bar on the outside, pulling down the upended stools and tugging them into place, I circle the room flipping on all the industrial
toggles. This is the part that feels like currying the bar to life, rousing
the aching drunk despite its groans: the heat, the ceiling fans, the
smoke ducts, the dishwasher, the coffee machine, the calculator, the
cash register. Out of the dead silence, everything is all at once abuzz,
whirring and flashing and blowing. The big red master switch that

controls the stereo goes on with a pop as the juice from the amps reaches the speakers. The salient feature of my bar is that it is constructed entirely on a lighted disco floor, of the variety introduced to public recognition by *Saturday Night Fever*. When I snap on the four breakers that control the floor lights, the crackling and humming of the light pattern bleeds faintly through the speakers, like the sound effects from the evil scientist's laboratory in a cheap horror flick.

I fish out my keys and head through the locked door to the gallery, which also contains my liquor room. In contrast to the spare white of the gallery with its skylights, the jumbled murkiness of the liquor room is comforting, with rows of kegs stacked like oil drums and my bike hanging from hooks driven into the overhead shelving. My office, inasmuch as I have one, is here. Papers for my perusal and files are spread among bottles on a corrugated tin shelf that holds the wine inventory. My desk consists of a box that I use for a seat, pushed up against the ice machine, which becomes the backrest. The choice of box is very important; it must be one that is an ergonomically comfortable height as well as sturdy. The double-walled Stolichnaya boxes make particularly good perches, and the Prosecco cases, when stacked, are also quite cushy. Balancing the ledger book in my lap, I go over the bank sheets and the drop from the night before and cull from that the opening till. I lock the safe back up and untie my shoes. I remove the khakis and blue button-down shirt I've been wearing and swap them for jeans and a black T. I layer an extra pair of socks over the ones I'm wearing and pull on the black Red Wing boots I've customized with extra-thick rubber insoles. I fold my daytime clothes and zip them into my backpack and then stuff my sneakers under the wine rack.

Long ago I learned I need to arrive well ahead of my shift's starting time, to give myself ample mental space to pull on the armor required to weather another night of indignities and inebriation. It has simply become part of the opening process, like anyone else putting on a uniform to go to work. If you remove fiberglass insulation for a living, you don a protective suit to go to work. Although the toxins inherent in my job are not quite as tangible, I find I need the same kind of protective remove, and it takes time to put it on. Drawing a deep breath, I lean back against the ice machine and stare up absently at the rows of liquor bottles extending almost to the ceiling. I sit this way for several minutes, my hands propped placidly on my knees, listening to the quiet. I'll be sitting back down on this box, putting my other shoes back on, in just twelve or fifteen hours.

o   o   o

Those summer visits upstate to see my dad in Eau Claire provided my introduction to hard alcohol, long before I was old enough to enter the Joynt. My brothers and sisters and I had always been allowed a trace of red wine mixed into a glass of water along with our pasta growing up, quite a goose for a kid. We were thrilled to be so trusted; it made us feel a part of the adult world. My father was born and raised in Italy and so never shared the American binge/purge ambivalence toward alcohol. Wine with meals was his birthright, simply a normal part of life for him, the way everyone else around us in Wisconsin drank milk with every meal. He saw no problem with treating his children like real people and including them in this custom. I haven't had that pale-pink dilution in almost thirty years, but I can recall exactly its flavor, the burr of the tannins roughing up my tongue.

Speaking in confused wonder still about Americans' juvenile relationship to alcohol, he told me a story from the end of the Second World War in Florence. Out walking early one morning, he and his sister came upon a crowd silently taking in a spectacle so incredible to them that many years later, he still marvels at it. Still up after an all-night bender, some American G.I.'s were lolling on the steps of Santa Croce, bleary drunk, passing a flask of wine back and forth, singing and carrying on like one would imagine G.I.'s might well be doing, away from home for the first time and flush from chasing out the Axis Powers. In Italy, though, he explains, wine isn't abused that way. Further, there a man measured his masculinity in many ways that might seem odd to us, but it simply went without saying that no man worth being called such would ever be seen as unable to hold his drink. You would never drink that much to begin with, but slurring? Singing? Carrying on like silly adolescents who had chanced across a bottle—and on the steps of a church!? The crowd couldn't conceive of what they were seeing; it was unconscionable. The G.I.'s had seemed to them the swaggering cowboys who stormed in on waves of adulation to liberate them. It would be like us witnessing John Wayne stumbling out of a drag bar, then stopping to take a piss on the American flag. But the longer my dad spent in America, he said, the more he understood those sacrilegious soldiers. Our puritanical backbone still heavily influences all of our views, alcohol not the least. Most Americans, he explained, aren't quite sure how to simply enjoy alcohol. They are like children, fascinated, so they abuse it, then they're afraid of it. A touch simplistic maybe, but not terribly far from the truth.

This, then, is the man who from the time I was fourteen on allowed me to partake in what became a beloved summertime ritual: the early-evening pitcher of gin and tonics on the screened porch. Despite his conversance with wine, he seldom drinks hard alcohol. His love, and characteristic alteration, of the great antimalarial reviver was, I've always been certain, due to an inexplicable but virulent anglophilia on his part. "When I was in Injah," he liked to joke, in his

Italian-inflected mangling of a British colonialist accent, "we would always take a cooler on the verandah."

My initiation into this simple, timeless ritual, the evening cocktail, was an important passage for me in several ways. First, having been included in civilized drinking from a fairly early age, by the time high school came about, I associated it rather mundanely with things you do with your parents. To most of my peers, freedom writ large on the weekends was driving somewhere outside of town to a quarry or a freezing corn field to slug down cheap, watery keg beer and syrupy fruit brandies in the headlights of a few cars, accompanied by wild whooping and followed, naturally, by hours of mournful vomiting. I went along, of course, lured by the prospect of Maple Bluff girls in Scandinavian sweater sets and Led Zeppelin pounding from the door speakers of Camaros, but, chastened by my father's disgust over the American soldiers, the goal of rendering myself falling-down drunk never held the fascination for me it did for my friends.

A more important dividend of watching my dad prepare his gin and tonic came in witnessing how he fearlessly took anything that came to him pro forma and, through curiosity and thoughtful application, altered it for the better. Aside from being an artist, he is an inveterate tinkerer and a skilled carpenter who, puttering between his two workshops and his painting studio, can build, fix, or invent nearly anything he needs. As well, he inherited his mother's, my nonna's, stately ease in the kitchen. He is a formidably talented cook, whom my siblings and I have spent far too much time trying to match, judging and comparing our dishes according to how close they come to his. He also worked for many years as a research chemist, giving him a firm grasp of how elements combine and affect one another. So it stands to reason he would turn his attention to even this unquestioned drink, simple as a Quaker prayer and written in stone.

One of the fondest running memories I have of growing up is arriving in his kitchen after the long, stuffy Greyhound bus ride from Madison and sitting to chat with him while he prepared drinks. He would take down a tall crystal pitcher and pour it almost a quarter full of gin. For years we had an ongoing polemic about which gin to use. He used to claim that all gin was simply grain neutral spirits spiked with juniper and that it made no difference which one you used. One visit, then, I brought up a bottle of Tanqueray and won that argument handily. Taking fat limes at room temperature, he would knead them in the ball of his hand against the cutting board, setting the intoxicating aroma tumbling through the room. This brings the citrus oil to the surface, he explained, and allows the gin to act as a solvent, removing and incorporating it into the drink. He would cut them in half, juice them, and set the juice aside. He would slice the rinds into thin strips, which he then dumped into the gin and pummeled a bit with a pestle. The juice was added to cause further extraction. At this point he would invariably swirl the pitcher under my nose and declare solemnly, "You could wear this as cologne!"

While that marriage was left to macerate for a few minutes, he would then take large ice cubes and, palming them lightly, thwack them expertly with the back of a heavy spoon, just once, whereupon they would obediently crumble into perfect shards, which he would scatter into the pitcher until it was half full or so with aromatic lime granita. I always marveled at the élan with which he pulled off that simple action; my efforts at duplicating this maneuver always end with me bludgeoning the recalcitrant glacier mercilessly as chips fly helter skelter.

He would remove the tonic from its chilling and pour it gingerly, on a slant, down the side of the pitcher, stirring it cursorily with a tall glass wand, just so the gin, which rises to the top, gets distributed;

you don't want to jostle that life-giving fizz out of it. We would take glasses from the freezer, garnished with fresh lime rounds for aesthetics, and carry the whole works like an Easter processional on a tray out to the front porch. In the late-northern twilight with my first drink as a young man, chatting with my dad, I could feel the tie to civilization, the history in this lovely laying down of one's burdens at the day's close.

This being my introduction to mixed drinks, it was a shock to taste what I was handed, years later, the first time I ordered a G&T in a bar. Gin, with flat tonic from a gun, some ice, and an insignificant little wedge of brown-edged, dessicated lime tossed on top. I was astounded, outraged that anyone could try to palm off such a thing as a drink. I remember thinking, if a restaurant tried to pass off food as slipshod and inferior as this drink is to my dad's, it would be out of business inside a month. I quickly came to learn that this was the norm in bars, and the artfully conceived drinks I was used to, concocted with the same strategic preparation as the best meals, were the aberrance to which I was privy. If only people knew what they were missing.

o   o   o

I don't recall ever being specifically aware of a bartender per se until I moved to France the summer I was nineteen. My first few hours there, feeling lost and bleary upon arrival in Paris, I washed up outside the Gare du Nord train station at the bar of the brasserie Le Terminus Nord with a friend. Struggling with jet lag and homesickness, I nonetheless couldn't help but gape with awe at the foreboding barmen behind the dazzling brass and cut-glass partitions. Unlike the lackadaisical bartenders I had known in Wisconsin, guys in flannel shirts who poured your draft and shot of brandy before slumping back over their *Field & Stream* in the corner, these men were professionals. Their triple-speed performance seemed like a mesmerizing ballet as they whirled about one another, their movements precise and rote and perfect. They never smiled, they never bumped one another. I noticed their eyes never actually met the customers' when, by way of taking the order, they barked in an impatient monotone, *"M'sieur?"* or *"Oui, madame?"* Instead, they would cock their head sideways, their eyes locked impatiently in some middle distance, like a football coach who has just demanded of one of his charges why he blew a play. A curt nod of the head was the customer's only assurance that his order had been properly conveyed. Their black grosgrain vests were tucked into their long white aprons and hid all their accoutrements: bottle openers, matches, pens, and wine keys. These they would whip out, employ, and repocket with consummate skill, often ambidextrously, lighting someone's cigarette, for example, while popping the top of a Pelforth Brune. I couldn't at that time comprehend that the indifferent flawlessness with which they held me in slack-jawed amazement was only the quotidian muscle memory of men who had moved in this same tight theater for years on end, performing hundreds of thousands, perhaps millions of times the menial tasks I now beheld. Their hands seemed to function apart from their detached faces, fluttering about like cleverly trained birds, as they chopped the foam from *demis,* whacked the grinds from the espresso machine, crisply plated change, and shouted orders with a perfunctory jargon I could only wonder at.

Outside the orbit of my father I paid little attention to alcohol, even eschewed it, until moving to France. After two tepid years of attending college in my hometown, I fled my townie status by securing a place on the Michigan/Wisconsin Junior Year Abroad program to France. The program was based in Aix-en-Provence, a breathtakingly pristine little diamond of a medieval town nineteen miles or so removed from the frank, blue-collar bustle of Marseilles, on France's southern coast. The town and the countryside could not have been more perfect—the shocking blue of the Provençal sky every day became almost irritating in its steadfastness. It was a rough place to be a student in, though. Aix is an affluent town and the Aixois are famously snobbish, jealous of the Parisians and anxious to distance themselves from the lowly Marseillais, their coarse neighbors. L'Université d'Aix-Marseille, the lion pit into which we were tossed to fend for ourselves, is one of the larger and more respected universities outside of Paris, luring students from all over the world. Coupled with that are a disproportionate number of smaller, private programs for foreigners who speak no French, cramming an already small, edgy town with more honorary near citizens than perhaps are welcome. The town's proximity to Marseilles' large Arab population means many of these students come from former colonies, are poor and barely tolerated within Aix's posh perimeter. I ended up warehoused in a huge, ugly dorm complex on the edge of town with most of these unfortunates. Africans and Arabs, fastidiously dressed in the western mode of the moment to better assimilate, kept fairly strictly to themselves, well aware that the sparkling cafés and haute cuisine just twenty minutes' walk away on the Cours Mirabeau were not intended for their delectation. My entire dorm floor was dominated by Corsicans, whose irrepressibly engaging demeanor and harddrinking swagger made me often reflect that they seemed the Australians of the francophone world—something about being raised on an island, perhaps? They made a breezy counterpoint to the Aixois' sour chill and helped me immensely in my navigation of the mores by which I found myself daily flummoxed.

Two other inroads helped me to break the Gallic ice while there. One was teaching English part time in a private, Catholic high school for girls in Marseilles, an adventure I barely escaped without diplomatic intervention. The other was an ill-fated "Cours de Cuisine et de Sommelier," a combined cooking and wine course offered as a time-filler to the students on our program. A paltry few of us signed up for it. I was one of the handful of students not housed in a cushy Aixois family home, so I fairly leapt at any opportunity to clear out of my shoebox of a room and speak some French. The instructor, Madame de Castiglione, was a wobbly, middle-age woman of great spirit, whose dramatically dyed red hair and chapped hands flew in opposite directions as she flailed back and forth in the enormous kitchen of the Ecole de Cuisine we used by night for our instruction. She wore a permanently befuddled expression, her eyes never quite focusing on one, as she dragged us mystified through impossibly complex, Escoffier-certified recipes for dishes we could never hope later to re-create on our own. We did some terribly unlovely dances in that kitchen. (There was a kind of unspeakable damage done one week to ducks, if memory serves, that may actually have been proscribed by French law.) The extent of our education in wine—the Cours de Sommelier part of the course—consisted mostly of our squinty discussion of the comparative vileness of the cheap bottles we were obliged to bring, and which we all bought or stole from Monoprix, the discount drugstore, on our way to class.

My true education in wine did begin that year, however, in a cramped and sparkling little wine shop called Bacchus on the tony rue d'Italie in Aix. I had gone looking for a nice bottle of wine to give my girlfriend at the time to welcome her back to town after a trip she'd taken to Switzerland. I had never entered this particular shop before as, impecunious as I was then, I could smell out an overpriced Aixois boutique at twenty paces, and Bacchus had precious written all over it. Knowing the occasion demanded something more impressive than the filched bottle from Monoprix, however, I marched in with gritted teeth. The proprietors were a fussy older man and his even older mother, an odd duo who became odder the longer you were in their presence. Two cats in a bag, they openly loathed one another but were somehow suspended in their patterns of petty commerce and oedipal entanglement, like characters in something that never quite made it out of Tennessee Williams's notebook. The son's imperiousness was perhaps the acme of the form, comical in its unflinching Gallicness. He literally oozed disdain for everything that crossed his store's threshold. But his mother had a chiding for every declaration of imbecility he would lash his customers with, and so the conversations would take on a bizarre, triangular course with none of the parties directly addressing any of the others.

"Bonjour," I began brightly upon first entering. "I'm looking for a very pretty wine to give as a gift to a very pretty girl."

"Yes," he responded gruffly, looking me up and down in a crazily hostile fashion. "I'm certain you are!"

"Oh, leave him alone," said Maman from her perch, "he seems a decent enough boy."

"Well," I continued, trying to feign vinous erudition, "I was thinking of maybe a Bordeaux or something like that."

"Oh yes, were you?" he thundered back. "A Bordeaux you were thinking? And why were you bothering to try to think at all, if you were going to give a Bordeaux to a girl?" He clucked his tongue and rolled his eyes, his lips pursed beneath his broad mustache in the fashion of a man who has caught an objectionable odor. We sparred back and forth for three-quarters of an hour about what might be appropriate as a gift, in which time he took into account not just her hair color, but also which country she was returning from, and whether by plane or train. It was as humiliating as it was exhausting. He declared and confirmed my varied unfitness—sexual, cerebral, and oenological—several times during the course of that first transaction, with his mother behind him clucking a dissenting refrain to each fulmination. More than once I considered turning on my heel, but I needed that wine. I escaped, in the end, clutching a sleeper bottle of Sauternes, buoyed by the wind of victory under my wings even while smarting from the sting of his disgust for my parting remark: "So, it is a Bordeaux, after all!"

That first time I entered, looking for the gift bottle, I was, being a self-respecting person, ruffled by his condescension. But I persisted, naively figuring something worthwhile had to be cloaked beneath such monstrous arrogance. That's not always a good bet, of course, but this time it happened to be. He was profoundly rude and mulishly opinionated, but also staggeringly knowledgeable, if you could stand the gale unleashed when you dared try to tap that reservoir. Over the course of the year there I began building the foundation of a deep appreciation of the complexities of wine, simply through his explanations of what he would not allow me to buy because I was not, in his view, yet worthy of it. I would show up inquiring after something I had heard good things about, gunning to impress him, only to suffer his *tsk*ing and chortling at my foolish bravado. "A La Tâche from Romanée-Conti, is it? *Mon fils*, at 1,650 francs a bottle, the price of that wine is only the third or fourth most prohibitive factor in your acquiring it." Instead, he would sigh and deign to guide me to something far cheaper that was local and that, being so, I might begin to appreciate if I could taste carefully and intuit all of the elements I could see and smell in the countryside around me that brought this wine together. My tutorial brusquely finished, he would send me on my way feeling stupid and insulted and having purchased something completely unlike what I had come for, and which was invariably excellent. By the end of the year there I had a handful of standout local vintners cataloged and a small foothold on understanding what constitutes a worthwhile wine.

I wasn't able to return to France for a couple of years, until the mid-1980s, when I glommed a scholarship to pursue a master's in French literature in Paris. I didn't leave there with the sheepskin, but I did find the first perfect bar I'd been in since the Joynt, and in retrospect that now seems more important to me than academia. It was called Le Fitzcarraldo, as in the Herzog film, and in several ways it could have been Passerby's prototype. It was a small two-room space in the Deuxième Arrondissement, near Les Halles but on the other side of Étienne Marcel, on the tranquil rue Tiquetonne, thus perfectly insulated from that area's tacky bustle. I discovered it by chance one day just wandering around, which amounted to my most sustained activity in that city while supposedly attending graduate school. Even my French friends hadn't heard of it. I don't know how long it existed, not long I guess, since it was shuttered when I next returned in 1989. For a brief couple of years, though, it so perfectly encapsulated for me the fleeting perfection of that city at that moment, it seemed less like a bar than a single clear voice.

The Fitzcarraldo was first an art bar, and put its identity forward as such by literally every month allowing itself to be entirely made over by a different artist. Walking in, you wouldn't recognize the place from month to month. The first time I came across it I believe the room was sky blue and silver, with plastic dolls' parts stuck into the walls and ceiling every few inches. A month later it was entirely clad in shiny black Mylar, with one squiggle of red neon in the back room that read simply in cursive letters, "Gros rouge," which is slang for a coarse, cheap red wine, and has struck me ever since as a great name for a wine bar: Fat Red. I subsequently saw it decked out in any number of different outfits, some of them requiring an amazing amount of effort on the part of whoever it was doing the making over. Whether completely covered in white chicken feathers or beige linen and bamboo or spent airplane parts, it was just a backdrop, and not really spoken of or acknowledged once in place, except for a sly smile if you asked about it. The owners and bartenders had that typical Parisian cooler-than-thou haughtiness, combined with an edgy kind of unwashed punk aesthetic that, though clearly a pose, was forgivable in that when pressed they were, in fact, quite pleasant. New Wave and punk were interpreted slightly differently there, with less political menace and more wry pop humor than here or in England. The artists and students and punk kids who hung out there seemed more at ease with one another than similar crowds packing the curbside at the venerated old Montparnasse and St. Germain haunts. Moreover, everyone at the Fitzcarraldo acted privileged to be a part of it, having stumbled onto a great secret. The wines and beers were more interesting than normal café fare and democratically cheap, a hugely important point to me at the time. There was a palpable feeling, when entering the place, that it was run by people who had an inkling of something that might be fun and decided to try it, rather than by an oligarchy that calculated what would be the most profitable thing to spin. That is, as an object lesson, why it no longer exists, of course, but to claim that it was thereby a failure means simply that you were never there.

o   o   o

I've always seen the creation of a slightly unsettling atmosphere as a proper goal of the bar owner. There used to be a place on 10th Street in the East Village called the Gold Bar. It was very tiny, with a bar capable of seating perhaps six people and standing room for maybe twelve others in the rest of the space. The entire thing was constructed of rusted steel plating, every surface, with some stark, Modiglianian steel stools with tiny round seats on them scattered about. Between the steel plates that comprised the floor ran a long crack through which poured an unpleasant shaft of fluorescent light.

Peering down into the crack, one discerned that the entire bar was suspended above an empty, brightly lit room below, which was inaccessible. It gave you the feeling of hovering perilously the whole time you were drinking. I read an article about it in the *Times* shortly after it opened that quoted the German owner's business philosophy behind this odd little fortress. New Yorkers, he reasoned, are people who put up with tremendous discomfort and crowding and, in fact, inexplicably in a country with as much space and resources as anyone could need, pay a premium to do so. In keeping with that, he tried to build the most offputting bar he could conceive of. In addition to being cramped and filled with hard, cold surfaces, every angle in the space was off by several degrees, imperceptibly to the innocent elbow-bender, but enough to exacerbate the awkward feeling already in place from the harsh materials and lighting. This was to make New Yorkers feel right at home, like being in an extension of their cramped, overpriced apartments whose floors and walls, covered with decades of slopped-on white latex and adhesive roach baits, canted with age at equally improbable angles. His philosophy struck me at the same time as humorous in its teutonically misguided kookiness and admirable in its straight-ahead charge at the nettlesome problem for entrepreneurs of deciphering just what in the hell people want and why they want it. Who would go to a bar conceived for the maximum level of discomfort it could offer its clientele? Except, having read about it, I became, for a short while, an occasional habitué of said establishment. For a while it worked, or seemed to, quite well. People secretly enjoy being told what they will like, to a degree that never ceases to surprise me. Simply stating "You'll get what you're given, you'll pay for it and you'll like it!" is far from the worst business proposition ever.

The Gold Bar idled along pleasantly (or unpleasantly) for a number of years, and I think it could have for a good deal longer, save for the fact that the owner grew to take his nostrums about New Yorkers craving self-punishment a bit too much to heart. The bartenders became self-absorbed, snotty kids who couldn't be bothered with the indignity of actually acknowledging your presence, much less serving you a drink. In my experience on both sides of the bar, I find people would willingly sit upside-down strapped into seats of broken glass, as long as the bartenders are snappy and pleasant and make good drinks quickly. My guess is that the place was just too small, or had cycled through its ability to draw crowds, and the poor tips chased the decent bartenders out, leaving the work to the bottom feeders. The last time I darkened the door of the Gold Bar was on my birthday many years ago, when I took a brood of friends there to imbibe after dinner. The place was empty, but we couldn't with the aid of a divining rod wrest a drink from the surly youth slumped in the corner of the bar reading a riffled copy of *The Tropic of Cancer*. After two hard-won rounds, accentuated by the bartender's dramatic eye-rolling each time, I asked for the tab. Young Werther was having none of it. I called more loudly, with still no effect. Finally I turned to my assembly, shrugged my shoulders, and we all filed out, with the bill unpaid. I did it simply for a jab, waiting outside the door for the languorous youth to come hurling after us, spitting injustice, but even then he couldn't be bothered. After a couple of minutes we exchanged looks of incredulity and loped on to another bar.

Still, the Gold Bar had its finger on something valid. I have often noted, throughout my years in this city, the proliferation of small gathering places, both bars and restaurants, into which New Yorkers will more than willingly wedge themselves, even queuing for an hour before to do so, while much larger and more lavish spaces that serve equally decent food go desperately begging for a few months before closing up entirely. The too-literal German owner of the Gold Bar was simply trying to exploit this inexplicable but much-observed urban phenomenon. That's no worse an idea than the delusions of most people starting bars in this city. So many ill-conceived spaces begin with the premise of creating warmth and luxury and comfort in order to foster camaraderie, only to have it backfire terribly. Camaraderie doesn't need luxury to thrive, it needs only an acknowledgment of the comfort of human foible and frailty. Why do people love their dingy, fusty, smoky dive bars, though the staff may be inept and the establishment drafty and dirty? Well, most would explain, just cuz! And that's more or less correct, insofar as people can't quite explain why they take more frequently and more deeply to a downtrodden space that reflects human use than an immaculately slick one that speaks equally of modernity and luxury as of sterility. Although the design of a space may have a great deal to do with how one feels there, it is not the arbiter of one's experience in a bar, an assumption I see far too often made by deep-pocketed investors in poshly banal spots all over this city. People come to my bar late, for the most part, to feed on the sort of dirty, frantic energy that suffuses the place when it's crammed to the rafters, when the DJs are hopping up and down egging people on, and god-only-knows what lurid transactions in human weakness are being carried out in the darker corners. It gets to a point of frenzy where all I can do is stand back, feeling vaguely Mephistophelean for my part in all this, and laugh. But there's clearly something immutably comforting in the lack of expectation one has in a space that mirrors one's own imperfection. If we have our demons, we want our bar to have its demons, too.

o   o   o

There is an ephemeral hour then when the bar, like a woman *d'un certain âge,* cleverly cloaked in evening light to conceal flaws she knows are beneath consideration, glows with an imperfect, hard-used loveliness. This is true of all bars I've worked in. The art deco bar at the Odeon, sold by the thousands in the 1930s and '40s as a kit offered by Brunswick, the billiards and bowling purveyor, still makes that room one of the most dapper in New York. The small, ill-carved wood bar found in a garage in Staten Island that we installed at the restaurant Kin Khao, after I sanded it down and refinished it, impressed even me with its splendor, in an otherwise cookie-cutter space. It is, of course, a subterfuge so carefully devised by the management to lure the customer in that, when you're that management, it can surprise even you. My bar at Passerby is a very peculiar beauty, to be certain; it will never be likened to the Bemelmans Bar in the Carlyle Hotel or the King Cole Lounge in the St. Regis. Though knowingly urbane, it is but a distant, scruffy cousin of those fabled rooms. It is a place, however, that pulls no punches, and its *jolie-laide* thorniness is precisely what becomes appealing about it. In the light of day it looks like a secondhand double-wide trailer outfitted with a plastic floor, some mirrors, and a scarred wooden bartop. The ceiling is a patchwork of old wainscotting, its paint blistered and smoke-stained, with dollops of black adhesive clinging to it from where acoustical tiles were torn off. One wall is composed of sky-blue gypsum board, unfinished save for smears of spackling covering the screws holding to the studs, while another, much larger, wall is made up solely of the naked studs themselves, with a battleship-gray cellular foam wedged between them forming a grimy, Mondrian-like grid. There are thirteen stools and five small Knoll tables, each one flanked by a couple of cheap folding stools, the kind you buy in Chinatown, with the fake wood veneer. A long raw pine bench runs the length of the room, the burn marks, carvings, and scribblings across its stolid planks attesting to years of insult heaped on it by the sophomoric and the inebriated.

After nightfall, however, the bar emerges from its dour cocoon. The Lucite tiles, lit from beneath, reveal a pulsing disco floor created by the Polish artist Piotr Uklanski. The bartop hums with warm lambency when the candles are lined up across it. This, like almost everything in the tiny space, also shows the hand of an artist. Japanese furniture maker George Nakashima, just before he died, chose and milled the magnificent two-inch-thick heartwood slab of an entire walnut tree, from roots to branches, that functions as the bar's surface. It lay fallow in the mill in Pennsylvania for years before we purchased it from his daughter. The long pine bench across the back wall is the work of Mark Handforth, a genial English artist who, in constructing this piece, followed the exact curve of an Eames chair he particularly loved. Collapsing oneself onto its spartan angles is a surprise in comfort. Floor-to-ceiling mirrors at the back of the room quell the claustrophobia that might otherwise quickly seep into the cramped environs. It's a mutt of a place, to be certain, but it has the mutt's ineffable, unpolished charm.

Loping fuzzily through opening, puttering around more than anything, I notice two women waiting outside the door with a little girl, an odd trio to be trying to gain entry to the bar an hour before we open. It turns out the mothers have been shopping at Jeffrey, the vapidly swanky department store around the block that moved in to fill Chelsea's haute couture void after Barney's went belly-up a few years back. They dropped their car at the disreputable garage a few doors down and now can't retrieve it for quite some time, as it's parked in and it will take a while for the slovenly attendants to unmoor. I agree to let them in, warning them I've just begun setting up. They seem sweet and reply that they don't care in the least, just a glass of pinot grigio and a place to sit out of the cold while their number comes up. But I should know better. I get trapped by this all the time. Setup time to me is almost sacrosanct, and I get tremendously frustrated and harried when I have to rush it in the least. Opening feels to me like going through a set of t'ai chi exercises, where each

must be executed in proper turn or the sublime order of things is ruined; if setup isn't carried through the way I prefer, the trajectory of
the night is marred and I feel I can never get on the right foot.

Tonight this disarming little girl ends up proving my point perfectly. She's plain and plump, not an attractive child, and because of
her weight and her bratty precocity I have trouble discerning her age;
between five and eight, I'd say. Although her mother is courteous and
attentive, this child is a nightmare, demanding in an exaggerated
nasal bray that I turn on the music, get her a Shirley Temple, turn on
the floor lights, and fetch her something to munch on. At first, because I often make the naive assumption that children are charming,
having never collected them, I accede to her orders with playful
flourish. Before long, though, I'm running to get ice and take the inventory of what's missing from the back bar and the coolers with her
right behind me whining for me to turn up the music and make the
floor go faster and brighter. I shoot a glance at the ladies, prattling
along unaware in the corner, then turn back to the little demon. "Do
you like to play with matches?" I ask solicitously.

"Noooo!" she replies in a tone of false ennui, no doubt aping a
Dawn Powell stance she saw her mother pull once that must have
gotten her loads of adult laughs and attention at some awkward
Upper East Side cocktail feed. "Would you like me to absolutely fall
off of my chair with boredom!" She's not sitting on a chair, she's
standing behind my bar, in fact, most unwelcomely, with one por-
cine little hand against the metal sink and the other braced se-
ductively on her cocked hip. Maybe, I reflect, she's one of those
uniquely awful specimens, the child actor. I consider dosing her with
a couple of shots of Everclear in her next soda. I have a bottle way up
on the top shelf, near the ceiling, that a friend of mine who's an ex-
terminator in New Jersey brought me as a gag. It's illegal to sell in
New York State, but I like the way it looks between the display bot-

tles of beer up there. It's pure grain neutral spirits—literally corn squeezin's—190 proof and highly flammable, the bottle warns in capitals. Many people, especially southerners, seem to associate it, somehow fondly, with disastrous black holes in their early drinking histories. The scramble up to the top shelf, however, balanced like an ungainly Calder mobile, with one foot each on the bartop and the cash register, as one must needs do to access that aerie, would doubtless attract maternal attention, which in this case would lead to more official attention. I sized up my adversary, now with her sausagelike digits thrust knuckle-deep into the glass of cherries I had put out for Manhattans, and figured it would *almost* be worth it.

"How about glass?" I offered cheerfully but *sotto voce*. "Do you like to chew on glass? It's like ice but it doesn't melt!"

"That's styoopid!" she countered, extracting a fistful of dripping cherries and popping two into her maw. "I hate this song! My dad plays this!" she opined through a mash of half-chewed cherry of the Beatles' "Yellow Submarine," which was all I could cull from my collection that I thought a kid might respond to. I went over and slipped in a Dr. Dre CD, swiped the cross-fader over, and turned up the refrain: "Bitches ain't shit but ho's and trix!"

o   o   o

Though it might be difficult to prove empirically, it turns out that the saddest place on earth to be is standing behind an empty bar. Often in the early evening there is a lull between the flight of worker bees flushing out of their hives, alighting for an hour or so to take in a beer with their coworkers, and the scramble that comes from the later prowlers who, in my bar, constitute the true crowd. In between there is an intermission that tries the publican's soul. At first it seems a welcome respite. The after-work crowd hits all at once, hard and fast, around six o'clock, and is desperate to chuff the fluorescent pallor from their skin. If you're not ready, you're in trouble. They keep you jumping for an hour or two, and by that time you need a moment to breathe and to replace your ice and garnishes. After that moment, though, as the early crowd starts leaving, the bar is all set up and glowing, it's night, you're primed to be hustling, and suddenly there is nothing to do.

A bartender abhors a vacuum. We are meant to be running, and running hard. Not only is that when you know you are pulling in money, but when you put on the outfit and step behind the bar, you are gearing up for battle of a certain type. When the wall against which you were meant to push turns out simply not to be there, you necessarily fall over. There is a feeling of foolishness that comes with standing behind an empty bar that, even this many years into the job, I find impossible to shoo away. The all-dressed-upness aspect makes it feel as if you're wearing a clown suit, or a sandwich board. It amplifies the feelings of servility incipient in this job and leads you down roads of despondency, regret, and panic that you might otherwise feel you have in control, or are entirely foreign to you. Other bartenders I know have confirmed this phenomenon. Where you might from time to time feel this kind of melancholia normally in life, the flare of gloom when the bar empties out and you find yourself wiping down the fridge or scraping the wax from the place on the back bar where the candles are stored is astonishing in its punctuality. It's simply a case of too much time for contemplation in a setting where you don't want it: dark, candlelit, romantically conjuring the tangled history of humankind communing over a draft or a dram, celebrating or fleeing, according to each drinker's impetus. The sink is gurgling its overflow into the extended drain plug, the music is mocking you. I invariably start retreading old guilts, regrets, and lost opportunities, wandering the road that led me to here, this moment behind this empty bar, wondering how other roads that I didn't choose would have looked. Each vignette shuffles by and takes its jab in turn, like rude strangers elbowing through a crowd: that bus I couldn't get on in Cuernavaca; that mosquito-riddled bench overnight in Paros; that huge boulder by the water in Cassis; the Ferris wheel, still turning somehow, high above the Tuileries. If I could just pay some money to shut these merciless thoughts down, the way you make an appointment to have a beauty mark that has turned precancerous excoriated, I would dial up that number, pay the nominal fee.

But while this existential purgatory can be demonic in my own experience, the universality of the phenomenon makes it for some reason hilarious to me when other bartenders talk about it. Every sailor has to pass the rock with the sirens on it, and it's always funny when it's someone else who gets shipwrecked. I've worked with people who find it so demoralizing slogging through those doldrums they refuse to open the bar, taking only the later of two split shifts. In part I find it funny because I see it as paying dues of a kind, the natural yang that opposes the charge one normally gets when the bar is packed and jamming and you cut a figure of envy as the guy in charge of the scene, through whom all currents in the room must pass. It only stands to reason that when that charge is removed, you feel deflated, even ridiculous, like an athlete on the bench, waiting for the chance to be let in the game to do what it is you do. This is to me just the logical flip side of all the good things that fall from above for a busy bartender, the great tips, the flirty attention, the temporary abatement of worry about what you might be doing with your life.

Every time I get beached by the dead time, my thoughts veer immediately to the same conclusion: It's over. The bar, that is. In New York the half-life of any given spot is a predetermined value, and the clock starts ticking the moment the paint is dry. When it's dead slow I inevitably start thinking, Well, it's been a good run, but it looks like that's it. Sad that it should end this way, without even a whimper, much less a bang. Such a nice bar, too. But you have to know when to bow out gracefully. I've had this thought at least a thousand times, dating back to the Odeon, a bar that is, I should point out, still very much alive and humming along. As soon as I start thinking how sad it is that my bar—whatever bar I'm in at the time—is a goner, passé, and left to be strangled by the speedy attrition of Manhattan land- lords, it is as if a gate is sprung that releases a hundred thirsty cus- tomers from a holding pen just outside the door. That very solipsistic thought, sopping with self-pity, is the cue for the mob to descend; it has happened to me so many times I don't even bother to laugh any- more at my own myopia. Besides, at that point I'm too busy.

o　　　o　　　o

These two black women who are semiregulars stop in. Pro- fessional women in their forties, I like them partly because they are slightly older than our crowd, which always makes me favor people simply because I get tired of talking to kids all the time, and partly because they're high-spirited. They never come with men, just the two of them, and they're loud and yakkety, calling me honey and sugar and sort of chastising me if I don't have what they want. What they want is rum, and not just any rum. They come in because from the time I started this bar I decided to carry some super-premium rums, for no other reason than that it seemed dorky to me, like, who drinks high-end rums? I quickly found out who does. Black people do, and from what I can tell, pretty much only black people do.

My first brush with this caliber of this spirit came a few years back through a Puerto Rican friend. Jorge is a thick slab of a man who was the floor manager of a popular brasserie-style restaurant in Soho. His sybaritic leanings closely parallel my own in that he doesn't blink at the thought of spending $150 on a bottle of wine he wants, or $200 more on the meal to accompany it, if that's what he's feeling like. Calmly striding the bustling floor of one of the city's hottest restaurants, he was always impeccably turned out and unfailingly intimidating, like a nose tackle in bespoke dress, guiding the wait staff with a firm, Brooklyn-tinged growl. Every time I showed up at his restaurant he would play the game of impressing me with some tidbit he'd discovered that I, he hoped, hadn't. That's how I first tasted the sublimely creamy Kumamoto oyster. More commonly it was something potable he'd uncovered. One night I stopped by late and he was holding a snifter of some unctuously dark cognac. I asked what he was drinking and he handed me the glass with his slack face betraying only a raised eyebrow. "You tell me." It was clearly some kind of XO or Hors d'Age reserve, I could tell just from the density of color. On the palate, however, it baffled me. It bloomed in my mouth with butterscotch and spice, at once deeper and sweeter than any cognac I'd ever tasted. "Christ!" I spluttered. "This is some kind of ringer, isn't it? Armagnac—no, a Solera Brandy de Jerez?"

Jorge snickered condescendingly. "Not even close, gringo. It's rum, man, Appleton Estate Reserve twelve-year-old. Better than anything for an after dinner." He let me finish it off.

Later, wading through the wholesale liquor catalog, I noticed these aged, reserve rums were far cheaper than their highbrow counterparts like single-malt scotches and vintage cognacs. Since taking a chance on them meant roughly half the outlay of a similar bottle of other premium liquors, I began to plunge in and experiment. I have very limited space in my back bar, unlike many places, so I can order only so many kinds of liquor. Still, with just three or four unusual reserve rums on hand, you are in a separate category from places with nothing but Bacardi and Mount Gay. My now-and-again regular ladies' favorites are Barbancourt fifteen-year Estate Reserve, the aforementioned Appleton's, and a nouvelle entry in a tall, slender bottle called Rhum Orange, which combines aged rum with an orange-based sweet liqueur, mimicking what B & B does with cognac. Not my kind of thing, but what these women want, they get.

Since I began stocking these rare-bird rums I've tried to extoll their glories to white people and each time I've gotten the same response: the warily cocked eyebrow as they mutter, "Rum, huh? I don't know. . . ." Even when I explain to them that these rums are a far cry from what they invariably got ill on at sixteen, no one will go near them. Maybe it's just a marketing glitch: Rum doesn't seem high-enough end when you're looking for high end. More frequently it's that anyone who has been to the tropics at some point probably survived some ugly night unwisely fueled by Palo Viejo, and that's what sticks in the collective memory: cheap sugarcane liquor. I agree, it sounds bad. But what the hell; cognac is all produced from a lowly, little-used grape called ugni blanc, which makes watery, sharp, unappealing wines. Bourbon is made mostly from corn, and those pedigreed single-malt scotches that are so knowingly swirled and discussed these days are distilled from fermented horse feed, more or less, with some swamp peat thrown in. Granted, from the lowliest sources frequently arise the most sublime elixirs; but still, in this company sugarcane starts sounding pretty highbred.

Since I buy these premium or unusual liquors only in small quantities, I will on occasion have run out when a customer is asking specifically for them. Due to my extreme liquor prejudices, if I'm out of something I deem unworthy of consideration, like Alizé or Malibu or Captain Morgan's, I shrug and say we don't have it. I always feel remiss, however, when someone requests something interesting and out of the ordinary, like Moscato d'Asti or a Palo Cortado Sherry, and I can't oblige them. This is completely arbitrary discrimination and unapologetic snobbery on my part, and I own up to it. Conversely, I cherish the moment of baffled incomprehension on the face of the customer who has just barked at me, "Gimme a Smirnoff Ice!" when they are gently told we have no such animal. My glee only ramps up exponentially when, as happens on occasion, that person just keeps striking out. My face, through arduous training, registers no trace of the elation surging through me as I rebuff their lists of Alabama Slammers, Alizé Sours, Red Bull, and on and on. I recall one woman, in a foraging pack of gals on the tear, who after trying to order an Apple Martini, a Woo-Woo, and something called a Purple Motherfucker, threw up her hands in disgusted amazement and, looking over the hundred-odd bottles in my back bar, yowled, "For Christ's sake, what the hell *do* you have here?"

It's a slippery slope, that. What you will or won't make, what you do or don't stock determines the personality of your bar as much as does the demeanor of your staff or the music, maybe more. One hopes the kind of person who orders Slippery Nipple shots, though otherwise clearly brain dead, instinctively knows to avoid a bar like mine, where that order will net them only a blank, faux-polite negative, in favor of the type of establishment that has chesty women bartenders who wear those ersatz ammo belts filled with plastic "shooter" glasses. Señor Alley J. Gator's Cantina, say. Occasionally they slip right through the hedgerows, however, especially on weekends, when invading hordes fill the city, pillaging in search of rare treasures like Coors Light and Goldschlager.

I might feel more guilty about my elitist sniffiness if I felt it was a fault unique to myself, but really it's just an occupational hazard of being a bartender. For the most part, you are what you drink in this demimonde. There is, I realize, nothing that inherently makes Smirnoff Ice, or "Appletinis," or any of a gaggle of drinks I consider offensive and off-limits inferior to drinks I happily concoct. It's all just alcohol, really, blended with other alcohol, or fruit juice. To the person who just wants that Smirnoff Ice, there is nothing better in the world. Nor would that person be happy with a Manhattan or a Negroni or any of the drinks I so loftily deem becoming and worthy. But therein lies the rub. It's not really the Smirnoff Ice I object to, it's the Smirnoff Ice demographically targeted customer. With each new product that pops up in the public sights, a tug-of-war begins in the mind of the bar owner or beverage manager, between simply selling what people are asking for and making your profit versus holding to some kind of model of propriety and tradition. It's a question of how far down that slope you're willing to go as the person running the bar. The unspoken assumption is that you're not just choosing alcohol, you're choosing the kind of people you want to frequent your bar. If your bar specializes in only Armagnac, say, with a smattering of other offerings, it may be because you love Armagnac and feel it should be elevated to a status of having its own chapel of sorts, where in-the-know imbibers can indulge in their mutual supplication. At the same time, you are sending an exclusionary message to others. It's not going to take long for Joe Smirnoff to wander in uncomfortably and fail to get first a Goldschlager shot, then a Rumple Minze shot, before finally settling for a Jack and Coke, the eternal fallback, and quickly checking out. This may be exactly what you want.

A bar's pitch and timbre, it becomes plain, is set to a large degree by the predilections of the owner. People respond to a specific pull in a place; the customer knows intuitively whether there's someone discerning at the helm or not. I acknowledge that the predetermined, hyperdelineated menu is unfair. It's unfair in the same way it's unfair that the music becomes the whim of the DJ, but it can also be good in that maybe the people in charge of picking that music, or that miscellany of liquors, know a fair sight more about it than the customer and are trying to set something interesting in motion. A thinking person, looking for an interesting space that doesn't insult her with pandering tomfoolery—happy hours and "specialty cocktails"—senses when a place is correct. Everyone else, used to being treated with the kid gloves of corporate obsequiousness, will come away thinking, What the hell was with that place, they didn't even have a TV!

I know what you'll order before you do. To a bartender, you are what you drink. It seems absurd on the surface to judge people by what they order, but we can't help it, it's what we have to go on. One isn't supposed to generalize, of course, it isn't nice. But to someone who has fielded hundreds of thousands of orders over a series of years, certain obvious patterns begin to emerge between types of people and what they ask for. This becomes so pronounced that drinks become important, sometimes surprising indicators of what you're dealing with in a customer. The customer's personality certainly has as much a hand in that decision as in any other. I grant you the research is skewed by geographical variances, demographic fluctuations, socioeconomic levels, and what kind of day the customer is fleeing. Still, it's fascinating how certain kinds of people all tend to order certain kinds of drinks. Not exactly so that you can predict the call, but at least so that when it's given you might say to yourself, "Of course you want a Pimm's Cup, you pretentious twit."

If you walk into a car lot to buy a new chariot, the salesmen there size you up and down according to your sex, age, dress, and demeanor. Then they judge you based on what you think you'd like to drive. You bore them if all you want is another Honda Accord. They'll obligingly sell it to you, but what they really want to sell is the new Porsche Boxster, at a horrendous markup past sticker, naturally. They want the customer who's not afraid of going beyond, willing to get gouged to find that newer, rarer experience. Bartenders are a lot the same. You want a vodka and tonic? Fine. You want a bottle of the Pol Roger Vintage 1990 Brut Rosé Champagne and two glasses, now you've got my attention. Naturally, a 20 percent tip on a $180 bottle of Champagne comes to a good deal more than the hoped-for buck left on the vodka-tonic, so the financial angle clearly plays in here, but that's not the whole of it. I'm going to make my money regardless what anyone orders just spilling pints out of the tap all night. But mindlessly filling glasses for people with whom I have neither rapport nor dialogue quickly goes from boring to actively aggravating. I begin almost to take umbrage by the way different drinks tend to fall to disappointingly specific categories of customers. In the face of all the current demographic targeting, one would prefer to think that people are, in fact, unique individuals with varying preferences and that, due to each one's infinitely mutable fickleness, a great bartender has to be able to conjure a back catalog of hundreds of zingy, frothy concoctions at the snap of a finger. Sadly, however, people are sheep, really, and the brains behind advertising have done their homework: We all just want the same things. There is a perfect ratio of backflips I've performed behind the bar to women who have ordered a Ward 8 from me ever in my career. That is, zero to zero. More to the point, the ratio of Ward 8s I've ever been asked to prepare to that of vodka and tonics is, currently, 1/879,954 and steadily counting.

This is so pernicious a truism that I am disproportionately charmed when a customer throws me for a loop. When a bunch of beefy trader types come in and actually don't all order dopey, imported bottled beers, matched with some kind of chest-pounding shot, but rather ask for the wine list, or when a woman and man order, respectively, a bourbon neat and a glass of Chinon Rosé, it makes me chuckle. What you order says something about the kind of person you are as decidedly as what you wear, what you drive, and what you read. With this in mind, it should come as no surprise that people are as odd about ordering a drink as they are about any other decision they are forced to make. One sees the gamut of human behavior here, as well. Some people walk into a well-stocked bar and see there a candy store, with each bottle representing a new adventure to be taken. Others are abjectly terrified of the dizzying choices and just want to take shelter from the obligation of having to make a reasonable selection in public, the risk of ordering something they won't like and that might bring derisive snickers down on their heads.

People who don't normally go out much find themselves in the position of needing to whoop it up some, and are predictably just as awkward at the assignment as they would be teeing off if suddenly shoved onto the PGA Tour. I feel bad for them, witnessing their wide-eyed perusal of the myriad bottles lining the back bar, as though a user-friendly libation will spring helpfully from its ranks, before they inevitably settle on a glass of chardonnay or, for the gutsy, a Margarita.

Americans have changed a great deal as drinkers. Awareness of alcohol's insalubriousness, combined with the shift in food toward lighter, health-complementing styles, has resulted in a similar shift in drinking. It's not that, apprised of the potential dangers of drinking, people are necessarily drinking less. It's that what has become popular now are liquors that hide their effect better. From the repeal of Prohibition through the 1970s whisky, brandy, and gin formed the ruling triumvirate in this country. Drinking any of those liquors to excess meant that you were driving yourself to do so, because the forcefulness of their flavor matched their strength. You know when you've had four bourbons. From the early 1980s on, vodka became the frontrunner, now perhaps fourfold over gin, the nearest competitor. Vodka's ability to hide itself in blended cocktails allowed people to drink with impunity, more or less.

The most common drink in New York is a vodka and tonic, followed, I suppose, by a gin and tonic or vodka and cranberry, then Margaritas. Nothing could be more generic and boring this side of IKEA than any of those drinks, yet people strain mightily to make them into important signifiers of savvy and position. This, many think, is best achieved by ordering the newest, most expensive vodka to come out of the chute, to then mix with their canned cranberry juice or tonic from a gun. It's ludicrous. I've tried not to cater to it too much, but the pressure can wear you down. After hearing the call two hundred times, it's sometimes just easier for me to order the damn Grey Goose and charge the absurd premium for it. Margaritas run about neck-and-neck with Cosmos for the after-work adventurers, and despite my admission of guilt in all of that (more on this anon), I must always choke back a frisson of disgust when fielding orders for either, they being both played out and time-consuming to prepare.

In fact, Margaritas up, with salt, recently tied Old-Fashioneds, in an informal poll of my bartenders, as the most irritatingly labor-intensive drinks we'll actually deign to make. There are worse drinks to prepare, certainly, as any bartender riding out the current Mojito and Caipirinha crazes will attest, we just don't make them. In the case of the latter two, it's not preciousness but rather a question of being able to make the drink properly, the way it's meant to be had. I can make you one of the best Mojitos you've ever had, but executing it—what with mulling fresh mint and allowing it to macerate in the rum while I squeeze fresh limes and mix the juice with just the proper amount of sugar, stirring it until nothing granular remains before combining the two to shake, pouring them over fresh ice, and garnishing with the mint blossoms and lime wheels—you're looking at fifteen minutes for one drink, ten minutes at best, if I have nothing else going. There's simply no way to field such orders when you're busy, it would be cutting your own throat. I love doing stuff like that if I have the time, but I routinely don't, and I can't possibly ask that of the other bartenders. It drives them crazy when customers then return and want them to duplicate it. We could make a far less labor-intensive version, substituting triple sec or simple syrup for the sugar, frozen lime juice, or Rose's syrup, keep a slurry of mint on hand, soaked in rum. Many bars do. But I've always felt that if you don't have time to do a drink correctly, don't take it on. A properly made Mojito when it's hot out is a thing that gives you wings, it's so good. A half-assed one is, by extension, twice the insult.

o   o   o

There are clear reasons why my favorite time at work is right when we open, when the bar has only its first couple of hours under its belt. The music is kept light because people want to talk to one another then. It has always puzzled me why people don't always want to talk to one another in a bar, but later in the evening, like clockwork, people start griping for me to make the music louder and louder. It's an odd thing for the owner of a business to complain of, but having the bar packed to the point of unpleasantness, normally an owner's dream, presents unusual problems for us. For starters, I'm decidedly a prima donna about being too rushed—my bartenders often make fun of me for it. I love working behind the bar when I have the time to chat with people, even strange people I may not necessarily care for. I don't really have to like them in order to gain from them some small other sense of what there is in the world apart from myself. Also, the platform of bartender gives one the opportunity to talk to anyone without needing credentials to get through their defenses and without necessarily getting involved with them. You can just strike up a conversation with someone, rally for a couple of minutes, and, if you choose, simply walk away to do something else. What I clearly want to do, so to speak, is direct. The reason I like tending bar when it's quiet is that guiding people to something better than what they ordered is one of the things I enjoy most about the job. I suppose part of it is just showing off and being appreciated for that. I think I know more about my wine list and my liquors than you do, and if you're ordering something I think you could improve upon for the same money, I'm going to let you know that. Most bartenders don't know or care enough to do this, and I admit I can't always be bothered myself. Sometimes I am just too busy, or I judge the effort would be wasted. When some half-in-the-bag coed slurs that she and her friends have been doing shots of Woo-Woos all night and what should they follow it with, my response is invariably "Water." Too, some people simply don't want my opinion on what they're drinking. There are plenty of times I try to broaden horizons, only to meet with the glacial whiff of New Yorker intractability:

He: A Jameson's, rocks, please.

Me: You like Irish whisky?

He: Yeah.

Me: Have you ever tried John Power's? It's quite nice. A little softer than Jameson's, maybe, a little more honeyed. It's been one of my favorite drinks for six months now, really excellent. Would you like to try it?

He (*staring*): No.

Me: Right, then. Jameson on the rocks.

But for every such exchange there are others where people are pleasantly grateful for having been led down a more interesting path, and it feels rewarding to play the omniscient publican who let them in on whatever it was they liked. A lot of the fun for me in working behind the bar is in connecting with people who might be looking for some pleasing novelty that they don't know about yet. To explain to someone what distinguishes a particular wine or liquor and then to see them utilize that knowledge in tasting it is a similar experience to an art historian filling in a painting's background before you view it. Without the guide you think, There's a frilly old painting of a guy with a tricorner hat playing a flute and a naked chick on a swing. Afterward, you can suss the nuances that separate Watteau from Fragonard in the thrust of French romanticism. Similarly, to know what you're putting in your blowhole advances your perspective from "red wine . . . tastes pretty good," when you know the wine in your glass is a Châteauneuf-du-Pape, which can comprise up to thirteen different grape varietals, several of them white, within the appellation laws for that wine, but that this particular vintner uses only five of them, the majority of which is Grenache, at 50 percent, rather than the usual Syrah. Or maybe it doesn't. Some people, of course, are just never going to care.

o   o   o

Early on while it's still quiet a couple sweeps in whooping and laughing. I eye them peripherally as they loudly storm two seats at the far end of the bar. The guy isn't actually being raucous, I realize, he's just along for the ride, with bright-red dyed hair and the requisite tattoos and piercings. It's the chick who's hell bent and wanting the whole bar to know about it. She's a lot of girl, stuffed precariously into a pair of red leather pants and some godawful black Lycra top, with large oval cutouts both above and below her breasts, which are clearly otherwise untethered. She's also got a black cowboy hat on, always a discouraging sign on this side of the Mississippi. She's talking loudly at no one in particular, to the whole room, really, in that amplified kind of stage voice, hooting and snorting with exaggerated laughter at her own witticisms. I know the type entirely too well;

she's a party gal, a man-eating tigress, five miles of bad road. Or so she desperately wants you to think.

Immediately they are asking my name and trying to buy me a shot, with an aggressive friendliness that sets off my alarms like a hot doorknob. I coolly tell them my name is Ezra and inform them I don't drink while behind the bar, which is nearly true. Finding the fishing poor with me, they decide to make nice with three amped-up French boys who have been trolling for girls for three-quarters of an hour. Shots are ordered all around and almost instantaneously Miss Outrageous is shaking her ample groove thing in a painfully ostentatious bump-and-grind, poorly disguised as a private lap dance for her dolt of a boyfriend, whose head is bobbing up and down like one of those backseat Goofys in a car. The French kids are mesmerized, as well; the water's thick with chum. I occupy myself cutting limes at the other end of the bar until I hear roars and look up to find Miss O. exaggeratedly miming a "Whoops-a-daisy!" as she tucks a naughtily AWOL udder back into place. "Ye gods!" I mutter, turning back to my limes.

When next I turn around, a few minutes later, the boyfriend is gone, perhaps to buy cigarettes, which I don't sell at the bar in an effort to, well, piss off smokers, mainly. Miss O. has moved to a table with the French boys and is getting into some kind of contest over who has more piercings or maybe just who's a bigger moron. One of the Gauls is hiking up his shirt to show he has rings in both of his nipples, while another of them has his hand in Miss O.'s chemise and is rooting around in there for decidedly filthy lucre. I'm trying to gauge whether it's time I step in here and enforce some decorum when I notice Boyfriend stopped dead in his tracks on the other side of the glass door in the entrance hallway, taking in the spectacle before us both with great wonder leaking from his ovoid face and a pack of smokes being strangled in his paw. It isn't until he pushes through the door and has been standing agape in the bar proper for thirty more seconds that Miss O. finally rouses herself from the languor of her gropings and leaps up with the fervor reserved for those pinched in flagrante delicto. In a hop she's all over Boyfriend, who stands stonily receiving her frantic cooings and caresses. He turns, opens the door, and shuffles out like a mummy, with her wrapped around him pleading. Her coat is still lying on the bar stool. I consider calling out to them: "Say, I might just take that shot after all, if you're still offering. . . ."

CHAPTER 11

Untender Tutelage

When I first arrived in New York in the late 1980s, I was, if anything, more lost than I had been in a foreign country. I came trailing a girl I'd met in Paris and, when that blew apart, found myself broke and broken-spirited, desperate to make some quick cash to return to France. In the process I fell unwittingly into the soup of money and ego that pooled in downtown Manhattan as that decade burned itself up. Having come directly from sleepy Paris, New York was terrifying and intoxicating to me in equal measures. Forced into the requisite blind march around Manhattan in search of lame odd jobs while sniffing at impossibly expensive digs, I spent a few miserable months painting apartments by myself, because it was one thing I knew how to do well and, I figured, work everyone needed done at one point or another. I proved terrible, however, at estimating the length and cost of a job, and so I ended up working seven-day weeks, often ten to twelve hours a day, scrambling to finish details under the foot-tapping vigil of the client, and sometimes losing money in the bargain. I quickly shelved that line and began the rounds at restaurants. Having put myself through college waiting tables, I find it simultaneously the greatest of evils and the ineluctable fallback. I was loath to return to The Life, but I figured it would be a grind I knew, a calculated compromise allowing me free meals and enough cash in hand to return to France in what I hoped would be a few short months. As well, the prospect of meeting new people in a town where I knew no one certainly beat out a paint roller and a boom box for company.

I flatfooted about for a couple of weeks without a bite before strolling past the Odeon one afternoon. I recognized the neon sign on the corner of West Broadway and Thomas Street from the cover of *Bright Lights, Big City,* and as I was taking stock of that a gorgeous black girl, bored with standing guard at the maître d' podium during the lunch lull, smiled beatifically at me through the double glass doors. I hadn't seen a pleasant face all day, so I pushed in and walked out an hour later gainfully employed. All I wanted was a temporary gig to make enough money to get me back to Paris and keep me there long enough to find work. I had no idea I would leave the Odeon four years later, a wholly changed young man.

At first I took a room in a dolorous railroad flat on the edge of Bed-Stuy in Brooklyn. I wound my way home late at night past the bodega on the corner where all the lids from the crack vials sold there had embedded themselves, like grim confetti, in the soft tar of the street. I was mugged six times while living there my first year in the city, somehow unable to rub out the glowing neon sign on my back proclaiming "white boy, fresh from the heartland!" Outside the subway stop on Flatbush it got to be like an automatic transaction, a simple reverse withdrawal: two or three glaze-eyed teens blocking the exit, one with his hand out, the other showing a knife or a gun. No words needed, just hand off your wallet, they walk away. The first night I was mugged, guilelessly walking home across the Brooklyn Bridge, I had somehow serendipitously tucked the entirety of my tips into a copy of D. H. Lawrence's *Women in Love* with which I was at the moment doing battle. While some thug held a bowie knife to my windpipe, I watched with vengeful glee as his nonplussed accomplice—clearly no modernist, he—pawed that volume from my knapsack while scraping for bullion and let it fall to the boardwalk unexamined, along with the rest of my belongings, before angrily emptying my wallet of seventy-odd cents and four subway tokens. Not trusting enough to rely twice on the repellent qualities of turn-of-the-century English mannerists, I considered more serious armaments: *Tristram Shandy*? James's *Little Tours in France*? Could I be arrested, I wondered, for carrying an unlicensed copy of *Beowulf*? I opted to stash my tips thereafter in my shoes before heading home, layering the bills flat on top of my insoles. How much I made on any given night determined how crowded the toes of my left foot would be during my commute. At home this emerged a damp, compacted wad, and for many years everything I paid for was embossed with my own personal frank, the bulbous curve of my heel mashed into the bills. I learned it was crucial, however, to keep twenty or thirty bucks in a dispensable wallet. If you had nothing to hand over, they might just shoot you out of frustration.

My building was a refuge for illegal Haitian immigrants, all of whom knew one another well. The hallways rang night and day with patois as the denizens stood outside their doors exchanging vivid gossip with the constant stream of guests passing through. Several of my helpful neighbors, when informed of my nocturnal difficulties, cheerfully offered to kill whoever had mugged me. One fellow, smiling broadly to reveal gold teeth, doffed his knitted cap to show me the pistol he kept stuffed amid his dreads. I thanked him politely, complimenting his resourcefulness, but elected to let my adversaries live.

There were large holes in the floor of that apartment, through which I could see the quiet older man who lived below me padding about and hear his French news programs wafting up. One day I arrived home to find that my bathroom, in its entirety, had inconveniently fallen through into his apartment. There was just a big square void, into which I almost tumbled, off the main hallway where it had been. It put both of us out of our bathrooms, in fact, since mine was located directly above his. We shared a nice laugh over it, and when the Haitian couple who owned the building came to fix it, they just fished my tub and sink out of the rubble and hauled them back up to reinstall.

Eventually I settled into a decent apartment in Park Slope with a friend who had also gone to Wisconsin. Christopher was studying to be a fashion designer and was equally impoverished. His mother is Japanese and his father an Asian studies scholar, so Christopher had grown up half in Japan. We alternated my gigantic Italian dinners with his unsettling Japanese breakfasts of dried fish and tofu cubes in soy sauce and broiled salmon with dried seaweed paper. My futon was in the living room, which was also the dining room, so on occasion he would come out clanging dishes and setting down little porcelain cups of some kind of vinegared sardine or fermented mush and rouse me on four hours of sleep to scoop hot rice, slimy beans, and cold salted plums into my yawning maw. It was so discombobulating on so many levels that I grew to like it.

To make a living, Christopher was designing and sewing custom-made leather jackets at the time. Half of the apartment was his studio, into which he had wedged a commercial sewing machine, one of those big commercial irons you see at dry cleaners', with the hanging water filter that looks like an intravenous line, and an overlock machine for seams and trim, all bunched around a vast table piled with sheep and cow hides and bolts of muslin and Bemberger linings of all hues. But we were both scraping by for money month to month. My lunch shifts at the Odeon, which one was forced to work before graduating to the lucrative dinner shifts, were netting me practically nothing, literally twenty-five bucks a day.

Despite the years I had already worked in restaurants through college and the years I spent in France, entering the Odeon was like sandblasting the scales from my eyes in terms of understanding how a restaurant actually functioned. At twenty-three I assumed there was precious little I could be taught about service, food, or spirits; I was quickly shown otherwise. By the time I arrived there, in 1987, the place was six years old, a veritable landmark in downtown New York nightlife terms. It had been much used and much touted in its first few years, but had passed into a kind of inertial doldrum, coinciding not surprisingly with the plunge in the stock market. Its owners, Keith McNally and Lynn Wagenknecht, the couple who had put it on the map with their vision and youthful pluck, had decamped to Paris, leaving the task of bringing revenues back up to the high-water mark of the early to mid-1980s in the hands of a cannily chosen lizard of a man named Jeff, whose near-complete lack of human affect perfectly fitted him for the task of trying to link the floor and kitchen as a single, finely oiled machine, albeit one whose by-products were human suffering.

I first took Jeff to be simply a humorously extreme version of the ubiquitous, pastel linen—clad Soho art world snob. It took me a very short time to realize he was evil incarnate. He ran the place like a prison camp, holding everyone who worked there in check with his reign of terror, punched home by the constant, random firing of anyone who failed to quake properly before him. At first his snits didn't bother me because he very much played favorites and, for a brief while when I first started working there, I held that golden position. He was monstrous, petty, and fickle. In the intervening years I have met other managers as despicable, but none more so, and none with the edge of intellect that rendered him even more perilous to navigate about. He was, on the other hand, a perfect foil at which the staff could poke fun for years. Tall, painfully emaciated, and sprouting the merest tuft of chicklike down atop his pate, he carried his overlarge head with the erectness and gait of a ballerina. His cheekbones were so prominent and his facial skin so taut across his nearly bald head that he resembled nothing so neatly as a skull. He peered at you appraisingly over a revolving collection of fantastically expensive, matronly spectacles and floated about in equally pricey, capaciously formless designer draperies, always hemmed to reveal a half foot of hairless shin. His mouth was a lipless, pinched sphincter, and he spoke with exaggeratedly crisp diction, in a high-pitched, schoolmarm's voice through which occasionally filtered a whiff of his native Virginia drawl. The overall effect was that of a disquietingly inquisitive machine, or a very large mosquito.

As horrible as Jeff was, he was clearly exactly what the owners wanted in place when they left the country, someone who wasn't afraid to crack the whip and didn't seemingly care that he was universally loathed. I do have to give him this compliment: He chose the staff purely on instinct and, although he was wrong plenty and there were some five-star freaks who moved through that place during my tenure, he had a predator's feel for what he wanted in the staff and he was often dead-on. Aiming for some ideal known only to himself, he stocked the floor with virulently outsized personalities and hungry achievers who fed equally off the energy of the scene as off one another. I have never been in a more dizzying assemblage of personality, motivation, longing, talent, and cunning than I found surrounding me on that staff in that era. I still have several close friends from that time—the pressure of coping in that battlefield having fired those rapports, kilnlike, to an obdurate glaze. It comes as little surprise that many of the alumni of that restaurant have stuck around New York and make up a veritable who's who of shakers and movers in this town, not at all confined to but certainly very strongly representing the restaurant industry in particular. Jeff liked to say that he didn't hire so much as he "cast" the floor. If he liked a certain aspect of a person, and he was relentlessly prejudiced in offbeat ways, he would hire them, regardless of their prior experience. Mostly it came down to looks and exoticism, though it was clear that coming from an impressive school seemed to garner his favor. We probably had more Ivy Leaguers carrying plates at one point than most mid-town legal firms employed. This made for a bracingly heterogeneous ragout of characters rotating through that room at any given time, an alternately hellish and wondrous cauldron of intellect, debauch-ery, and jangled nerves, with everyone trying to make his or her mark along with the tips. Even now, at the remove of more than a decade, it is easy to conjure, but difficult to summarize, the atmo-sphere of that floor, its peculiar combination of superfluous terror and incestuous, striving kinesis.

The unexpected bright spot in the Odeon's managerial viper pit, and my one true mentor in this profession, turned out to be Paul, who was then the bar manager. At first, occupied with getting my sea legs on the floor, I never noticed him. At six foot three, two hundred pounds, and almost albino blond, he wasn't an easy guy to miss, ei-ther. He went about his duties in an understated way, which set him remarkably apart from others in charge of that restaurant. Quiet, thorough, and dauntingly intelligent, he moved in a permanent aura of long-suffering disgust for the vapidness surrounding him on the floor. In response, the wait staff hated and feared him and his little oligarchy; he ran the bar as a guild, completely apart from the rest of the employees, with its own rules and bylaws, on an apprentice sys-tem that culled the best and the brightest from the floor when he had a space to fill.

In contrast to the waiters, who came and went speedily and were so expendable as to be nearly beneath consideration, the bartenders seemed ordained. There were relatively few of them, they were all older than the wait staff and held themselves with a wizened, lofty omniscience that put any young, cocky waiters on immediate notice as to who called the shots. They never bothered joining the wait staff in the early evening for the uniformly repulsive "family meal"— scraps of leftovers, meat and fish too old to serve to paying customers, baked without seasoning on institutional trays and gobbled cheerlessly over rice or pasta with corn oil. Instead, while we wrestled down this filth they nonchalantly continued their setup, secure in the knowledge that they would later have a fifty-minute break to sit at their own table and order from the menu, sipping on a glass of wine and picking idly at the day's specials while thumbing through a magazine. Although in principle everyone on the floor was required to wear the same uniform, which in the 1980s meant the ubiquitous white button-down shirt with a tie, black pants, and black shoes, a clear schism emerged there, too. The greater part of the wait staff invariably wandered in sporting a similar dog-eared ensemble, cobbled together from thrift stores and army/navy outlets, which had us all limboing by a hair's breadth under the required dress code: cheap cotton pants faded to gray from overuse, frayed at the cuffs and torn at the left rear pockets from extracting wine keys; crumpled shirt pulled hastily from the backpack where it lay reeking still from two prior shifts, the chevron of its pocket dotted with a constellation of ink and its underarms and collar a perfectly matching, vivid, greasy yellow; some castoff tie still knotted from its last service and stained to a degree where it could functionally substitute as the menu; surplus postal carrier's shoes, dull and streaked, with the toes upturned and the heels ground flat from wear.

We were required to purchase two short, white butcher's aprons, made of coarse synthetic canvas, the top half of which was folded over to leave a kind of humiliating marsupial pouch, in which were thrust our checks and order pads. In contrast, the bartenders strutted around like swells. Their jet-black wool trousers were crisply pleated and held up by silk braces, their freshly laundered shirts immaculate and pressed, having been drawn from a serene grove of them that hung in their part of the dressing room below. They were allowed to stuff their florid cravats cavalierly into their shirt fronts and wore long, clean white tablecloths knotted about their waists. I most envied these dashing improvisations, which draped to their neatly polished boots and flowed dramatically like a *torero*'s cape as they pounded up and down the raised wooden lattice on a busy night.

Not only did bartenders make more money than the wait staff, drawing a percentage of the floor's tips on top of their own, but they also seemed to profit from some invisible force field that shielded them from the constant needling and testing the waiters were subjected to. It was clear that Jeff didn't have the appetite to query one of those stalwart figures behind the bar as to what type of coulis today's fish special arrived on. It wasn't that they knew, either; it was simply acknowledged that their time and talents were too valuable to waste on such trivialities, an inequity that made toiling on the floor even more humiliating. If it was difficult to score the lucrative dinner shifts as a waiter, and if it could be over a year before a recruit saw a ferociously coveted late-supper shift, I couldn't even imagine how these exalted beings behind the bar had secured their positions.

I watched them work with equal parts fascination and envy. The best of them displayed a flair and showmanship that seemed the very life juice of urbanity to me. On a busy night, that long bar with its deco curves and terrazzo floor, cozily lit by little more than the neon of the old clock above it, would thrum with the energy of downtown Manhattan. Spinning to keep up with my tables and barely able to pause long enough to dump a drink order, I could only take in the bar in hungry flashes: all the cavorting, well-shod men with glinting drinks and plates of appetizers before them, the beautiful girls perched on stools with their skirts hitched up. I felt like a child staring open-mouthed at a carnival from which I was uncomprehendingly and cruelly excluded.

Happily enough for my circumstances, if I had failed to notice Paul while scurrying to keep myself employed, he had somehow noticed me. I was astounded when on a lunch shift he called me over to where he was ticking off inventory on a sheet and asked if I had any interest in training to work behind the bar. I stammered that I would love to but that I had never made drinks, really, and didn't much know how. He laughed in a slightly deprecating way and said he didn't want people who thought they knew how to make drinks, he just wanted people who knew how to work and were honest. The making of drinks, he continued, he would teach me, and he told me to come early on Monday of the next week.

That following week I began to be drilled in the various liquors we carried and, just as important, those we did not. Paul explained that there were other kinds of bars for people who simply wanted to go out and get sloshed, and ours was not that. The bar had to choose its clientele, and that meant setting the parameters of what would be appropriate to serve and not. The Odeon adhered to the tradition of a classic bar, he said, and in so doing specialized in making the best possible versions of classic cocktails. There is a sort of canon of these old reliables, and it is not especially broad, but it must be executed perfectly and uniformly. That is enough, but that is also quite a lot. If someone asks for a Long Island Iced Tea, he continued, we simply tell them we don't make those here, and then that kind of person goes away, seldom to return.

"Why would we want to make them go away?" I gasped, horror-stricken at this apparent lapse in democracy. I had no concept of the snob appeal of certain beverages, or why others were seen as tacky and unfit for the skills of a knowledgeable barkeep. I couldn't imagine that a bartender wouldn't fairly bend over backward to make whatever his customers asked for. "Does a Long Island Iced Tea contain ingredients that are too complicated or expensive for us to make here?" I inquired.

Paul furrowed his brow and snorted. "It's a combination, basically, of every white alcohol out of the speed rack, vodka, gin, tequila, rum, and triple sec, with a splash of fresh lime juice and then filled with Coke to make it look like iced tea." Why, I then wanted to know, would we specifically refuse to make drinks we have all the ingredients to make? Aren't serving the customer and making money the dual goals here? Paul turned to me with a look halfway between disdain and amusement, a look I would come to know quite intimately from him over the years. "Look," he said, "if people want to drink something—a pint of hard alcohol, that's what that drink is! It's a way for idiots to get fucked up as expediently and cheaply as possible. If that's your goal, then I don't want you in my bar, and I'm going to make my bar as uncomfortable for you as I can. If you insist on getting messed up like that, then I'm going to make you do it on three or four ten-dollar Martinis, instead." I still didn't exactly get the guidelines. It seemed to me just as offensive to be getting smashed on Martinis as on anything else, but clearly there was a hierarchy I would have to come to understand.

There was, it turned out, a great deal I would have to come to understand. One of the best aspects of moving to the bar from the floor was that Paul used his position to protect his bartenders from the ravages that Jeff and other managers inflicted on the wait staff. There were periodic buffalo slaughters, where five or six waitpeople would be fired at a time. These functioned to keep everyone there aware that they could lose their job at any given moment over any of

Jeff's innumerable whims. Though the restaurant didn't necessarily function well as a result, the purgings gave Jeff the impression he had an iron grip on all proceedings. But if Paul was low key as a person and kept us well insulated from those sideswipes, he was as tough a taskmaster in his own way as anyone I've ever worked for. He held a very clear idea what was proper in the bar and what was not to be done there. His disdain for the impure in bartending went much deeper than simply allowing Southern Comfort but not Rumple Minze. He taught us that when you are behind the bar, you must take a proprietary stance: It is *your* bar now, and you take care of it as such. You have to project confidence and control always. If you show hesitance or indecision, especially here, on this level in New York, where people have zero tolerance for novice bungling, the customers will eat you alive. If someone asks for a Circus Cup, and you don't know what a Circus Cup is, you don't apologize and say you'll attempt it if they can tell you what's in it. Never. You look at that person as if they are fresh from their high school senior skip day and tell them, with only the faintest sneer, that we don't make those drinks here. At first I was appalled by this kind of snobbish pretense, but I quickly found, as with every hoop Paul had us jump, that he was ahead of us all and had proven reasons for everything in his rule book. Hesitation is not rewarded behind the bar, and particularly not in New York. The turnabout is truly remarkable when a customer senses you may be confused or lost for a moment. Instantly there is the incredulous rolling of the eyes, the exaggerated sigh, and the impatient shaking of the head before the dismissively barked replacement order: "Forget it, just forget it! A white wine's fine. That'll do. You do have white wine, I take it?"

But the downtown attitude we were schooled to project was balanced by absolute attention to detail in the drinks we poured. The drinks we made we were taught to make perfectly and to execute in exactly the same way every time. Paul stressed the importance of flourish in presenting a drink, even when the customer isn't aware of it. You ice the glass for their Martini and fill it with soda water and then place it casually in their view while you tend to the making of the drink. Somehow those cubes, those bubbles, are subconsciously already chilling the Martini for them, laying the groundwork. When you shake a cocktail, you do so crisply, militarily, no fey three-second slurring of ice and drink, but a vigorous, two-fisted, over-the-shoulder assault that will leave precious shards floating on the surface of the pour. Garnishes always get done last, not dumped in beforehand out of expediency, but utilized as dramatic tools to finish with panache while making the customer salivate—wrenching the twist, peel-side down, just above the drink so that the citrus oil fans out iridescently on contact with the surface, then slicking the rim with the rind before dropping it in nonchalantly. Paul trained me to pour a uniform shot, first by revealing the secret of how to count off a correctly measured pour into a very quick ten, achieved within the five seconds it took to hit two ounces, so I could more accurately divide my counts of recipes. Once I had that down, he tested me rigorously, making me upend two bottles at once, in staggered counts, blindfolded, until I got the volumes dead-on. He stressed that a bartender never had free time. You use both hands as much as possible, you consolidate and file drinks in your head as the orders come in, expediting them in order of the quickest to the longest to prepare. You do only one task at a time and you finish it completely before turning your attention elsewhere. You greet all customers immediately when they enter, even if you can't get to them, because you must know at all times precisely what's going on in your bar. You clean and restock constantly when you're not serving customers. You put every single thing you touch behind the bar back exactly where it goes— and there is a correct place, and only one, for everything we use. The other bartenders are your support, your brethren, and so you always do right by them by leaving the bar impeccable at the end of your shift, cleaner and better stocked, if possible, than when you arrived. Paul strove to hammer into us a fundamental awareness of how everything back there came down to us; making a drink can be a poetic exercise, a choreographed set of practiced reflex motions every bit as moving and pure in its efficiency as Chinese opera. Or it can be a careless, offensively hacked together maelstrom of stop and start, poor preparation and wasted motion, with predictably shabby results. Most people would never stop to consider the difference, but many are struck by the former and irritated by the latter without quite being able to formulate why. It gets expressed only two ways: "Wow, that bartender's great," or "God, that bartender sucks!" What's it gonna be, then?

It all sounds draconian, almost silly, but in practice it worked impressively and in fact was what was necessary to keep the gears churning on this lumbering, filthy machine that must function nearly around the clock. When I first stepped behind the bar, even the initial round of stocking that the lunch bartender had to perform during the quiet daytime shift made my head swim with its endless niggling details. Paul had warned me that making drinks is almost the least of a bartender's duties, but I hadn't quite believed him. How much more could there be to tending bar than standing there chatting and making drinks? Now I became terrified I would never be able to do all this by memory, let alone field the litany of drinks while holding down the crowd at night. Every day I would scramble to make sure I had every last detail in place for the night bartenders, whereupon Paul would pass around and point out ten or twelve things I had neglected. While cleaning the mirrors I had reversed the positions of the Kahlúa and the Chivas, a seemingly nitpicky observation until you consider one of the night bartenders grabbing blindly for the bottle and ending up with a Black Russian consisting of Scotch and vodka. The rag that hangs from the pincers beneath the soda gun is the same one from yesterday. The salt in the bowl for rimming Margaritas is clumped, and so needs mulling. There are fingerprints on the number window of the cash register. The silverware we bundle into napkins and roll into a tight cylinder for diners at the bar has corners sticking out all catty-wumpus. Glowering, I would stamp around for another hour putting out these sizzling little fires before Paul would let me take my thirty-seven dollars in tips for that day and leave. For a long while I doubted my capacity to ever get this maddening little space under my control. The human effort required to give that bar the sparkle, spit, and polish that kept customers wowed was, when I consider it, almost unconscionable. I don't expect I'm enough of a dupe to ever again work so hard for so little. But in retrospect, though I certainly can't say I would do it all over again, I have no rancor; if the tips were often less than stellar, the tutelage inflexible, and the hours almost inhumane, I learned very thoroughly what was important and what corners could be cut in a profession for which the only real classroom is just this kind of forge. Like a good coach, Paul was constantly pushing us, challenging us to compete with him, exhorting us to live up to the reputation of our profession. That didn't always take with staff just hoping to pay the rent while shopping their head shots around, but if his sincerity and dedication were misplaced, that only made them more admirable. It was clear he hated the Odeon and the brutishly arbitrary arrogance that was law on the floor there. But he squared his shoulders to do his job beautifully despite where he was, simply out of personal and professional pride, simply because it was him doing it.

If, in moving from the floor to the bar, I found myself knee-deep in new drudgery for which I wasn't certain I had the patience, one astonishing perk became apparent to me immediately: the remarkable difference in the way customers treated me as a bartender. I continued, in fact, working as a waiter on the floor for years after becoming a bartender, retaining my Thursday dinner and the following supper shift, and so was able to gauge this phenomenon on a weekly basis. Where many people are by nature offhand and supercilious to a waiter, I found they became jovially deferential, often seeming to be seeking some kind of approval from me, the moment there was two feet of mahogany separating us. Sometimes the same customers whose jerky behavior made them the bane of the wait staff would be the exact ones joshing and flattering me behind the bar, offering to buy me a drink every night and tipping me a crisp Benjamin come Christmas. It was a welcome peculiarity to me after years of schlepping food to ungrateful omnivores. Whereas in the thirteen years I put in waiting tables I could count on one and a half hands the times someone lauded my service or stuck a twenty in my palm, I suddenly, and quite undeservingly, found myself with what could only be described as a sort of fan base. It wasn't just me, either; everyone who tended bar, I noticed, had their coterie of slightly too friendly acolytes. I have never been able to properly explain this double standard. Bartenders certainly work very hard, but so do waiters. Bartenders, however, are seen as exercising a degree of mastery and personal control over their domain that waiters are not perceived to possess. This is almost entirely unmerited, of course. There are plenty of clueless bartenders, as there are plenty of waiters whose knowledge, expediency, and professionalism enhance your meal immeasurably. Bartenders, though, work singly, or at most in pairs, which tweaks people's instinctive preference for the lone wolf, the individual shouldering the load himself. Like chefs, bartenders are viewed as knowledgeable artisans, hands-on fabricators who create an actual end product, a task somehow intrinsically more valued by customers than merely taking an order and then hauling out something prepared by others, even though a competent waiter or waitress is obviously doing a great deal more than just that. You can't underemphasize the candy factor, either; as a bartender, you hold the goods, you are the keeper of the hooch, through whom the hopeful and weary must all pass if they wish their thirst slaked, their daily burdens unknotted. A bit oversimplified, perhaps, but in effect that's the way it works. As when dealing with bouncers and bank tellers, it always just seems more prudent to show a smile and a tip of the hat to someone holding the purse strings, even if it's their job to open those to you. Equally, there is some play in the cliché that bartenders are, given their position, five-cent psychologists, by definition wise to the world, having heard and seen it all. If we aren't exactly available to hear and solve your problems, it's still taken for granted that we *could*, if there weren't all these other people around asking for drinks. After all, you've got to have some qualification for being back there, right?

To be honest, I can't pinpoint exactly why it works the way it does. I can say that as my newfound status first began unfolding to me I found the experience nothing short of an epiphany, and while sounding in me a terrible sentiment of injustice for waitpeople, including myself over the course of all those years, it also made me resolve shudderingly that I would never again wait on tables.

o   o   o

I did not invent the Cosmopolitan. Not technically, at any rate. I've had to reiterate this position to someone or other every year or three since 1987, whereupon that person invariably writes me up as the Inventor of the Cosmopolitan. I did invent what you think of as the drink, the version everyone means when they order it, last decade's instantly understood signifier of crass, table-hopping New

York privilege. Perhaps it's better to say I *re*invented it. But a drink called the Cosmopolitan existed in name before I took my hand to it, and so, by strict definition, I am *not* its creator. By every other consideration, however, it's my drink, for better or worse.

I worked Friday nights at the Odeon for years with this great girl, Melissa, whom we called Mesa. She was very sweet but had an imposing mien, which worked very well for her behind the bar; a tall, athletically built rocker chick, she had been through rehab, favored gothishly dark makeup, loved guitars, and played in an all-girl group. People thought we looked alike and often asked if we were brother and sister, to which, being smart asses, we replied that we were, but in truth it actually felt like there was something sibling in our friendship. We backed one another up so fluidly on those crazy-busy Fridays, intuiting one another's ballet with the glib precision borne of familiarity combined with pressure. In the midst of battle we had a lot of fun goofing with each other, too. I was always doing this stupid thing to her, because the Odeon was such a celeb hole. When some shlub would walk in with a fedora on, I'd whisper urgently, "Check it out, it's Frank Sinatra!" Or when an actual minor celebrity came in, some fool like Mark Kostabi, I'd say, "Check it out, it's Iggy Pop!" For a while it always made her spin about, looking for the icon in question, before curling her lip and throwing me the drop-dead look. But you never actually knew that Iggy Pop wouldn't surface, either. I recall, one night, singing along loudly to a Velvet Underground song while walking back to the bar from the rest room, and an entire corner table stopping dead and staring at me peculiarly. Taking stock, I looked down square into the face of Lou Reed, who was clocking me with cautious opprobrium, trying to gauge whether I was somehow mocking him. Another night I remember serving a Maker's Mark to a skinny, faux-cowboy slickster who was hungrily scanning the bar crowd for ass, and as I was ringing him up I whispered to Mesa, "Check it out, it's Sam Shepard!" Instead of rolling her eyes, however, she fliply replied, "I know, I saw when he came in."

We were constantly messing about with drinks, partly to kill time and partly to quench the insatiable alcoholic thirst of the wait staff, who in turn were all drinking to kill time. One night Mesa showed me this drink some girl from San Francisco had made for her at Life Café, where Mesa had worked before. It was called the Cosmopolitan and she made it with vodka, Rose's Lime, and grenadine. It looked pretty but tasted awful: jarring and artificially sweet and just wrong. I liked the presentation, though, up in a martini glass, so I decided we could take this and make it much better. Absolut had just come out with Citron, so we wanted to use that, for no particular reason other than that it was the new, cool thing at the moment. We naturally substituted fresh lime juice for the Rose's and put Cointreau in it to soften the citric bite. To stand in for the grenadine we added just enough cranberry juice to give it a demure pink blush. We decided it had to be shaken extra hard and long, to make it frothy and opaque, and garnished it with a lemon twist for color and flourish. We found it was surprisingly good, like a high-end, girlish Kamikaze. Cute. We didn't think anything much else about it, it was just another drink we made up in a long line of them that we concocted to amuse or gross out one another, which were then palmed off on the wait staff. No one ever drank them, aside from a couple of insane waiters who would down anything in their endless struggle against the ennui of the floor. But this time when we sprung it on the wary guinea pigs, there was a much more serious reaction. They went uncharacteristically nuts for our new potion and immediately began requesting we make them exactly that way, soaking up dozens during their after-hours binges.

For a few months the retooled Cosmo became our private staff drink. Everybody was happy. Mesa and I felt cool as hell, having conjured a drink everybody wanted, even over the aggravatingly constant stream of Margaritas, and the waitresses were being much nicer to us as a result. But soon enough the staff started raving about them to their friends and some of their favorite regulars, and from there the floodgates opened. The diaspora into the downtown night set was shockingly rapid, like anthrax on a stiff breeze. Ghoulish people dispensing air kisses at the door started slithering in and barking out orders for rounds of them for all their friends. I recall clearly the feeling of turning to Mesa in utter puzzlement, asking "Who the hell is that? How do they know about Cosmos?" Word was out and traveling fast. Each time someone I didn't know ordered the drink, it made me wrinkle my nose and eyeball them suspiciously. Our pride at having fashioned a slick house drink that people seemed to adore was quickly pushed aside by the annoyance of having to sling a couple hundred of these labor-intensive pink monstrosities in a night. They soon became the bane of our existence. We pushed the price of them up to eight dollars—a relative bargain now but which at the time seemed like a slap in the face—just to try to stanch the flow. It made no difference.

Friends began reporting they'd seen other bartenders making Cosmos, as though I should *do something* about it. I chuckled, citing the difficulty of procuring a patent on a drink recipe. But the first time I actually witnessed someone order one in another bar, and a bartender I didn't know trying to make one, was a peculiarly gut-wrenching shock to me, like suddenly overhearing two strangers bandying about the name of one of your siblings. It was probably a year or more after we'd come up with ours. My wide-eyed voyeuristic fascination edged from rank disappointment into proprietary horror as I watched this bartender toss together a ham-handed imposture of what we had so carefully elevated. Crappy rail vodka, tons of cranberry, a little squeeze of lime; it incensed me that this is what some unsuspecting customer was going to carry off, thinking she was tasting the much-heralded Cosmopolitan. I've since witnessed so many awful variations on the drink I don't even flinch anymore, but that first time it was such an affront it felt like someone was mugging me in broad daylight.

Customers began coming in asking if I'd ever heard of a drink called the Cosmetologian. Others, who had been cued by the wait staff, or by a regular who had witnessed the drink's rise, tried to take me to task. "People say you're supposed to have invented the Cosmo?" they would query vituperatively. "So how do you account for the fact that I was drinking Cosmos in San Francisco in 1977!" Sick of trying to defend something I truly didn't care that greatly about, I would play dumb and mumble, "Um, you were maybe just, like, way avant-garde?" After a few years of this my reaction was ground down even further, to where I would just sigh, raise my eyebrows, and say, "No. That's incorrect. I don't know who said that, but I did not invent the Cosmopolitan," only occasionally adding, *sotto voce*, "I just perfected it."

The other day, walking down Seventh Avenue, a friend of mine nudged me, grinning, and pointed up at a billboard. It was an ad for Grand Marnier, which is, by the way, repulsively cloying in a Cosmopolitan. The tagline read, "The Grand Marnier Cosmopolitan: official drink of the beautiful people."

"You should fucking sue them, man," my friend quipped. "That's your drink!"

It still hits me kind of funny each time someone approaches me and asks if I make a good Cosmopolitan (the time having long since passed when they would first probe inquiringly whether I knew the drink). Several different responses flit immediately through my head.

Whenever the same question is posed with a Martini, for instance, I like to playfully reply no, adding that I only fashion great ones and refuse to lower my standards for anyone. For the person in search of a really cold, lovely Martini, overlooking that kind of insufferable joke is worth it, I suppose, as it points out the proper level of hubris they're looking for in someone striving to fulfill their high expectations. I wouldn't dare take the same tack with the Cosmo question, nor, God forbid, aver to my personal hand in its inception, having at this juncture fought way too many verbal battles with the outraged, incredulous, or just plain daft. I can only vaguely recall a time when I would sniffily refuse to make the drink if someone referred to it snappily as a "Cosmo" rather than a Cosmopolitan. But such tempests in a teacup are far beyond me now, as the drink and its nomenclature have long since passed into the public vernacular. I now just smile and nod in mute affirmation or, lowering my eyes, reply in a measured tone, "Do I make a good Cosmopolitan? Yes. Yes I do."

Funnily enough, in the fifteen years I've been making them, during which, McDonald's-like, I've easily churned out well over a hundred thousand, I don't think I've tasted the drink once since that first year. I don't believe I've ever had a whole one. It's not my kind of drink, honestly. I tend not to drink mixed drinks in general. That's not to say I look down on anyone who loves them. Strip away all the hokum you've come to associate with the drink—the Manolo Blahnik slingbacks, the orangey-tan sixty-year-old, ascot-wearing Euroslime cruising waif models at Au Bar, the hideously constant and mortally dated appropriation of it by *Sex in the City* (which I've never actually seen, but am routinely chided for)—and you find that, far from a malevolent symbol of hyperentitled wretched excess, it is actually a benignly simple and, I still must say, fetchingly balanced drink. I like to remind its myriad detractors, who often seize the occasion of meeting me in the flesh to unload their vitriol, that the Cosmopolitan is not responsible for the loathsome crowd that has adopted it over the years. I invented it, to the degree you could say I did, for a bunch of waitresses. How much more proletarian can you get?

I was surprised to read in an interview with one of the all-puissant pooh-bahs of comestibles in this city promoting his cocktail book that he professed a preference for "classic drinks," noting how the old faithful cocktails were well constructed and balanced, unlike confections like today's Cosmo. I felt as though I'd been plinked. I found it disappointingly myopic in a man pushing a book on the history of cocktails. There is no greater booster of the classic drinks than myself, and when I remade the Cosmo so long ago I did so with the base knowledge that many of those timeless mixes—the Daiquiri, the Margarita, the Whiskey Sour, the Sidecar, the Old-Fashioned—are appealing because of their triangulation of liquor, which gives body and punch, with the sour and sweet elements. The Cosmo so neatly adheres to that bedrock formula, with no added frippery (save for a harmless dash of cranberry for color), that even this many years later I have not been able to improve on the drink's respectful balance of these three elements. I have made many other, different drinks, some of them excellent, but none exactly better, because it is hard to define what would be specifically better than something that effectively simple. There has, happily, been no similarly stormy response to any of those other libations, created before or since the Cosmo. No one stalks into my bar sneeringly demanding to meet the "supposed inventor" of the Part-Time Geisha. I'm never kidded about the endlessly galling supporting role the Sanchesmo plays in the hands of actors on *The Sopranos*. I've never had to endure any articles ridiculing the done-to-deathness of the Pomme Soixante-Quinze or the

Ginger/Ginger, notable for the sleazy, trendoid crowd that surfs waves of them from L.A. to Cap d'Antibes. More's the pity.

For a time during the frantic Cosmo-hell grab-fest period in the early 1990s there were a slew of offshoot "Cosmos" surfacing one a week or so. They came and, appropriately enough, went in thankfully record time. The most flogged of the lot was the incorrectly named Metropolitan, using currant vodka in lieu of the citrus. The name Metropolitan, however, had already been given a drink. It is a gin Martini made with the old proportions of two-thirds gin to one-third vermouth, but with Lillet Blanc substituted for the dry vermouth and garnished with a half-slice of orange. It's an unexpectedly lovely drink, far worthier of the moniker than the bizarre, medicinal-tasting interloper no doubt dreamed up by some not terribly inspired marketing team at Absolut to capitalize on the second inexplicable windfall to strike their mediocre brand.

o   o   o

Having come from Wisconsin, the celeb thing in New York was kind of a kick to see, for a very short while. You deal with it to some small degree anywhere you work in this town. Bill Cosby comes in for a hot dog. Saw Laurie Anderson at the gym. But in certain places it becomes the buzz, and it's rarely because the people in charge of those places have arranged it that way. The type of bars and restaurants that celebrities themselves open in New York are, as a rule, abysmally ill conceived and overfunded ventures doomed to failure, where from the opening day the staff wanders about in a state of perpetual embarrassment until one day you read in the Dining section of the *Times* that it's been mercifully closed to make way for a Starbucks. If restaurateurs and bar owners could put their finger on why certain places create their own vortex while others, seemingly more worthy, go wanting, well, they would kill for such alchemy. Why Max's Kansas City in the 1960s? Why Elaine's in the '70s? And why on earth the Odeon in the '80s? The food, after Patrick Clark, the first chef, left, went through serious ups and downs, even hard-core fans of the place will agree. The service, what with all that personality running about, could be spotty and begrudging. The wine list featured cheap bottles marked up in proportion to those mid-'80s bonuses. Granted, the room is lovely and clever, a former '30s-era luncheonette expansive enough to still wear its art deco trimmings elegantly. But none of this accounts for how many of the famous and their admirers found their way, like expectant *pelegrinos*, to that shrine.

When I first arrived at the Odeon the go-go years were still in full bloom. My welcome to the upper tier of staff working the night shifts there was perfectly representative of the era. On my first night shift, as the dinner waiters broke from the floor to let the supper waiter take over, I was told by the salty redheaded waitress I was trailing that there was a surprise for me down in the men's room, in the second stall. The door, she added, would be locked from the inside, so I would have to crawl under. I begged off, sensing some kind of ugly hazing coming down the pike. She persisted, giggling, and pushed me toward the stairs, warning that I'd be sorry if I didn't. I crept into the men's room below on guard, expecting a shower from a Champagne bucket of water perched on the door, or three waiters hiding out, ready to pounce and upend my head into the toilet, God only knew. But the room was empty. I tried the second stall, which was locked as promised. I peered under it to find no one there. I slid under and stood up to find a mirror and two sharp lines of powder next to a rolled-up twenty. Dumbfounded, I laughed out loud. Back at the top of the stairs to the dining room I blushingly accepted a flute of Champagne as the rest of the wait staff hooted and cheered my arrival.

Waiting tables and tending bar there at the time sometimes felt like being in an absurdist play. Living in a hovel in Brooklyn and riding the F train to work to pull the occasional hundred-dollar tip from people I didn't even know. Long tables of unlikely parties would stuff the place late at night. I love to recall waiting on an older gentleman with a Texas drawl and the accompanying, immaculately blocked, cream-colored ten-gallon hat, whose party of fifteen or so consisted mostly of surgically modified blondes cracking gum. Straight off he wanted to know what our best Champagne was. Well, I told him confidentially, everyone goes for the obvious Cristal, Roederer's *tête de cuvée*, which for some reason has come to symbolize the high life, but my preference was for the far superior Krug Clos du Mesnil, a delicate single-vineyard rarity flush with tautly balanced fruit and toast. It's not cheap, I warned, in fact it's a hundred dollars a bottle more than Cristal, but it rewards the discerning drinker. I had, in fact, only ever tried a sip of the Krug once. "Splendid!" he cried, clapping his hands. "Six bottles to start, some glasses, a couple pitchers of OJ, and a bucket of ice." They wanted Mimosas, he clarified, and wondered if we had fresh orange juice. Stunned, I told him we did, but perhaps for Mimosas he would prefer the Gruet brut, from New Mexico, at twenty-eight dollars a bottle. No, no, he barked, bring what I told him about, the French one, and they would take it from there. They went through almost a case of it, mixing it with orange juice and ice. At first I tried not to wince, but as I brought out bottle after bottle and removed each from its lined box to plunge into the ice bin I thought, What the hell. To him the price clearly couldn't be less of an object, and they're certainly enjoying it, which is supposed to be the point, right? Clutching bimbos on both wings, he bade me try one myself. I laughed and accepted the glass, shaking my head as the wine foamed out over the ice and pulp stuck to the flute. They left almost three whole bottles opened and tipped exactly as one would suspect a man of that kind of hedonistic abandon to tip: three crisp Bennies.

Though revelers from all professions blew through that room in those years, the Odeon was the de facto playground of the artists who had colonized the surrounding factory loft spaces of Soho and Tribeca and the Wall Streeters who shuffled the few blocks up after trading closed to blot out the paper trail with a steak and Scotch. Not surprisingly, then, when the stock market went bust at the end of the decade and the art world, whose frivolity was tied directly into the magnanimity of its index-funded patrons, went reeling, the rivers of Cristal slowed to a trickle and then seemed to dry up overnight. The managers, already a vile lot, became even more pinched and bellicose as the owners leaned on them to keep the course. They increased the hours of operation, opened tables on the sidewalk, desperate to appease anyone coming through. But the heyday was over and it was palpable. The politics on the floor became asphyxiating as the poisonous tension trickled down from the managers. Paul was given the option to continue on at half his salary. The tips had crashed earthbound after the stratospheric profligacy of the years prior. Waiters and bartenders were quitting or being fired in droves. Even longtime customers seemed to echo the doom. Warhol would straggle in blanched and emaciated, his wig akimbo, looking like a ghastly satire of himself. Keith Haring still traveled with his coterie of tough-looking homeboys, but now they fairly carried his frail frame, his head bobbling above as though his oversized glasses weighed too much to bear. Jean-Michel Basquiat took a rear booth one night by himself, nodding so furiously I could barely understand his order. He went down to the men's room for the longest while and when he returned, he just sat smiling and peering through heavy lids from the steak that lay cooling in front of him to the room around him, rocking almost imperceptibly in his banquette. I asked my friend Betsy if he was okay and she, having seen it plenty, replied nonchalantly, "What are you gonna do? He's a total sweetheart, but he's just always fucked up." He paid up, never having touched his meal. I can't recall if it was the next day or a couple later that I read in the paper he was dead.

Finally it was my turn, too. I was fired, like everyone else. Despite knowing for over four years that it could happen at any moment, that in fact no one ever left the place before he or she could be fired, I thought I had somehow leapt the barrier, that I had been there so long they couldn't possibly dream of firing me. Jeff never gave me a specific reason, because there seldom was one. He simply said, in his inimitably insectoid way, "Well, it's just kind of time to go, don't you think?" adding, to cushion my shock, "It's not like we were ever friends or anything." I often have wondered what the exact wording was when he, the following year, was himself turned out to gentler pastures.

It turned out to be a serendipitous turn of events, as reverses often are. A former floor manager was moving to open up a hip Thai place in Soho and wanted me to put together and run the bar for him. I was hesitant, but after having watched Paul for several years, I thought I could step up and take my turn. It was right when Asian fusion cuisine was hitting its first strides on the East Coast, having been the rage in California for several years prior, and Kin Khao took off like a comet. Being at the Odeon as it began to sag was more depleting than I had been able to gauge, until I simply stepped over to someplace where the energy had moved. Like quicksilver, it just flits about this town from chosen spot to chosen spot, bestowing its cornucopic favor on those who can correctly read and mirror the moment. Kin Khao's subdued wooden interior and stripped-down Thai food offered repenting downtowners the faux hair shirt they felt fitted in the early 1990s adjustment to all that greed generation hubris. Of course, this being New York, no one wanted to deal with actual privation when they spoke of the need to change our ways, to reject the venal and spendthrift '80s, so the revelry just needed to be cloaked a bit differently. Kin Khao's owners hit that mark perfectly and I was back on the ride, this time in charge of the bar.

CHAPTER III

Barbarians at the Gates

Most days Stephen is the first customer in the door, and he never stays too long. He's grumpy about the crowds and the noise, so he slurps with an alarming efficiency, often going through the better part of two bottles, then gets out before things amp up too much. He is sitting before me even now, nursing his fourth glass of Menetou-Salon, gobbling the fat Spanish olives out of the condiment tray and piling the pits meticulously into a neat pyramid in the center of a beverage napkin, his Pall Mall idling in a full ashtray next to his bony, liver-spotted hand. He's chattering on about the way to tell oak trees apart by their bark, cueing the constant nod from me and prompting the occasional, "Oh, yeah?" He'll talk to anyone, more or less, and truly to any woman. It's grueling to witness how baldly he yearns for female company, smiling with tobacco-stained teeth and gesturing with shaky hands at some wary girl who's arrived early to meet someone. You get old, I guess, but that never changes, you're still young somewhere in there, you remember what a lion you used to be.

Before I met Stephen I had only ever known women to fuel their alcoholism on white wine, but that's what keeps Stephen propped up, seven or eight glasses nightly of Chablis Fourchaumes, or Meursault or Sancerre. Though he requests his whites to be French only and very dry, in a heartbreaking stab at wine savvy that, circa 1972, would have been very well regarded, in reality he doesn't really care what the wines are or what they cost. He clearly appreciates that I root out nice ones for him and elaborate on why I'm pouring him what I am. Occasionally when I'm doing the ordering and cross something that floored me at a tasting but that's too expensive for me to pour, I'll get one case of it just to serve to Stephen. I know what a sad waste it is, really. He's touched, but the regal wines are just a means to an end, like insisting on using a Beretta silver-plated target pistol, with scrolling and a carved walnut grip, to shoot yourself in the head with. It's clear he can't tell the difference between a Bâtard-Montrachet and a cheap pinot grigio, but he is immensely warmed by the gesture.

Stephen tries my patience and principles every day. His constant neediness pushes my buttons, and his drunkenness, though quiet, can stand out appallingly in the light, early crowd. I routinely feel more like his nurse than anything else. Several times I've had to help him up after he has fallen from his stool. He wanders out wordlessly without paying sizable tabs, and the next day, arriving hale and re-freshed, he'll argue tenaciously that that's impossible and that he must have paid. He accuses me of stealing his cigarettes, when he knows I don't smoke, and I'll have to go around the bar to fish the pack up from where he's dropped them for the hundredth time. He'll call over and over for another glass when I'm running crazily, trying to serve the after-work crowd. He has no concept of others. Even on his largest tabs his tips are embarrassingly picayune, the more egre-gious for a man who, if he has little else, certainly has made a great deal of money in his life.

I can't be angry with Stephen, though. He's a formidably sad fellow, and even if he has a nice house on a lake upstate and a former wife who was a renowned beauty in Hollywood, and a daughter by her somewhere, he leaks desperation and fragility from every pore, and so I can't begrudge him, even when he's driving me nuts. I don't know what it's like, yet, to feel like you've placed solid bets and then watch as all your chips get raked cruelly in. He was one of the most influential men in the fashion world in the 1960s, in New York and internationally. You know his name, perhaps it's been on your dad's socks or belt. But bigger fish came up in the '70s and '80s, he'll eagerly divulge, and that world not only eats its young but picks its teeth with its elders.

Returning from serving some beers downbar, I find him elaborating some point about John F. Kennedy to a trapped couple, a story I've heard him trot out easily a dozen times to illustrate how he knew, in a cursory sense, the president. Ashes float about them as he stabs the air with his cigarette to punctuate his story, his long body unfurled over them like a broken awning. He begins coughing violently, which erupts into the usual red-faced choking and finishes in him hocking up an oyster into a handful of plundered bev naps as the horrified couple capitalize on the interruption to slink off to a table.

o   o   o

There was a day in my mid-twenties when I had gone up to wander about the galleries of the Metropolitan Museum. It happened to be a Monday, however, and when I got there I found it closed up tight. My absentmindedness was vexing enough, but having walked up sixty blocks and across the park, a more pressing issue was relieving my bladder in what any tourist knows to be the hospitality-bereft salt flats of the Upper East Side, with its pricey shops and ladies-who-lunch restaurants on constant vigil against any interlopers who might attempt to employ the facilities without having first dropped a few hundred. I crossed Fifth Avenue and, with teeth clenched, began the twenty-block trek south to Barneys. Scuttling past the crisp linens and boxwood shrubs outlining the tables on the patio of the Stanhope Hotel directly across from the Met, I realized I was never going to make it that far and swerved in past the liveried bell-hops to fall on the mercy of the front desk. They were perfectly congenial and pointed me directly to the men's room. That emergency averted, I decided to poke around for a moment or two on the ground floor, unfamiliar as I was with the concept of the Grand Hotel. No one appeared to mind me nosing about. Guests wandered in and out and the porters and bellhops swept past unconcernedly. Sneaking a bit farther down a black marble hallway, I turned a corner and was amazed to find tucked there a lovely wood-paneled drawing room, or small library of some sort, set about with large leather wing chairs and mahogany tables, the walls hung with equestrian hunt prints. I chuckled at the staginess of it, as though a curtain were about to go up and a Wodehouse farce to blow in. The room was empty, but as I stood drinking it in, suddenly feeling inadequately clad in jeans, T-shirt, and high-tops, an older gentleman maneuvered around me, padded across the emerald carpeting clutching a newspaper, and flopped onto one of the striped-silk settees as though it were his den. He smiled and nodded benevolently at me, cracking open his paper. Out of a door I hadn't noticed in the rear right of the room appeared a waiter in a tuxedo, his hair shiny with pomade, who strode up to the older fellow and took an order for a scotch on the rocks. As he then turned to take me in, I prepared to turn tail and shoot out, certain that security would be fast on my heels. To my amazement, he nodded deferentially, made an expansive sweep across the room with his arm, and said, "Anywhere you like, sir."

You're kidding me, I thought. I was sure this had to be some kind of private enclave and that at some point I would be found out and swept from the exclusive premises, no doubt with half the staff being summarily dismissed for their breach of duty in having failed to intercept me. But, heady with the buzz of novelty, I decided to go along with the game, as far as it might go, and so tiptoed into the room and perched myself cautiously on the edge of one of the green leather chairs.

When the waiter returned with the older gentleman's glass, balanced on a silver tray, he placed down a coaster and delivered the drink without asking for money or a room number. Turning then to me, he asked what I might like. Blushing, I tried to make up for my lack of sartorial correctness by going for instant cachet, and so stammered that I'd been thinking of a glass of Champagne. "Absolutely, sir," he replied crisply, and vanished like a whisper.

In the few minutes he was absent I sat in the posh quiet of that room titillated by the soothingly patrician surroundings but terrified at what I'd somehow gotten myself into. He didn't give me any choice about the Champagne. What if he brings me a bottle of Champagne and it's two hundred dollars? What if he brings it and then discovers I'm not staying in this hotel and kicks me out? I wanted to peruse the books along the walls, but I was afraid even to get up to do that. Still, part of me was getting a tremendous kick playing the part of privilege. Even if I got booted out amid the disapproving stares of the paying guests, I was determined to see how far this caper could go.

My unease was replaced with awed delight as it became clear to me my subterfuge wasn't a caper at all. The waiter brought me a very pleasant glass of Champagne, which cost roughly what a glass of Champagne costs, and after I drank it and declined another, he brought me the bill, on a silver tray. No one sent for security, no cops barged in and clamped me about the elbows in midsip. I paid as I would anywhere else, save tipping enormously out of relieved gratitude. Sauntering out of the hotel I felt springier than I had going in, expansive. Could it really be that simple, I wondered, to broach these fortresses of the *ur*-affluent? What in reality was nothing more unusual than stopping somewhere for a drink inverted, in one solitary transaction, a great deal of what I took for granted about New York and my place in it. Being a downtown denizen and casting a fishily envious eye at the cavortings of the monied beings up in these lofty parts, I had simply assumed that the ranks were closed and applications were not being accepted. Access to sanctums like the one I had just crashed was a function of having been born in the right families and attending the right schools. Or was it?

It makes sense, I realized, reflecting on it for a bit. These places are open game, they have to make money just like everyone else. In fact, they have to make a lot more than everyone else, given their operating costs. Why would anyone throw you out? Unless you're dressed in rags and acting like a buffoon, their whole gig is hospitality, and they've doubtless seen everything. They can't take the chance that you might be a rock star or Johnny Depp. There are no velvet ropes uptown; if you want in, they'll take your cash. But I found it interesting that I had assumed these places, on account of their luxury and history, to be so exclusive that I dared not pass their portals. I couldn't be the only person who thought that way, and I suspect, in fact, that these places rely on that intimidation factor to keep hoi polloi at bay. As it turns out, then, they do have their ropes, they're simply of a finer type of velvet.

Experimentally, I began showing up alone on the occasional Friday night at the Stanhope, greeting the desk clerk, and strolling back to take a seat in the library bar. At times I would decide to dress the part to perfection, curious to see if it changed anything about my reception. It pleased me to be donning a suit and tie in what I saw as ironic turnabout. Just when most young men in this burg were gearing down, shedding their weekday sack suits for the obligatory grunge uniform and heading south to get some play in the meat-market singles scenes in the Village or Soho, I contentedly doffed the T-shirts and jeans I wore to a fray in the pounding gristmill of Kin Khao during the weeknights. Wearing a suit, I've always thought, is pleasant only when there's nothing in particular compelling you to do so. I had no motive other than simply to sit and have a Scotch or two, lost in a novel. It was like being out while staying in your living room, provided you had somehow grown up on an estate. Fully aware of all the Friday night frenzy I was blissfully missing, churning away south of me, I recognized another aspect of my life running counter to that of most other people in this city: While they were sitting at their desks all week, I was running around on my now-bludgeoned feet. It only made sense that when they get off work they migrate to the smoke and noise, where they can meet, in standing room—only boîtes. For me the solitude, the solicitous peacefulness, and the conservative exclusion of the Stanhope's rear bar was a balm for my entire being. Here was everything I couldn't access in my workaday life, played out at that time between a cramped one-room apartment and a blustery, smoke-filled bar.

Though the fabled snobbishness of the Upper East Side had always been anathema to me, my forays to the Stanhope, where I was never treated offhandedly, always left me feeling calmer, more humane and optimistic about my life's possibilities, society, my fellow man. To many of my friends, it sounded as though I had turned into a Ralph Lauren toady. The question is not one of whether they'll allow you in, one remarked, but why you would want to go to some overpriced, hoity-toity hotel bar filled with post—opera-going dinosaurs puffing Cubans and swirling snifters. But did I have to be rich, I argued, to have a drink in the Stanhope? It's very obvious that poor people don't go there. What's interesting to me is why they don't, when in reality they could. What you spend on shots of Jack at the Cross-Town Lounge in the Bronx could just as easily get you the same drink at the Stanhope. I'm not saying the drink at the Stanhope will be the same price; it may be double. Still, if you have enough money to drink, you could in fact choose to go wherever you like and drink whatever you can afford there. Drinking, as a pastime, is relatively democratic. One can advisedly drink only so much, and drinks can vary only so much in price. In a cheap bar a pour might be five dollars, and in the most expensive places double that. Is it not preferable to have two drinks in a place you enjoy to four in a place you dislike but is cheap? Not for some people, I'm aware. Still, clearly it's not exactly economics that determine where people dare enter.

Once at ease in my ritual at the Stanhope, I began to wonder about other venerable old hotels in the city. Did they all have lovely bars, as well, seemingly exclusive but in fact open to the discerning or intrepid public? I began making rounds and fell headlong into a world I could hardly believe still existed, though I had a great deal of trouble convincing my friends—who saw no point in venturing north of 23rd Street for anything, under any circumstances—to accompany me on my forays. Discovering one after the next of these proudly intact rooms, I felt at first like an archaeologist stumbling upon long-rumored cultures hidden right in our midst. These were not some swankified remakes, drawn up by an overpaid architect to simulate Old New York, with a few Restoration Hardware leather chairs strewn about and some Rosemary Clooney blaring for atmosphere. One could feel instantly that these magnificent old rooms, some languishing in their dotage, were the real thing, direct pipelines to the New York of the 1930s and '40s and '50s, when men checked their hats and taxis the size and shape of Airstreams ferried the bright young things from these hotels to the Stork Club and on down to Sheridan Square. Walking into them, you can imagine every writer who ever drew from these spaces the stuff to create and the tonic to shut it off at the end of the day, from Thurber in the '20s up through John O'Hara and Tom Wolfe.

I began to pride myself on what I came to think of as my collection. Often I would hear about where might be another glorious old bar from the patrons or waiters at the one I was in. The waiter at the Stanhope told me about Mark's, a snug little jewel box tucked into the ground floor of the Mark Hotel, not far away on Madison Avenue. An older couple there, in turn, told me about the incomparable Bemelmans Bar in the Carlyle Hotel just a block south. Ludwig Bemelmans, the writer whose best work has sadly been ushered out of print while he is remembered solely as the creator of the "Madeline" series of children's books, lived in the hotel and painted the cartoon murals of Paris that line the smoke-yellowed walls. Having giddily thrown open these doors, I began to find similarities in a number of these bars, particularly the presence of just such lovingly kept murals. The much-used Oak Bar in the Plaza Hotel has its murals, just recently restored, by Everett Shinn, the once-heralded student of Degas and early member of New York's Ashcan School of painting. Befitting the room, they are as masculine as the Bemelmans filigreed work is playfully feminine. The indisputable acme of bar murals is at the King Cole Lounge in the St. Regis Hotel on the corner of Fifth Avenue and 55th Street. Hovering imposingly above the bar in the dark, high-ceilinged space is the famed Maxfield Parrish painting of Old King Cole, flanked by two attendants. Originally commissioned in 1905 for John Jacob Astor's Knickerbocker Hotel at Broadway and 42nd, the painting hung for years in the Racquet Club on Park Avenue before finding its way to its present perch in 1935. In it the king is seen trying to stifle a devilish little laugh, as one of the banner bearers flanking him wrinkles his nose while the other cracks up. The inside scoop on the tableau is that Parrish depicted the merry king as having just farted. A similar but not quite as impressive Parrish mural of the Pied Piper, painted three years later, still dominates the bar of San Francisco's Palace Hotel, for which it was commissioned. Maybe I just feel the King Cole mural is more impressive because of my love of the room that surrounds it. An imposing, wood-paneled amphitheater with low-slung leather chairs and quiet corners, it is the consummate grown-up bar, like a cathedral to alcohol, with hypercompetent bartenders and a prevailing mood of calm, restraint, and order.

My favorite murals, however, are still those sly monkeys and other animals disporting themselves that encircle the beloved Monkey Bar on the ground floor of the Hotel Elysée on East 54th Street, even if the bar itself is no longer my favorite. In fact, the murals on the walls aren't the originals, either. All that remains of those are a few framed fragments kept nearby, but the cavorting simians pouring drinks, smoking cigars, and playing cards between the wall sconces were faithfully reproduced from old photographs, like the caves in Lascaux.

A fabled 1950s-era romper room for the literary set, where Hollywood intruders like Marlon Brando were tolerated perhaps more gaily than at the Algonquin, the Elysée, like the Carlyle, had its famous residents, as well. Tennessee Williams lived, dissipated, and died there. Tallulah Bankhead is said to have descended from her room on her birthday to perform for the assembled an impromptu torch number clad in a fur coat, with nothing underneath. When I first discovered the Monkey Bar, it was like opening a sarcophagus. The room hadn't been touched in what seemed decades. Wisecracking old waiters in threadbare gold jackets greeted you with thick Eastern bloc accents and, shuffling across the worn zebra-print carpeting, ushered you into a sticky, leopard-spotted banquette that might have been the rage in the '60s. A garishly lit white piano would very occasionally accommodate some warbling F-list tinkler. The place had settled into its senility perfectly, though, and it became a revered haunt of mine in the late '80s, not least for the fact that it was almost invariably empty. That was then, of course, and this is now. Naturally, the owners weren't as keen as I was on the place's atmospheric dilapidation keeping crowds at bay. In the big takeover and renovation a few years back that turned the bar into a spiffy, nouvelle-hip lounge servicing a pricey, chef-driven restaurant there, the only survivors were the monkeys. The drinks are solid now and the waitresses buxom, but I miss the dusty Lithuanian waiters cracking wise and the soiled charm of the place as it was. The drinks back then were terrible. It is the only bar I've ever been in where I could instantly tell the liquor had been watered down. But I'll take personality over potency any day.

To say that my discovery of these history-drenched, old guard East Coast haunts changed the way I think about people and altered my perception of the possibilities open to me in this world is not as vast an overstatement as it sounds. For several years it became a low-key obsession of mine to uncover the lost genteel New York watering holes still churning right alongside the city's more obvious, glossy veneer of searing hot spots. Ironically I happened to work at some of those hot spots at the time, maybe a submerged part of why I was drawn to these holdouts from another era. I love all kinds of older bars in the city, especially those like the Cedar Tavern, with its 1950s-era abstract expressionist peccadilloes, and the Old Town Bar, both with ornately carved back bars to match anything I've ever beheld. The Subway Inn, the prototypical Manhattan gin mill with its gallery of black-and-white boxing photos from the days when that was still a sport, squats tenaciously still on the corner of 60th and Lexington, making no apologies to its more delicate neighbors. The dark back tavern of the Oyster Bar in Grand Central, separated from the bustling main room by swinging louvers like a cowboy saloon, has doubtless been far more seasoned by dealmakers and heartbreakers than the upstart Grill Room in the Four Seasons. But it is particularly the old hotel bars that draw me in consistently and inspire my reveries. At the time they were built, these hotels were the apotheosis of luxury, and their creators were clearly looking to make impressive spaces that suited the types of worldly wise travelers passing through New York. They had little way of knowing their goal would provide these rooms the insulation from New York's voracious appetite for novelty that would allow them the longevity to become cherished time capsules, as well. All the luckier for us.

o   o   o

Despite my growing fascination with and cataloging of the species, I never wanted to own a bar, never planned on it, and would, in fact, have scoffed had I been informed prior to Passerby that I would soon be a partner in one. Having worked for so many years in restaurants, and loving to cook and being a wine geek, I'd been asked countless times by friends and acquaintances when I was going to open my own place. I would always grin ruefully at the naiveté of the question. Those years on floors and in kitchens scrubbed from me any illusions of the bucolic, enviable high life of an owner. I routinely hear people talking about how they're going to someday just give up their job as a professor or an attorney and open a restaurant. I look at these people cross-eyed, as though running a restaurant is some kind of retirement idyll for those who have just had their fill of working so darn hard. To my ears, what these people are actually saying is "Damn it all, I've had enough of this life as an associate design editor on a monthly magazine—I'm going to follow my dream to work in the coal mines!" Restaurant work is grueling, fickle, and thankless.

The margin for error in any direction is so small and so mutable you can lose your customer base, or fail to establish one, without ever even knowing why. It is not to be undertaken lightly and, really, not to be undertaken by sensible people in any event. Bars are slightly different, and perhaps only slightly. But there's a clear correlation between the type of person required to weather this business and the fact that almost every restaurant owner I've ever known has been an out-and-out maniac, one or two even dangerously so.

For a moment in my twenties I considered going to Peter Kump's or the Culinary Institute of America to start on the road to chefdom, but my friend Stephen Lyle talked me out of it. He was the executive chef of the Odeon when I was there, and has since gone on to start several restaurants of his own, the most recent being Village on West 9th Street. We used to play tennis together on occasion, the best part of which was always talking afterward. Stephen, an autodidact who is consumed by philosophy, grew up in an American family in the south of France and made his way into the cooking world through arduous apprenticeships in several Michelin-starred restaurants. When I told him my thoughts on attending cooking school he asked me, "You like to cook?" I answered yes, of course, and he replied, "Good, great, then cook, and enjoy it. Cook for your friends, whatever, but don't ruin it for yourself by trying to become a chef. That's like deciding to become a prostitute because you like to fuck." He went on to explain that being a chef often has a lot more to do with keeping schedules, hiring and firing, training, ordering, and doing inventory than it does with cooking or experimenting with food.

Maybe he was simply feeling beaten down that day, but his words reverberated in me. Everyone in the restaurant business knows the ironic trap of management. If you excel at your job as a waiter or bartender, you get the choice shifts by outlasting everyone else and climbing the seniority ladder. Once you're at the top, cock o' the walk and pulling in the most money, naturally the owners want to make you a manager. Dangerously enough, however, everywhere but at the very uppermost echelon of restaurants, managers get paid salaries that often pan out far below what the top waiters can make in tips in three or four nights. While you think you're moving up, you're being had. Worse, once on salary, you're at the restaurant or bar's beck and call. There's no limit to the hours you must be available. When there are no lids for the teapots on the brunch shift, the linen doesn't arrive in time for the dinner shift, and the beer delivery slobs leave all the empty kegs they were supposed to collect sitting in the stairwell to the rest rooms, do you think the wait staff has to worry about it? Not a chance of it. They complain to you, as do the managers above you. When you take into consideration the fact that most young people working in the service industry are making a trade-off to facilitate other interests, waiting tables or tending bar being jobs that pay less money than full-time professions and have no benefits, but leave you time to paint or act or write, you see even more keenly what a horrible misstep "promotion" becomes. Now you find you have no time, no benefits, and, somehow, are earning less than you did on the floor. Since owners must pay managers directly from their profits, they are seldom willing to shell out decent salaries, ones matching what tax-free tips come to. I watched so many of my friends fall into this morass that when my turn came, I politely declined, three times: once at the Odeon, once when the owners of the Odeon moved to open up Lucky Strike and asked me to manage that bar, and finally when I moved over to Kin Khao, where I agreed to help open the bar, but made it clear that once it was up and running I wanted only to tend bar. Later I made an uneasy truce in agreeing to manage the bar at Kin Khao when the position came open. The owners savvily cornered me thusly: "Do you want to take the position and get paid a bit extra to do the job you're basically already doing, or would you prefer to answer to someone we have to then hire to be above you, who doesn't know half of what you do about the place and will drive you insane?" It seemed like a valid point and so I caved. It really did feel like I was making a deal with the devil, though, not at all how one should feel when moving up the ladder, and I was always mistrustful of languishing there.

I was just rounding the turn from my sixth year at Kin Khao into my seventh when Gavin Brown first approached me about helping him start and run a bar in his art gallery. We had met years earlier when he first came to New York from London to participate in the Whitney Art Program. He somehow snagged a job at the Odeon in his first couple of weeks here, having reeled off to Jeff a short list of the better-appointed restaurants in London in which he had presumably tenured before being forced to jump the puddle. As I was one of the people charged with training him on the floor, it became immediately apparent he had never waited tables in his life, didn't know the sharp end of a fork. He was hopeless, but we were all imposters in the same way, and once someone was on the floor we all helped to cover it up as best we could. About two weeks into his appointment Gavin did something that indelibly endeared him to me. We were sitting around having our "family meal," as it's known, prior to a Sunday brunch—a dreadful, low-paying shift foisted onto the new recruits scrapping for seniority. Our breakfast was restive, as we were being grilled on the menu by a loathsome, ass-kissing gorgon of a floor manager. Attempting to intimidate and stump us, in the manner of the head manager under whom she quaked, she trolled the special drinks sidebar and turned to ask Gavin what was in a French 75. Hung over, his curly hair springing out, his eyes bloodshot, and his unshaven face drooping above his plate munching eggs mechanically, he swallowed and said affably, "I haven't a clue." The manager absolutely exploded, shrieking on and on about how we all needed a lesson and were all going to lose our jobs. In the midst of her harangue, as the rest of us were eyeing one another in annoyed disbelief, Gavin shrugged his shoulders, set down his napkin, got up, and walked out the front door. Just like that, a half-hour before service. It was one of the most perfect moments I have ever witnessed in a restaurant. She stopped as though her throat had been cut, realizing that through her harping she was now down a waiter on a very busy shift. Her head snapped back and forth like a bird's as she barked nervously, "Where'd he go? Does anybody know where he's going?" We all shook our heads, our gazes just hiding smirks.

Somehow a week later he snuck back in, I suppose having pleaded with Jeff that he needed the job. Jeff knew the manager was being unreasonable, as she ultimately admitted to not knowing herself what was in a French 75. (A slug of cognac or gin in a glass of Champagne, with a bit of sugar and lemon juice added. A surprisingly lethal sort of Gallic boilermaker, it was named after the caliber of cannon the French were pounding the German lines with in World War I, the 75-mm. Modèle 1897, by troops returned on leave to Paris where they were downing lagoons of them in a concerted effort to forget they were headed back to those same trenches.) But Gavin was back only for a few months before his basic unsuitability to the task got him fired for good. It wasn't so much that he couldn't wait tables—an art for which none of us truly had any noticeable gift—it was more that he couldn't properly pretend as though he cared about any of it. While he was there, though, we got along well. I was wasting a lot of time and money shooting pool down at the now-departed and keenly mourned Julian's poolhall on East 14th Street. One day in response to my bragging about my technique, Gavin mentioned he liked to "play a bit of billiards," as well. I recall thinking this was going to be easy ducats, stripping the limey of his lunch tips, before getting my ass handed to me on a platter. I was so furious and dismayed I literally stopped playing from that point on, saving me any amount of money and perhaps starting the pebble rolling that would eventually lead to Julian's downfall. Gavin's girlfriend was back in England, he told me, a lovely redhead from Newcastle with what I found the improbably Dickensian name of Lucy Barnes. She arrived eventually, they were married, and he started working in galleries. By the time I had moved on to running the bar at Kin Khao, he had his own minuscule gallery in a shallow storefront space on a dumpy street west of Soho leading to the mouth of the Holland Tunnel. There was virtually no foot traffic whatsoever, but he began building a reputation as a kind of peripheral bad boy of the art world, just when the YBA, Young British Artists, thing began in earnest here. His gallery was close to Kin Khao, so I would stop in occasionally to ridicule the artwork and rib him about the charlatanism of his profession, selling the emperors of the art world all their new finery.

Things came to a pass at Kin Khao when the owner asked me to take a full-time position as beverage manager for all three of his restaurants. I knew to mistrust this brevet, which would obviously spell the end of my days behind the bar and the start of my days in a dank cellar office, dealing nonstop with vendors on the phone and plotting profits-versus-liquor-costs graphs on computers. The managing part of my job was already the pill I had to swallow. Tending bar, talking to people, and hanging out with the wait staff were the only enjoyable parts; I didn't want to give up the better part to do the worst part times three.

Just then an opportunity blew in from a completely different direction. I received a phone call from Christie's auction house regarding a position they were trying to fill. They were looking for someone to launch the wine-at-auction and online wine auction programs at Christie's East, their lower-priced venue for lots up to $100,000 or thereabouts. Someone in the wine world, they wouldn't tell me who, gave them my name, and they wanted to interview me. I laughed, assuming wires had gotten crossed and they would soon discover they had meant to contact someone else. I had for years followed wine sales at auction through the catalogs, simply out of spectator interest, but I'd never even been to a live auction, and the kinds of wine I could afford to deal with in my job were a completely different breed from the top Bordeaux, Burgundies, and blue-chip Californians that traded hands back and forth at these affairs. Thinking it a lark, however, I went to the interview and things went swimmingly. I spoke to two young women from human resources who assured me I was indeed their candidate, and I was asked back a second, then a third time, to talk to various wine-level bosses in the organization. The job sounded plum, but huge and intimidating. Basically I would be operating from scratch the whole wine program for them: starting up an online auction program, managing the warehouse up in Westchester, assessing major lots all over the country or world as they came in, running or helping to run the auctions. Could I take such a job? It sounded like it could drown me. It could also open up a whole new level of the wine world for me and turbocharge my education and contacts.

While I was debating whether I could actually take this job, Gavin dropped by and told me he wanted to start a bar, attached to his new gallery in Chelsea, and asked if I would give him some ideas on it. I told him immediately I had a very good idea on it: Don't even think about it. He laughed and told me that in fact he had already taken a lease on the space, where a fetid rice-and-beans joint that catered to the cabbies next door had moved out, unable to pay the rent. Groaning, I agreed to go down and look at the space for him, warning him again that he was making a huge mistake and that he should see if he could still back out of the lease without a penalty. I seconded that advice when I actually saw the space, which was even worse than described. An old fryer stood against the wall with its pu-trescent oil gathering a surface layer of multicolored mold. A horri-ble soundboard dropped ceiling crowded an already claustrophobic space. Every surface was covered with yellowing grease. An ugly modern juke box filled with salsa and merengue was still plugged in to one of the wall outlets. Whoever ran the place before had clearly fled, and that's what I suggested Gavin do, as well. He was implacably upbeat about it, however, saying it was going to be great, that all of his artists were going to chip in to make it unique and lovely, a con-cept that reminded me of the Fitzcarraldo in Paris. He asked me early on to take part in it, but I declined, though I told him I would donate my small store of knowledge gratis to do what I could to insure he didn't lose his ass on it, seeing as he insisted on pushing it forward in the face of all good advice. He already had most of the room laid out, the disco floor and mirrored walls and the bench. I told him where I thought the bar should go, how high it should be, how to set the back bar and shelves, and where to place the cobras and the ice bins to set up two drink-making stations for separate operation on busy nights, all without the remotest idea I would one day be manning them myself.

Talks progressed at Christie's. The people I was interviewing with said they wanted me to meet their master of wine, who would be com-ing from London shortly to oversee an auction. Meanwhile, I was grow-ing tired of Kin Khao. Gavin kept after me, no doubt sensing my unease with what I was doing. He pooh-poohed the auction house, imploring me to come and join the bar. "C'mon," he enthused, "you're going to kick yourself if you don't do this. It'll be great, ten times as much fun as that stale lot, and you'll make more than you do now!"

"I'm not sure it will be great exactly," I countered. "I suppose it could be kind of funny, though, for a while, maybe. . . ." He offered me a generous percentage of the business in exchange for my opening and running it. His idea was to create a little clubhouse, basically, where he could expand his gallery openings and where his artists could have a place to play that could be more or less their little secret. There would be no sign, no address number, no listed phone number, no matches or cards telling where it was, and no publicity of any kind. If others found it, splendid. He didn't care if the bar itself made money, he explained. It wasn't exactly conceived as a vanity project, and if it turned a little profit, so much the better, but that wasn't really the driving idea. More important was simply that the bar cover itself financially and take on a momentum of its own, thereby reflecting something interesting, he hoped, back on his gallery. This, I conceded, was a more admirable goal than most people set out with when starting a place—and perhaps well more realistic—but how exactly were the other bartenders and me supposed to make money if no one knew it existed? "Never mind that," he countered. "You'll make money."

The quizzical thing is how sound this starting premise has proven; strangely enough, I think Passerby has done as well as it has in part because we never set out thinking we would make money on it. In this town, with first-year failure rates of new bars and restaurants famously hovering around 95 percent, low expectations are a wise precaution. Gavin has since admitted to me that in the back of his mind he suspected the bar might last a year or so. I considered that if I could work three shifts a week behind the bar and pay myself a small salary out of the rest of it, I could make out slightly better than I did at Kin Khao and perhaps have fun in the bargain. The thought of no longer having to answer to perennially clueless owners, a species that occasionally turns up only to fling out inane ideas that make them feel in charge, appealed greatly to me, even if the idea of *being* an owner, of even a tiny, hands-on enterprise like this one, slightly terrified me. I anxiously asked everyone around me if I should do it, in a way I have of always liking to collect the consensus on tough decisions, even if I know which way I'm leaning. My friends and acquaintances told me resoundingly I should go for it. I warned Gavin that if I agreed to take his offer I was going to run the bar my way, and that included maintaining a wine list that would be so over-wrought and out of place in a dive like ours that we would most likely lose money on it. He was delighted. Over a lunch of cheese-burgers we cemented the agreement, after which his gallery assistant Kirsty said to me, "Oh, look out; Gavin took me to lunch once, too—just the once, mind you—and I haven't been out of this office since!"

Preparing for the opening didn't feel any different from other projects I've started for people: hectic, unending days held together with duct tape and bad take-out coffee. The defining moment of re-alizing this was going to be different for me came when I went to buy glassware at the restaurant supply store on the Bowery I'd been using for years. I was choosing carefully to avoid having any of the same glassware I'd used at either the Odeon or Kin Khao. Comparing wine-glasses, to me the bar's most telling vessel, I instinctively put down the majestic 16-ounce, broad-bowled, long-stemmed beauty I was ad-miring, reflexively thinking I would love to have those glasses, but given their price, and bartenders' propensity to overpour with such a glass, I'd never get that past the owner. It took two beats for the bub-ble to pop in my mind that there's no longer anyone to get past: I *am* the owner. Standing alone in the middle of acres of dusty glassware in Balter Sales Corp.'s showroom, I grinned moronically considering this improbability. We use those gorgeous Libby Perception Tall glasses to this day. They are far too expensive, they are so impressive the customers steal them constantly, and the bartenders often pour twice the amount they should in them, since what is considered a generous pour in a dinky glass looks niggardly in what is effectively a pint on legs. I grumble about all of the above incessantly, and I wouldn't change them for anything.

I'm aware this flies directly in the face of all of my earlier caveats about abandoning all hope ye who enter into the service industry, but in a certain sense I was amazed by how surprisingly simple it was to open this bar. As the preparations were going on and throughout the first few months, I was overtaken many times by the feeling that we were kids playing at opening up a business. It felt sort of fake. I kept waiting for the inevitable adult intervention, where some higher authority steps in and makes us take down the tree fort because it actually broaches the property of the old lady next door. I don't mean to imply it wasn't tons of busywork: aggravation galore in terms of jumping hoops laid down by the municipal authorities to keep exactly this type of business from flourishing. There's the inevitable ocean of regulations and bylaws, forms to be filed, banks sniffing about, contractors and suppliers to be rounded up and goaded into fulfilling their promises, which they by no means do. But you simply set the entirety in your mind as a lump sum, a mountain to be climbed, then find out in turn what each hurdle is and start jumping them, one by one.

The facet that most seems to fascinate people is the fabled difficulty of attaining a liquor license. Obviously, these things vary wildly from state to state, even city to city. I know that in some places—San Francisco, for example—getting a liquor license is like finding a great, cheap apartment there, more an insane stroke of luck than an everyday occurrence. They apparently have a quota system, like taxi medallions in New York, whereby the city allows a set number of liquor licenses. To start a new bar you have to wait until an established one goes belly-up or someone decides to sell theirs. In fair Gotham, however, people can't wait that long for new bars to open, especially given the stupendous rate of their failure—they want their drinks now. Getting our liquor license amounted, really, to little more than handing a specialized attorney a check that should have been one of those throw rug–size ones you see the sponsor of tune-up tournaments foisting onto a sheepish Andre Agassi. Wait six months while the liquor lawyer does his pirouettes and when the bell goes off, you're open. People find that hard to believe, but that's simply because the proverbial bureaucracy tying up the process is virtually impenetrable to the unfortunate layman who thinks he's going to just wrestle this gator himself and save that lump of gold. You yourself cannot obtain a liquor license, in this state, anyway, but the liquor lawyer can. This is all he does. He's arrogant and creepy and he always talks to you on speakerphone. He pockets an enormous chunk of your opening capital and then treats you like you're an idiot. Just resolve yourself that it all goes through him, and you'll recoup your investment within a couple of years if things go well. I've talked to people who have tried other ways. It simply doesn't work. In this case, if you want that framed piece of paper, you pay the man, end of story. I should add that the situation can be complicated, sometimes mightily, by location. Neighborhood groups and churches can completely squelch the prospect of getting a license, if you have the wrong plan for the wrong neighborhood. Serendipitously for us, our godforsaken block is contiguous to absolutely nothing for a huge radius except slaughterhouses and industrial buildings. We could blow the roof off the bar and there are virtually no neighbors to complain about it. So our license, once all the gods of inspections and regulations had been given proper sacrifices, arrived without incident.

My mistrust of leaving the bar in others' hands led me to caution Gavin that I fully intended to be working behind the bar the whole time I was there. He agreed that he wouldn't have it any other way. I spent too many years watching exasperated owners trying to run restaurants and bars from a chair in the basement, grasping for a hint of what's going on nightly on the floor from the receipts and written reports of the managers, a precaution not unlike reading tea leaves to follow your stocks. It makes them bitter and paranoid, thinking everyone is ripping them off, simply because in most cases everyone is. If you don't dig in and get your hands dirty, if you aren't physically present in your place, you are not going to know what's happening there and abuses will run rampant. There is no such thing as being an effective absentee owner. Bars and restaurants need constant attention and monitoring, and dilettantism is decidedly not rewarded. Sadly for those people who think having their own restaurant or bar would be a lark, simply throwing money at something is not going to make for success in the service industry. You have to throw yourself, and most of your time, energy, and ideas, into it wholeheartedly if you want to even have a hope of still having a place two years down the line. Even all of that is no guarantee; some people just start out wrong-headed, with bad concepts, bad location, bad execution— there's no end to the potholes in this business. I tell people who ask me for advice on opening a bar, as a surprising number do, that you have to look at most of the job like you're embarking on being a glorified janitor. It's really more maintenance than anything else. You set the thing on its course and, provided your opening gambit was a sound one, from then on you're simply involved in maintaining it in working order. That means maintenance in every sense, including actual maintenance. I'm constantly puzzled by how many restaurants start beautiful and quickly get run down, or start with extraordinary flourishes in service or ambitiously high-shooting wine lists that they simply can't or won't maintain. It's all of a piece; customers perceive these changes instantly and make dire interpretations therefrom. Granted, bars and restaurants fail for all kinds of reasons, even if the people behind them are seasoned in the trade, but often I see places started by people in other professions who are eventually over-whelmed by the relentlessness of the upkeep and the unforgiving fickleness of the customers. People sometimes just don't want to have to work that hard. If a customer who comes in ten times and loves your place chances in on a night when you're not there and your employee is being surly or inattentive, or doesn't produce quite as frothy a Kamikaze, chances are they won't be back. It can be a merciless way to make a living, and a mirage to those who think it's going to make them rich.

I find, oddly, that I love working hard. I took Wednesday nights solo years ago at Kin Khao and have kept them straight through. When I opened Passerby the first shift I assigned was my Wednesday alone. Through the week there are different setups of bartenders and busboys, culminating in the weekend shifts, which can have several of both. Wednesday is my one night of working purity, where it's just me against the bar, *mano a legno*, no other bartenders to bump into, no busboys underfoot. This setup can make for a punishing ride if the night gets even mildly busy, but I anticipate that ride in the same way a rodeo cowboy loves to see how long he can sit the bronco trying to upend him. Having to do everything in the room myself also gives me the perfect read on the bar from week to week. How busy is it? Who's coming in? What are they drinking? What are they saying about the place and the wine list and the service? It sounds simplistic but, if you're there you know, if you're not you don't, confirming Woody Allen's line that 90 percent of success is simply showing up.

There is, of course, that problematic other 10 percent. If you're working alone and there are no cherries out, no limes cut, no clean rags, no cold wine stocked, a keg empty, and not enough ice in the bins when you open, and then the room immediately fills with kids from the neighboring galleries, photography studios, PR firms, and dot-com companies, the ensuing carnage can make for Lucille

Ball–inspired scenarios, while removing years from your life. But tonight begins the way I like. There's plenty of time to set up, it's empty for a bit, then it builds slowly, with a scattering of customers I don't know.

It was originally as a means of controlling these solo nights that I fashioned Sad Disco. At a certain point during the bar's first year, the crowds were reaching a critical mass. While pitting myself against the onslaught, I made a game out of holding down everything while spinning music on the two-deck CD mixer, DJing while tending bar and striving to miss nothing. On the mixer there's a digital readout that counts down the time remaining on each track, so the trick is to line up two songs in advance and keep one eye on the deck while taking orders, making drinks, and doing dishes. When you've got to clear tables or get ice, the strategy is to insert longer tracks, like the Stones' "Sweet Virginia," or Pink Floyd's "Fearless," to give yourself the necessary minutes. I realize that simply putting on an album and tending to business would be much easier, and often when beaten I did just that, but where's the challenge in it? The problem with playing music to suit your taste, of course, is that your taste is not everyone's, and once people become aware that somehow the music is being altered to preference, they instantly want that preference to be theirs. The disco floor is something of an ironic statement; there's no room and no license to allow for dancing, and, at any rate, disco is not to be found in my repertoire, nostalgic or otherwise. Still, the floor being the draw, people naively assume we're trying to make ourselves out as an intimate dance spot. Women, in particular, will query plaintively and repeatedly as to why you're not playing "dance music," whatever exactly that means. My response to this, one night when a particularly invasive young lady kept haranguing me about "upping the tempo" because she and her friends were trying to "light it up," was to canvass my CD collection carefully for the most threnodic

dirges I could wring out of it, stringing along one aching acoustic bal-
lad after the next for hours. I found it not only pleasingly perpendic-
ular to the floor's bouncy throb, but useful in that it helped restrain
and confound the crowds that were beginning to overwhelm me. I
continued it for several weeks running, as a counterpoint to the din
of the other nights and to allow some thinking people an entrée back
into the bar. Gavin had briefly displayed a poster in the gallery de-
picting, in Chas. Addams–style black-and-white washes, a maudlin
DJ spinning Nick Drake, Cat Stevens, the Smiths, Simon and
Garfunkel, and the like, above whom floated in ghostly balloon letters "Sad Disco." I co-opted the name for my Wednesday night
morose-fest. Now when customers would wail, "Don't you have any
Fatboy? We're all about to commit suicide here!" I would simply
reply, "It's Wednesday, love. Sad Disco. Feel the pain."

After the first few weeks I began to notice a recurrent character
during Sad Disco. He was a stout, bald-headed, light-skinned black kid
who, rather than joining the tirade on those nights, seemed to be as
amused as I was by people's consternation, frequently sidling up to ask
where I got the version of Steve Lawrence and Eydie Gorme doing
"Black Hole Sun" or whatnot. Very quickly we struck up a musical
friendship. Jesse became something of the bar mascot. Falstaffian in
both appetite and mien, he is a big drinker and an imposing presence.
He first gained my favor by brilliantly and unflinchingly dressing
down a few discophiles berating me one night, rabidly painting the
portrait of their venal inability to recognize the inherent worth of Sad
Disco. Jesse has the unusual quality of truly not caring whom he of-
fends, without being an offensive person himself. This combination
can be very useful here, and it's likely due in no small amount to being
born and raised in racially polarized Brooklyn to a white mother and a
black father. Unlike most kids his age, his intelligence and curiosity
have carried his musical preferences far beyond contemporary pop

and hip hop. He began bringing in offerings to include in the Sad Disco lineup, surprising me with both the wiles to dredge up 1950s and '60s esoterica I never would have found and the honesty to pay homage to top 40 songs so common that no DJ would ever go near them.

As the bar became progressively busier, I found my game of trying to keep all the plates spinning atop their sticks while balancing a bowling pin on my chin and juggling three oranges was not the most productive course for me or the customers. Jesse moved directly from popping in the occasional cut to helming the night. What began as a lark for me, however, became a mission and eventually a calling for him. He began burning customized CDs that were subsets of Sad Disco, then incorporating those with albums on the turntables. As his collection grew, his take on Sad Disco refined. Now, smirking like a café-au-lait Buddha behind the console, he began to play cat-and-mouse with the anxious patrons, slipping in the occasional danceable track early on, only to jerk it back to Joni Mitchell or Cat Power in the next few songs. In this manner he would incrementally tease it up to where the dance-starved were gratified, if temporarily. He would yank the place from a pensive, almost tearful distraction to a shirts-off, ass-wagging, sweaty mash before letting it back down to earthbound drear, in a two-hour span that left the entire bar breathless and drained. I gave him rafts of grief over wussing out to whiny girls demanding Prince songs, but in reality it became impressively clear that he understood better than any of the other DJs something I've tried in vain to emphasize to them from the start: It's crucial to take the measure of, and then follow, the energy of the room. I had to admit Jesse did it better than I had been and, in taking Sad Disco to a new level, characteristically made it his own. Now he spins at several other places around town, having quit his graphics and film work to take this ride, though he's still about most nights. It has occurred to me that he probably loves the bar more than anyone, more than I do.

Tonight, early, it's a lot of gay men. One of the things I love about my bar is its ability to chameleonize from a rock-and-roll dive bar to a wine geek tasting post to an annoyingly elitist art world clubhouse to a fashion model/coke whore hang to a gay bar to a bridge-and-tunnel frat party, sometimes incorporating three such incarnations in a night. Sometimes this makes me laugh aloud, sometimes it makes me cringe and wonder what the hell I'm doing here. It's like having a child and knowing what you'd like to mold it into but having to acknowledge that the child has a will of its own and naturally becomes whatever it must, irrespective of your wishes or guidance.

I once schemed semiseriously with a friend about opening a gay bar. This had nothing to do with either of our proclivities; I'm straight and, though he was gay, he loathed gay bars and never went to them. It simply occurred to us, having both tended bar for over ten years, that as a pure business prospect, a gay bar represents your surest bet. As a bartender, the things you cannot fail but notice about your clientele are how they act, how they spend, and how they tip. This trifecta comes across the line in the highest common denominator with gay men. Simply put, they are the best customers. They go out more than anyone, they spend like demons, they are hands-down the best tippers, and I've never had to boot one out of any bar I've ever worked, for any reason. The gay bars here in Chelsea are packed wall to wall most nights, so somebody, we reasoned, is making all that money. Why shouldn't that be us? When I informed my friends of this whim, they queried why I would ever want to open a bar where I would never get to talk to pretty girls. That might, I replied, actually be a sort of blessing. I also never said I would necessarily work behind said bar, though not to do so would be flying in the face of all my earlier theories about hands-on ownership. But who, in their working life, tries to perform in an atmosphere that is as continually and distractingly sexually charged as the bartender's? Maybe the bouncers in a bordello. It sometimes gets so aggravating that you feel like it's actually unfair. I frequently bring to mind a quote of Genet's when piqued by the jealousy of watching some couple intertwining lasciviously, either ignorant of all eyes around them or perhaps performing for them: "Still I couldn't accept the idea that people made love without me."

A year ago at Halloween I had a strangely pointed example of this epigram unfold before me. There was a young couple who wandered in with the other revelers. I didn't notice them right off, as on that night especially, there are some fairly attention-grabbing characters in attendance. I recall we gave a little prize for the best costume to an Asian girl who looked perfect done up as Frida Kahlo, monobrow and self-tanning gel, the whole bit. Meanwhile, there were quite a number of geishas in attendance. Big year for geishas, for some reason, which became somewhat interesting as a large group of Japanese girls, along with one older gentleman who turned out to be their boss, mapped out the bar from some guide they had and descended for the night. None of them spoke English, but the boss was this explosively effusive fellow who spent the night pounding on the bar, demanding shots and drinks of whatever he saw being made or going by. At a point there were six or eight geishas dancing on the bar around this flabbergasted group of tourists. Imagine arriving in Fukuoka the night of some huge, ill-defined celebration and going out to get a drink and finding yourself surrounded by Japanese Marilyn Monroes.

One of the geishas caught my attention, a lissome brunette with short-cropped hair and a spray of freckles. She wasn't on the bar, she was just dancing by herself on the floor, slowly, kind of swaying about absorbed in her own rhythm. She was, in effect, just another pretty girl, but like Salinger's girl struggling with the umbrella on Jones Beach, in just that frame where you happen to be, she conjured something more remarkable, she seemed to carve out her own silent applause. Then I noticed her boyfriend was back sitting on the bench across the room contentedly watching her and realized she was actually performing for him. I found this a very fetching scenario; it made me smile to have somehow stumbled, in the midst of this bugling crowd, upon these two lovers clandestinely playing out their private game. She turned to see me smiling and I quickly looked away, like a peeper caught in a bedroom window.

When next I looked back she was dancing directly in front of me. Every now and again she would look back at her boyfriend and he would give her a nod of the head, to which she would shake her head no. His cue became more insistent, until finally, with a self-conscious shrug, she pulled the sash on her kimono and let it slide to the floor, revealing an awful lot of sinewy flesh, clad only in a black merry widow and panties above black fishnet stockings with leather pumps. The crowd dancing around her fanned out a little instinctively and people started cheering her. I looked immediately at the boyfriend, to see him laughing and clapping on the bench, then back at her, swaying away unconcerned, smiling at me through her bangs.

He slid off the bench and picked his way through the crowd, wrapping his arms around her torso and sinking his lips into her neck. She lowered her head but never broke her gaze from me. His fingers pried under her corset and across her thighs. He bit into her shoulder and I saw her panties move from his hand snaking around inside of them. Still she stared directly at me, with a look on her face like a calculated dare. Jesus Christ, I thought, what is up with these two? A little taunting exhibitionism? Looking to make a sandwich, maybe? Or just a little game, perhaps; knowing I was clocking them, they were toying with me, to make me jealous or have a bit of a mutual laugh: "Did you see that bartender staring at us?" I had to admit, too, it was working damnably well. Standing with an empty glass in one hand and the ice scoop in the other, I couldn't take my eyes off of this languid scenario. I was willingly playing into their hands, in part because I wanted to figure out what they were up to. But there also wasn't much else to do right then, and when people start making a spectacle in front of you, you tend to look. I went about my chores and served people as they came, but every time I looked up, there they were, locked up like octopi, with her deep brown eyes burning holes in my retina as he pawed her from behind. Licking and biting her arm, he unhooked the top of her corset. I began to feel like Margaret Dumont: "Good heavens!" Acknowledging their little joke, I smirked and she smiled back lasciviously, at which I felt myself actually blush. I had to literally pry my gaze away and go robotically pull glassware from the dishwasher and stock it on the shelves.

A very titillating instance, I thought. Funny, and kind of wearisome, too. Occasionally there is this kind of evanescent pain associated with this job. It's a pain for which there is not yet a correct term. Regret and envy are too strong, and jealousy doesn't properly define it. I certainly didn't wish I were him, but I did want to know what it was like to be kissing her the way he was right then. Who wouldn't? You'd have to be dead not to acknowledge that she's a peach, and I'm only human; their naughty little game found a chink in my armor, and it worked on me. I envisioned them leaving, laughing at their slinky charade, maybe using it as fuel for a further romp. Good for them, I thought, God bless 'em. They're doing no harm, just playing with what they have. But why, then, did it make me feel ever so slightly strained, or cheated, like someone just took something from me, a small thing, insignificant, and that I can do fine without, but that I was kind of attached to, anyway? There should be a term for the feeling of loss for something you never had, and never thought you wanted. When they picked up their coats at the end of the night to leave, he waved laughingly to me while she blew me a kiss. I nodded and smiled to them, feeling like someone who has just somehow been beaten in straight sets.

o   o   o

Different groups of guys are chatting across the bar, someone has brought in fresh-roasted cashews and is passing them around, everything is amiable, and I'm wearing my jolly publican guise. I finish up the opening chores, cutting and stashing extra fruit for later, lighting and setting out the candles and filling bowls with "cat food," my name for the organic sesame snacks we dole out to the post-office crowd early on.

A groan is forced from me and I look quickly away as the door opens and emits two sometime habitués, tortuously awful barflies I refer to as Frick and Frack, or sometimes, less prosaically, "those loser fuckwads." They push in all red-faced swagger and bouncy expectation, sizing up the room with empty little half-smiles, like two hungry dogs. Both Englishmen, these two embody much of what I revile in their patrimony. Frick is older, perhaps in his mid-sixties, though the combined ruinous effects of alcoholism and perpetually bowing and scraping his way up the food chain have weathered him mightily, and he could, I suppose, be as young as fifty. He is supposedly a journalist. I couldn't verify it. Though he is routinely scooped up in the gill-net hauls that are those horrid magazine spreads of parties around town, the ones with each reveler frozen, pasty and astonished, in a more awkwardly unappealing grimace than the next, I've never seen any printed proof of his occupation anywhere. Having never encountered him even remotely sober, I can no more imagine him penning so much as his signature than I could expect a tip from his perfidious ass.

Frack is a good deal younger. His youthful bloom has only begun to be displaced by the bloat of drink, despite his complete inability to pay for one. Sporting the same tongue-in-cheek shag cut every Oasis-inspired Brit hipster clones of late, he orbits nervously about Frick like a remora on a shark. He is, by his own telling, a mixed-media artist, which is what it's called when you assemble piles of cast-off junk and then set out to find someone to, hope against hope, sell it for you.

I have watched these hateful parasites on far too many a night in their pathetic game, trading on the basic New Yorker's inexplicable fascination with and thrall to all things English, whereby they wheedle drinks out of anyone who will listen to their drummed-up pontifications. They are maddeningly successful at it, as well, to the point of making me openly hostile to them, a condition neither one has ever, I believe, noticed. Frick, pallid and jowly, is simply too drunken, his eyes perpetually unfocused as he yammers and gesticulates to whatever captive he's taken, and Frack's goofy self-absorption, as he floats along like a nodding, has-been rock star, doesn't permit much room for outward perspicacity. I've often wondered why they pal about, so disparate in age and profession, if not in condition. My guess is that it's easier to clutch at the rungs of the social ladder while presenting a father/son-like front of lovable Anglicism. The real reason may just be an unwholesome symbiosis: glomming free drinks, with each one slurping up the other's windfall. As ubiquitous as roaches, as sycophantic as dogs, they'll attend the opening of a closet if it means blessedly free drinks. Not surprisingly, they have a method of evasion when it comes to paying that sets every bartender's coals ablaze: all bright-eyed greeting and lip-smacking attentiveness while ordering, they suddenly feign deafness when the drink is put before them and the price announced. Sweeping up the glass while guffawing at some vapid joke or bombastically making some ersatz point, they'll quickly try to snake off to a table or a corner, like children hoping their parents will somehow magically forget about their bedtime. This forces you to step around the bar and pursue them, an action they hope you simply can't be bothered to perform. When then cornered, they will eye you with perturbed affront and, waving a dismissive hand, tell you to put it on their tab, a laughable if unfunny notion. When told that if they want to start a tab they will have to put down a credit card, like anyone else, they will then pat themselves down dramatically, confounded by where on earth that damnable credit card from Barings could have gotten to. Inevitably by this time whatever dupe they've been buttering up will whip out his or her wallet, frowning at the intruding barkeep over this trifle of mere money when two such distinguished guests from the sceptr'd isle are concerned. It never fails and it rankles me like nails on a chalkboard.

One of the most depressingly squalid dioramas I ever hope to witness came to me courtesy of Frick, a sour scenario in two acts that unfolded one night among himself, a famous German photographer, and the photographer's heavily bibulous and dumpy wife. The three of them fell out while talking, apparently breaking into contest, incredibly enough, over the prized frau. Eric the timorous was tending bar alongside me and, as the drunken shouting moved into opiated lunges and missed punches between Frick and the photographer, I had to move in and quell the prizefight. The photographer angrily loped out of the bar and we considered the fracas settled enough as Frick collapsed in victory onto the long bench directly opposite us, next to the reprobate wife.

After a few quiet minutes I glanced up past the customers lining the bar to behold Frick and the photographer's wife zonked on the bench side by side, grappling and fumbling at one another strangely, both with heads thrown back and mouths drunkenly agape. Confused, I squinted to look closer and received a slap: the photographer's wife, I now perceived, was moaning in terrible, rhythmic heat as Frick diddled her before one and all. I stared in horror for a moment, not quite believing what I was seeing.

Rushing up to Eric, who was down the bar filling a shaker at the main station, I whispered frantically, "You have to look RIGHT NOW! It's the most disgusting thing you've ever fucking seen in your life!" Squeamishness being Eric's defining state, his eyes bugged large with the urgency I imparted.

"What? I'm not looking, whatever it is—"

"No, you have to go look now! Frick is openly fingering Rita right in front of us. It's like a geriatric porno flick. Go see, you must go look immediately!"

"No she is *not!*" he squealed, grimacing. "You have got to be fucking kidding my ass . . . she's got that pickled clam all flappin' in the breeze?" He stared deliberately at the drink he was making, even though simply looking up from where he stood would have verified the offending spectacle in all its grisly detail. "I am *not* looking at that shit for anything in the world!"

I stood next to him, running color commentary and goading him in hissing revulsion. "It's truly the most horrible thing. You're going to kick yourself if you miss this. Their heads are bent together now—ack! They're kissing, or trying to . . . what happened to her underwear, anyway? Eric, look quick, it will turn you to stone, man, I'm not kidding. You'll turn to a pillar of salt!"

"I'm not looking!" he remonstrated, shaking his head staunchly while straining out the drink for a woman at the bar. "I refuse to look."

"Look, look, my son, behold the ugly, ugly truth . . ."

"Stop! What are you doing anyway? Go over and make them stop that foulness! You fucking own this bar or what?"

"Are you nuts? I'm not going near them. I'm not even taking any money from them without a hazmat suit on."

Shortly the star-crossed dalliance was terminated and they pulled themselves together. Eric still wouldn't look over at them, though, for fear that I was trying to trick him into witnessing a vision the relief from whose horrific imprint might take most of a lifetime. It was so pathetic that I thought at the time it was hilarious, like watching two dung beetles carousing. Now, though, every time I see Frick wobble in, it immediately comes back to me and I just want to launch a javelin cleanly through one of his eye sockets.

Tonight Frack is in fairly good shape, but Frick is explosively drunk from the get-go. Informing all within earshot that they've just come from an opening at MoMA, he starts his usual act, weaving and shouting inanities about himself to anyone who will hold still long enough in his sights. Somehow, without fail, people find this amusing, smiling permissively as he crashes their groups and wrenches the conversation over to himself. I tell Frack he had better take Frick out of here and he nods, telling me he'll see to him and make sure he doesn't drink any more. His own first beer he uncharacteristically pays without quarrel, producing four balled-up dollar bills and nothing in the way of a tip. I give him a long look and he raises his glass up genially, winks, and says, "Cheers then, mate!"

Cheers at your burial, I think, scooping up the pile and unwadding each bill.

As soon as I turn around, Frick's bulbous, red-veined nose is there to greet me. I recoil slightly and regard him without inquiring whether he'd like anything. He raises his hand and asks for a pen and a pad of paper. Fine, I think, and put down a dupe pad and a pen. He seems to know enough not to ask for a drink from me, at least.

Several minutes later he waves me over as I'm walking down with a pint. He thrusts several sheets of the dupe pad at me and says, slurring, "You know who I am, I take it?" I again regard him aloofly, without answering. "Good, splendid. I'm quite a famous illustrator, you know. These should cover a month or so of drinks easily. You'll be able to sell them for several thousand dollars. Take these and open a tab for me, then. Get me a bottle of Champagne to start with."

This is a new twist. I cock my head to try to look into his empty, unconnected eyes, wondering if he actually cannot remember the times I've had to cut him off and send him out. He's waiting like an old dog tied to a parking meter, rocking slightly back and forth, staring at nothing, his thin hope circling above us like a swarm of flies. I pick up the scribblings he's made, pages of preschool mush, and make as if to appraise them. "Hmm . . . I'm afraid these will only get you water here. But I'm not really in the art part of the business, you know. You might try some of the other galleries."

His face reddens and he spits out ferociously, "You're a fool! You're an ass!" Laughing, I turn and walk down the bar, amazed that I was almost starting to feel a little sympathy for Frick, just for a second or two.

The episode makes me wonder if I would hate Frick and Frack as deeply if they knew enough to tip, at least. I conclude I would; despite the astounding palliative powers of the well-placed ducat, they're too annoying on too many levels. Besides, it's an entirely moot consideration: it ain't never gonna happen.

Tipping remains something of a mystery for a surprising number of people who should know better. In a restaurant everyone knows to tip 20 percent on food and liquor, but in a bar the breakdown becomes a little different. It's clear, when you now see tip cups sprouting at every counter where opportunistically cheap business owners are trying to augment wages for their underpaid employees, that the tip thing is a bit out of hand. Knowing whom and how much to tip people can seem kind of complex, but many people use their lack of awareness to justify not tipping at all. This is a big no-no. I've clarified the situation for myself like so: If someone is performing a service for me that requires them actually to create something on my behalf, I should tip them. People ringing up my purchase on a cash register, therefore, do not merit being specially tipped, whereas people making me a sandwich or frothing me up a cappuccino do. It's not a perfect rule, but it does streamline the process for me.

Bartenders live on their tips and wits alone, quite simply put. There is no salary we receive from the house. If you find the bartender a bit lacking in social graces, it may be that you prompted that gruffness by not tipping on your first or subsequent rounds. We are not standing back here sucking up smoke and insult for your edification or our health. You should leave a minimum of a dollar per drink on every drink, regardless. Water is, by the way, a drink. You should never leave less than a dollar for anything, ever. Change on the bar is an insult. If you run up a big bill, keeping a tab on a credit card or being served a pricey bottle of wine or Champagne, then the 20 percent rule becomes appropriate. You can't grouse that because you paid $350 for a bottle of Gaja Barbaresco you shouldn't be expected to shell out more on top of it. The money you're paying for your drink goes to the house. Only the tip goes to the bartender. You have to look at it as though you're renting space at the bar, and regardless what you're drinking, you have to pay your rent. I've often told friends who embarrass me by not tipping well the same thing I tell people who try to justify their cheapness by claiming they've only enough cash for the drink: Brother, if you don't have enough to tip, then you don't have enough to drink, and you've got no right walking in. Tipping, whatever you may think, is not optional, it's only made to seem so. If you think I'm wrong, see how far you get stiffing bartenders before someone makes a very hairy scene for you.

Not long after first stepping behind the bar at the Odeon I was working one Saturday night with an older guy, Matthew, a bitter actor type, washing up on the far side of what you might term his prime career years. He was a sympathetic enough fellow with me, overlooking my novice gaffes and stepping in to show me the ropes, but he had way too short a fuse with the customers. I saw him get in a lot of shouting matches, in his clipped Brooklyn accent, over things that seemed truly trivial. He was a perfect example of how not to react to the quotidian deluge of minor outrages heaped on you by bartending.

On this night he was serving a foursome ordering fairly labor-intensive drinks, and the guy paying each round, as they went, kept leaving exactly a dollar on a thirty-two-dollar round. Matthew was pissing a stream of curses about it, his ears enflamed, until the guy ordered a fourth round. Matthew steamed past me, latching onto my arm, and pulled me down the length of the bar. At the far end of the bar Matthew turned his back to the customers, picked up a rocks glass, and plunged it under his apron, fumbling about under there and then making some kind of lurid swirling motion.

"You know what I'm doing?" he barked at me, his eyes burning weirdly. I replied that I didn't.

"That asshole down there, I'm rimming his fucking cocktail with my dick! How do you like that shit, buddy? I'm giving that fucker a cock cocktail, right?" He roared with laughter and clapped me on the shoulder. I shook my head cautiously, but because I was new and didn't want to make waves I just watched as Matthew made a Dewar's Old-Fashioned in the glass and brought it, along with the other drinks, to the guy. The guy paid up and floated a dollar once again, unwittingly missing what might have been his final reprieve. As he took his first sip I tried to look away, but Matthew kept jabbing me in the ribs, waving the dollar triumphantly between two fingers and hooting at his cleverness. "Look, look at that fuck, Toby! Do you absolutely *love* that shit, man? That guy's sucking my dick right now, bro—he's sucking my fucking cock! I'll give you a prick cheese swizzle stick, you cheap motherfucker!" On and on.

I can't tend bar like that. Worrying about that kind of crap will kill you quick in this profession, having that kind of hot head and trying to strong-arm people. Still, I don't see why, as a customer, you wouldn't hedge your bets and get chop-chop service by tipping well. It's one of the few areas in life that are truly reduced to black and white; you can be the most absurdly condescending, insulting ass, and if you're tipping like Croesus, you're golden with me. Conversely, even if you're Mr. Amiable, polite as the dickens, talking this and that, maybe even wringing a goodwill drink out of it, if you tip poorly or not at all, you're getting daggers from me. I'm not going to spit in anyone's drink, because I'm just not going to lower myself to that and risk the trouble it could cause. But I've known plenty of bartenders who would do it in a second if you stiffed them, and would court the ensuing trouble. Just pay your buck a drink and we can all play together nicely.

o   o   o

I look up again to see Chief pushing through the door, looking quarrelsome and bent out of shape a bit, which is to say, looking not unlike himself. He is a wonder, is the Chief, and watching him waddle in, wrinkle his nose at the volume of the music, which is not at all loud, and then finally get settled sort of unspools all of the aggro-ness that filled me and turned my eyes slitty in having to deal with Frick and Frack.

"I'm amazed you're not off on some exotic vacation," he barks, always starting out on the attack. "Aren't you heading somewhere?"

"I hadn't planned on it, Chief," I replied, shrugging. "Why, are you offering?" Years ago at Kin Khao the Chief began coming in for dinner, eating at a table but always winding up at the bar for a smoke and a coffee. I had him pegged several times. At first I thought he might be one of those guys on the verge of homelessness, living in a room somewhere nearby that he has rented for $112 a month since 1957, heating up cans of Dinty Moore on a hot plate, porn photos and old greeting cards tacked to the walls. But he seemed to have plenty of money. He's an old drunk, I then thought, I've seen the type a million times—hides it perfectly—probably here to cruise the little Asian hotties, a roué, they used to call it. But he only occasionally had a drink, and never more than one. Also, he was far too crotchety to try picking up the waitresses, and at any rate he couldn't have been less interested in them. I couldn't figure him out.

What he couldn't get enough of, it turned out, were the cats. There were two cats who lived in the restaurant and were kept down in the basement during service. He loved them, literally came to the restaurant to visit them, and would gruffly demand they be released to come up and see him when he was there. He had several cats of his own, he explained. The other managers just treated him like a lunatic and would tell him the cats were to remain downstairs during service, particularly as one of them was very fond of biting the customers. I would always go fetch the cats for him, though, in part just because I relished the mayhem caused when Mommy would sink her fangs into some unsuspecting diner's hand. The Chief was outraged about the condition of the cats, and lobbied long and hard on their behalf. They were too fat, he would complain, and they don't like it down in the basement. How he knew this I never inquired. He hatched elaborate plans to spirit them away, and confided them to me. He was quite serious.

It wasn't until I had for several months been indulging what I took to be this harmlessly crazy old man, who had nothing better to do than rally for the downtrodden cats before going back to his empty room, that I chanced to ask the Chief if he did anything.

"Do I *do* anything?"

"Yeah, like as in a profession. Did you have a job ever, or do you have a job, I mean?"

"Well, yeah," he muttered, "but it's kinda winding down now. I'm getting ready to retire."

"Oh, really, retiring is it? And what is it you do?"

"I teach," he bit off.

"You're a teacher! That's amazing. What do you teach?"

"Surgery," he replied innocently, picking up his coffee.

I stopped for a moment. I had been trying to be a wag, just baiting him to see what he would come up with, but this I wasn't prepared for. It seemed just too terribly sad to me that this poor fellow was going to try to pass himself off as a professor of surgery. I wished I hadn't begun the conversation. "Uh, yeah? Surgery, huh?

"That's right. At Columbia."

"At Columbia Medical School?!" I asked, volubly embarrassed for him now.

He looked at me as though I was an idiot. "Well, yeah, that's where they teach those kinds of things," he said nonchalantly, turning his attention back to scratching Tiger between the shoulder blades.

It evolved, over the course of a long cross-examination, that he was not only a professor of surgery, but in fact a professor of *neuro-*

surgery at Columbia. He breezily crushed my pathetic attempts to trip him up with tricky questions concerning the location of the "sella turcica" and the function of the hypothalamus, recalled from my high school human anatomy courses. I didn't believe him for the longest time. What actually made me realize that he wasn't lying was his dismissal of my incredulousness; he didn't care if I believed him or not, and neurosurgery was the last thing he wanted to talk about. His wife, which I was also astounded he had, was, it turned out, also a surgeon, though just a practicing one. They don't seem to live together anymore, in one of those kinds of amicable arrangements older couples sometimes quietly come to, though they're not separated or even remotely contemplating divorce. They seem to split time among the three houses they share. All of this he revealed in the ingenuous tone of a distractedly cranky child, which is how he speaks of just about everything.

That was probably seven or eight years ago. He found Passerby when I moved over here and shows up intermittently to rattle my cage. We sort of talk at one another rather than to, but he's one of those people I just love to see walk through the door. Everyone in the room seems to have their MO for being there except the Chief. He doesn't fit in at all, which of course is why I like him. He's technically neither a barfly nor a regular. He's an irregular. We jaw about golf, about wine, some politics. He still talks about how unhappy the cats are, and has elaborate plans to kidnap them. Catnap them. Whatever. The weirdest part about my rapport with the Chief is that I'd been treating him for so long like he was just a crazy homeless guy that, even after discovering his professional standing, I just went on treating him the same way. I've never known his name, actually. At Kin Khao the waitresses used to call him the cat guy. I'm certain I could just ask him and he would tell me, as bluntly as he does anything else, but I think it works out fine this way. I've been calling him Chief for so long it would seem kind of odd to have to attach another name to him. I like that he has never acknowledged one way or another my calling him that, either. It started out being kind of facetious, when I just thought he was a nut, but it ended up being a perfect fit, and now it's stuck. He just is the Chief.

"I'd like a beer," he growls, "but I don't want any of those damn nouveau beers that taste like a loaf of pumpernickel! I just want a beer beer."

"A beer beer, then. Okay, Chief. A wee pilsener on tap, maybe?"

Ignoring me, he settled in for a grumble. "What's up with beer these days, anyways? It used to be just beer. It was good. I liked it that way. Now I can't find any regular beer anymore. I go to the store to get a six-pack and it all looks like molasses. And it costs a fortune, too. Who the hell wants that? Who wants to drink a bowl of fermented granola when you're thirsty?"

Uh-oh. Chief was, as it happened, sitting one seat away from M.C., who is something of a regular, is perhaps one of the most intransigently opinionated people I've ever come across, and just happens to be the brewmaster for a local brew pub. He's an interesting fowl but, not unlike Chief himself, a prickly character and quick to take umbrage. Though he can rub some people the wrong way, I like his black-and-white take on the world. There is simply no middle ground with M.C. Three things consume his attention and it is the entirety of that obsessive attention he devotes to them. They are: the Beatles, Hunan Chinese food (the making and eating of), and beer (the making, drinking, researching, judging, and everything else of). Beer geeks are different from wine geeks in some fundamental ways, the primary one being a lack of the highbrow affect—and patience for same—that the wine world cultivates like a Grand Cru vineyard. But what we share is that same absurdly microscopic tunnel vision in regard to our obsession. There is not a thing, for the most part, you could tell M.C. about beer that he hasn't already lectured on in Scotland or California. And his opinions, once he has carved them out of stone, are not to be swayed.

Pulling Chief's pint in apprehension, I smiled at M.C., hoping he hadn't been listening or had been distracted by the music. But he was already shaking his head sadly as he bent his frame across the seat separating the two. "If you don't mind my saying so," began the irresistible force to the immovable object, "it's not that anything's wrong with the beer these days. It's actually just that Americans have never known what real beer tastes like, so they have trouble when something that isn't colored water, something that actually has strength and body and flavor of its own merit, is put in their mouths and they have to make heads or tails of it!"

Chief, no blushing flower, pushed his glasses up his nose a bit farther and jumped right in. "Well, strength and body and flavor are all fine. I like those in my whisky. A beer I like because it's supposed to slake my thirst, not compete with my dinner!"

I moved slowly away laughing. This would be tantamount to M.C. barging in and somehow starting a conversation: "What the hell's up with brain surgery these days—where do these guys get their licenses, at the D.M.V.?" In a sense, it was a delicious matchup, but being so I could tell if I got too close I was going to be refereeing it still tomorrow afternoon. As I moved off out of range of the fireworks I could hear M.C. ask if Chief knew what a cask-conditioned ale was, to which Chief replied patently no, and that he didn't want to, either, if it was one of those bitter things the English drink warm.

I'm still cutting fruit and hurrying through other small chores when I look up to find Beth seated almost directly in front of me with a girlfriend of hers I've not met before. She has that quizzical, slightly mocking smile on her face that I've never quite figured out, and which to be honest kind of scares me. I still don't know how she does it, but she always makes her entrance this way; I never see her actually walk into the bar, she's always just suddenly there, which makes it even a little scarier. I greet Beth and shake her friend's hand, feeling as though I'm being passed through a security scanner at the airport, so intense is their combined scrutiny. I gather Beth has spoken of me to her friend and this is the dog and pony show. I draw a long breath and instantly feel a deep psychic exhaustion setting in. I get them both a glass of wine and turn back to cutting fruit, but Beth's not having it. Wine you can get anywhere. "Darling, I thought of you," she says floridly. "Have you seen that series they're doing with writers talking about their favorite cities? They've got Edmund White doing Paris, I wondered what you'd think."

Beth is problematic. She first began coming in a couple of years ago. I noticed her for the first time chatting animatedly one night with a thin, rabbinical-looking fellow. She would subsequently show up with any of a number of other guys, none of whom was her boyfriend at the time, though eventually she did bring him in, as well. I was attracted to her, as most men are, right off the bat. I've now witnessed Beth's personal magic at work on so many of them I've lost count. She's slightly heavyset, in a voluptuous way, with wide hips and athletic shoulders. Her hair is an arresting silver gray, having prematurely turned that, she says, her sophomore year in high school, and she keeps it in a short, boyish bob. A pretty girl, by any standards, she makes deft use of her inviting smile and her galvanizing intellect, turning men to pigs in short order. She puts on the femme fatale persona rather heavily, drawing a bit too hard on the Dorothy Parker blueprint. But it can be charming if you're feeling indulgent.

Beth's problem is that she needs male attention the way vampires need blood, and will descend to scary depths to get it. Having known me for only a short time, she began imploring me to have an affair with her. After putting her off a number of times, I had to take her aside and make clear that she could not come into the bar any longer because I have a girlfriend, and she was being annoying. She apologized and promised she wouldn't harp on it any more, adding that she would like for us to remain friends. Problem was that she didn't exactly stop the haranguing. It only picked up after she and her boyfriend split up. She would sit drinking for hours, at the end of which she would ask if I wouldn't just like to come and sleep at her place, just sleep, that's all. Or she would ask me repeatedly if I wanted to go away with her for the weekend. That failing, she would end up just lurching home with whatever guy happened to start up a conversation with her. I watched in horror as she shambled off with some of these derelict losers actually fearing for her safety. Several of them, hoping for lightning to strike again, still troll disgustingly through on their lecherous rounds.

I watched months of this Jekyll and Hyde show turn into years. Beth became a fixture that every bartender in the place dealt with, but none as much as me, because she just wouldn't give up her insane crush. She would arrive coked to the tits, chattering away on all cylinders at once. Often she would bring in men she met elsewhere, or had picked up through work, and moodily prop the unsuspecting pigeons at the bar, taking my temperature to see if there wasn't just a whiff of hoped-for jealousy. She would pull me aside, drunk and crying, and demand to know if I found her attractive when we first met. It was mortifying to deal with, stomach-turning, and I felt horrible for her. I wanted to backhand her and tell her to wake up and stop being a goddamn doormat. It became confusing. As a bartender you can't tell people anything, but had I in fact become a friend through extended contact? Did I have some kind of moral obligation to this girl simply because she alighted on my bar and chose it to play out her tawdry dramas? The obvious answer, shouted in chorus by a number of my friends, was certainly not, her problems are hers. Still, inexplicably, I like Beth. She can be by turns undeniably clever, cattily funny, lively, and engaging. A financial analyst by profession, she is extremely well read and loves to talk about literature. When not in her cups and being depressive or manipulative, she is as charming a person as you'd want to be around. Then again, not only do I rarely see her sober, but I just happen to be the purveyor of the potions that transform her into an embarrassing monster. I've often found the most problematic people among the most engaging, however. At the same time that I have little patience with misconduct and invented melodrama, I also have trouble simply ruling a person off-limits because of a character flaw or two.

In a sense Beth is only symptomatic of a larger malaise, a two-way problem for me or, I should say, us behind the bar. Girls create a gigantic, perpetually churning conundrum. I've never had a girlfriend who didn't abjectly loathe what I do for a living, and who could blame them? I cannot offhand think of another job quite exactly like mine, where part of your job, it could be said, is actually flirting, in the sense that being a good bartender, among many other things, entails making all the customers feel welcome and included. That gets construed in many ways by many people. Everyone flirts, and flirting is lovely ego food for people, it's true. Many people flirt at work, too, it only stands to reason. Imagine, though, trying to get difficult work done while people are looped and coming on to you heavily. Having that be, in fact, an unspoken part of your job. It can be joltingly stimulating and uplifting; it can also be crushingly frustrating, perplexing, and frightening. Inarguably it fucks with you. People make you their plaything, their immediate goal, their object of lust for the night. That type of intensely focused personal attention can be a far more intoxicating elixir than anything I can pour. Even if you think you have your priorities straight, it can be treacherous terrain. It is equal opportunity, as well; my gay bartenders struggle as mightily with it as the straight ones do. In fact, there is a certain amount of implicit cross-pollination going on, wherein the straight bartenders must inevitably field the attentions of gay men and the gay bartenders have at times found themselves flummoxed by the ardent push of randy women. Recently George, a man who hasn't said boo to a woman since he was ten, pulled me aside wide-eyed to confess that there had been a particularly serpentine young lady dancing in the bar the night before, and he had awoken startled from a dream that night wherein he was, you know, *doing it* with her!

Having a proper balance of men and women in the bar is a crucial sign of the bar's health. Therefore, making women feel safe and not like they're being preyed on is partly the bartender's concern. As such, he becomes the touchstone, the safe guy for women to talk to. But there's frequently more than just that in play. What is it about being behind a bar pouring drinks that makes women who would never even look at you at a party, or in passing on the street, strike up conversations or simply start grabbing at you playfully in placing an order? What is it that then makes some of them stay all night, or return late, to take you home? Beth herself once said it's because bartenders have one of those well-regarded blue-collar professions, like firemen, that combine a certain flashy machismo with the familiar and welcoming: nonthreatening, dependable servitude. Who doesn't like a bartender, he gets you drunk?

I worked for a long while at the Odeon with this Irish bruiser of a guy named Tommy who had quite a history. His dad had been in prison for murder during Tommy's childhood in Hell's Kitchen. Tommy and his brother both had survived a decade-long drug habit, and Tommy himself had pulled a stint in prison for beating the hell out of some guy with a bottle. He was, nonetheless, a surprisingly decent fellow. He was very kind to me and had a keenly developed sense of humor that, although quietly cruel, was devoid of the scary overtones you might suspect from a 250-pound ex-felon who could crush your skull like a walnut. Well, almost devoid.

Tommy used to love to take advantage of the girls we called "bar rags," who hang out until after closing, at which point you, in principle, scrape them off the stool, drape them over your shoulder, and head home for some ethanol-fueled squalor. I'm no puritan myself; I can easily see the amateur thrill involved in that kind of *nostalgie de la boue,* but I also know just how it comes back to haunt you in the worst way behind the bar. You're the stationary one. People know where to find you, and they make your life grotesque. No one has to live with their mistakes like bartenders do. As a result, I have long adhered to a protective clause whereby I can't go home with anyone I meet at the bar. Tommy had no such qualms, and he was constantly pushing the envelope of salaciousness with these girls. It got so that he didn't even want to be bothered with taking them home anymore, he'd just have his boff there in the restaurant and send the girls reeling off in a cab. He would take them down to the women's room, where there was a divan of sorts, and return with this creepy wink-and-nod demeanor, while the girls hastily tried to pull themselves out of that casting couch kind of dishevelment. You see these things, late at night when the rules are all getting bent, and sometimes you don't know where to file them. Often the girls would return. Tommy would take them down to the office and hand me the proverbial Xeroxes he'd made of their coupling.

For women bartenders, it is in a sense worse, in that the slavering attention is more constant, but there are different factors at play. Male customers see a girl behind the bar and start hitting on her immediately, as well. But guys are as conditioned to being snubbed in that situation as the woman tending bar is conditioned to deliver a fishy look and walk away. Male barkeeps have to play it slightly differently, because if you put women down brusquely, even if they are being wildly inappropriate, you're seen as being some kind of bizarre heavy, the spoilsport, and they can turn on a dime and become slashingly unpleasant. I've always found it more advisable to laughingly play along, while keeping my distance clear. Sometimes that two feet of walnut between you and the customer feels like crucial insulation.

People have very little compunction, when you are servile to them, adopting outlandishly presumptive and rude courses of questioning that would draw shock in any normal social setting. It's as though, once on display, you are the assumed plaything. Men, taking in the fray of the full bar and translating that into dollar signs, will ask you outright how much you make in a night. Women have other interests in mind. It always begins very formulaically. They prod you first: "Do you have a girlfriend?" Then they probe further with either the direct "And do you cheat?" or the very slightly camouflaged "Are you faithful?" From there, with the increasing boldness that successive drinks produce, they can home in on you with a persistence and directness that makes you fear you might accidentally have wandered onto the set of a porn flick.

A couple of years ago I was working alone on a Wednesday night when a gaudy group squeezed through the door. The whole bar stopped and craned its collective neck for a moment before settling back into a murmur. There were five leggy young women, clad, despite it being midwinter, in what appeared to be some strategically draped handkerchiefs. They were surrounded by a protective phalanx of six gay men, with whom they were out tearing up the town. The assemblage blew in like a nor'easter, clearly already having been to an establishment or two. The alpha female among the girls was a particularly Valkyrian blonde who, it was immediately clear, was running the show. The boys she brought in were all buzzing around her, whispering little risqué asides and cackling maniacally. She called for shots right off, actually snapping her fingers. Smiling, I was reminded of the early Updike story "A&P," where the narrator, a stock boy with mouth agape, loses his job defending the blond apparition who comes strolling in a bikini through the supermarket where he works. Through the story he refers to her only as Queenie.

She was clinging to one of the men in particular, the pair of them casing the place and whispering, laughing to one another. Eager to get some trouble started right off, the two of them waved me over frantically. As I approached, Queenie grasped my forearm, leaning over the bar.

"We love your hair!" she gushed, pulling me in uncomfortably close.

"My hair?"

"Yeah! We love your hair and we love your ass!" I looked from her to him. The fellow watched on closely, grinning and nodding.

"I see. Thanks. What kind of shots would you like?" I asked.

"We think you have a really cute ass. Which of us would you prefer to think you have a really cute ass?"

Still eyeing them both, side to side, I took a deep breath and exhaled slowly. "Neither, actually. What is this, the Penthouse Forum? You want a drink or what?"

He abruptly reached around her and pulled her shirt up over her belly, showing a diamond stud pierced through her navel. "Yes, we'll have shots," he said brightly, "whatever you want to make. You wanna see her tits?"

"No, thank you." I laughed. "I've seen my share of those. My sisters all have them. You keep those things in their holsters, okay? What are you freaks drinking, please?"

I had to admit, as stupid as they were being, I was finding them amusing. They confided that Queenie and her girls were Rockettes. I asked, "You mean like as in Radio City Rockettes? I didn't know they still made those." I didn't believe them, never having seen a Rockette but assuming them to all look like chunky 1930s Busby Berkeley gals, over-the-hill actress types. They insisted they were, in fact, Rockettes, and their walkers insisted, too, so I didn't push it any further.

As the night got busier, I was dashing back and forth and ignoring them for the most part. Several guys in the bar tried angling their way into the group, cluelessly trying to sniff out which girl was with which guy. Queenie was getting more lit and brazen as the night went on, grabbing at me as I went by on my rounds and calling me over to try to embarrass me in front of her shrieking cohorts. I was relieved to be busy, and kept a smiling distance.

At one point I needed ice, and so I grabbed the buckets and dashed into the hallway to unlock the gallery door. I left that ajar and proceeded to unlock the liquor room door. Once inside, I heard the gallery door slam shut. Queenie strolled into the liquor room with a feral grin on her face. I put down the ice buckets and began, "Darling, you're not allowed back here . . ." when wordlessly she hooked her thumbs in her waistband and dropped her skirt and panties. She then pulled the straps off her shoulders and let her blouse fall, wriggling it down over her hips before stepping out of it and her sandals at the same time. In two neat moves—like a basketball player off the bench shedding tearaways—she is standing before me smirking, naked as a lima bean.

I stood for several moments like a dumbstruck child, riveted to my spot, before uttering flatly "Oh my." I couldn't help but gape. She was incredible looking, but that wasn't the whole of it; her presence was so bizarre and visceral, as if someone had just plopped an albino porpoise down in the dingy confines of the liquor room. She padded over to where I stood and, still without a word, reached down and began undoing my belt. My brain was reeling. Finally I snapped to and said, "No, no, no, this isn't going to happen," removing her hands and moving her gently away. She had remonstrations of her own, a very headstrong girl, shall we say. After a brief tussle I ended up ordering her to get dressed and come back into the bar and behave. I was so flustered that it wasn't until I had wandered back into the bar that I realized I'd just left a complete stranger, albeit one you could say I knew somewhat intimately, in my liquor room, with all the money and alcohol. I had to let myself back into the gallery and ask her to step out of the liquor room, whereupon I locked it back up and left her, now mad as a cottonmouth, to clothe herself in the empty gallery. Clicking the gallery door softly closed behind me, I paused, hidden in the dark hallway to the rest rooms, to collect myself a moment before reentering the bar. Her snarky friend in crime was waiting expectantly for me with a sly look on his face. "What were you two up to in there?" he shouted teasingly above the din, making the preschool shame-shame gesture with his index fingers. Queenie stomped out a few minutes later and made instantly for the door, without so much as a glance in my direction. In like a lamb . . .

∘   ∘   ∘

The bar begins filling with the later crowd, couples taking tables and the first spray of tomcats headed out for the night, better dressed and looking fresher than those who came directly from work. With every seat taken, there are still groups of five and six pushing in, and I'm seeing the shift in the customers like watching ominous clouds rolling in. I steel myself with my longtime mantra for pulling myself through the weeds: "Set 'em up, knock 'em down, set 'em up, knock 'em down . . ." I'm taking orders as quickly as I can, keeping sets of three and no more in my head at once, so as not to lose any and have to ask again. I'm trying to make eye contact, a quick nod to acknowledge those I can't get to yet, but it's no longer a well-mannered crowd. Every time I look at someone, they begin blabbering their order or, if they're down the bar, waving the ubiquitous twenty, behavior that always leaves me just shy of winging an ashtray at the offending rube.

I'm kicked into hyperefficient mode now: head down, no smiles, no quarter, passing over people who flag me but don't have their orders together, delivering drinks without flourish, making change curtly. Pretty soon I've reached critical mass. I want to be pleasant to people who are pleasant, or whose faces at least register empathy for my predicament, but in the end I can't even do that. It all breaks down at once. I'm tripping around on the rubber hex mat like a wounded animal, grabbing at glassware and bottles, staring dumbly at half-filled orders I've iced up on the station shelf but can't now remember. Unattached arms poke imploringly at my peripheral vision, several waving urgently or snapping their fingers. Searching frantically for a Champagne flute I know I just took down, I become so enraged by the loss of the ten seconds it takes to locate it that upon finding it, I smash it into bits against the sink. I'm bellowing curses that I hope are drowned out by the blaring music. It's as though I'm in one of those excruciating dreams, where even as I become mired in quicksand and my actions slow to a maddening crawl, those around me cavort monstrously unaware, their faces frozen in hideous ricti, all horsey teeth and corpulent lips agape in piercing laughter.

As soon as there's a lull I bolt from behind the bar to reclaim some glassware. At the nearest table are five art scenesters who have been there most of the night, the whiff of clove smokes hanging over them. I begin clearing the table and notice several Champagne flutes filled with red wine. I'm thinking, What are these dorky kids up to, splitting up glasses of wine? Then I notice several wine bottles lying on their sides under the table, when no one has purchased any wine by the bottle yet tonight. I shift to my avuncular scolding voice: "Hey, look, you guys can't just bring your own wine in here and expect to—" Looking closer, I see the wine bottles are, in fact, the type of merlot I serve. I don't get it. The whole table is actively, nervously trying to ignore me. Then like a bus it hits me: the Champagne flutes are kept at the end of the glassware shelf, closest to them, and the merlot is kept just below, on the back bar, the closest wine to the customers. They reached over the bar while I was crazed in the weeds and filched a mess of booty, and this is the remainders. The entire night seems to bend in on me and I go off like a Roman candle. I begin hurling curses at the top of my lungs. The girls look up, terrified, but the three boys increase their volume, trying to buy some time with forced ennui. I'm yelling, "How fucking *dare* you come into my bar and steal from me, you art-worm cocksuckers?!" While customers at other tables look up, wide-eyed at my insta-rage, this crew goes on with their strained conversation, feigning nonchalance. Gnashing my teeth now, I lean in and sweep the tabletop with my forearm: candles, ashtrays, and wine all raining down together. The kid closest to me, with a blondish fall of bangs and tiny round wire rims, turns to face me. He takes an exaggerated drag of his cigarette and says contemptuously, "You need to fucking chill out, man," then blows the smoke in my face.

Unwise of him. I don't even think, I just explode. Snatching his hair up in a big handful, I yank him off his stool and begin dragging him through the bar. He lets out a muffled howl and flails at my hands and arms, but his feet are trailing behind him and he can't stand up. His friends all leap up from the table and begin pulling at me, but I'm not letting go for anything now. The whole improbable cortège lurches toward the door like an indecisive mastodon. Other customers are jumping up from their stools as we push through, some of them hooting and cheering. One of the girls in the party is crying, fumbling with a wad of money, trying to push some twenties at me. I shriek that I don't want her fucking money. Oblivious to the cause of the fracas, the other customers break into applause as I heave the assemblage through the door. One group of regulars follows outside to scream at the retreating kids, "We hate you! Stay out of here!"

After throwing them out, literally—something I've never done before—I'm trembling and clammy. People are cheering and clapping me on the back, which only makes me feel worse. These kids ripped me off, true, and so it could be argued that I was justified. But I know, in a grand-tally-in-the-sky way, that I wasn't. Granted, these kids were in their twenties and knew they were in the wrong, but I've done tons of stuff in my life for which I should have had my ass kicked and didn't. Equally, I've dealt far more humanely with far worse infractions; over the years I've had I don't even know how many drunks trying to pick fights with me. I've had drinks thrown in my face, and I've always made a point of talking down trouble without resorting to violence. Part of that is just common sense: I'm a skinny guy and I know if I start going off on customers, even ones who are egregiously out of line, someone's going to break my nose, and then it doesn't matter who was wrong or right. Clearly, my adrenaline was running from being so busy and it amped my outrage. I am shocked, though, and a little scared by my own reaction. I know in the pit of my stomach that I am somehow partly responsible. I like to think I'm all-seeing and holding down the whole fort under siege, but in fact these kids snaked the vino right out from under my nose while I was lathered.

I begin picking up the broken glasses and empty bottles, moving slowly between the tables, feeling idiotic and gripped with remorse. Several customers pitch in and help me, a couple of them patting me on the back or pounding me on the bicep, saying "Way to go, man!"

which only increases my shame. There's one good thing about my job at times like this, when you really need a drink: take your pick.

∘   ∘   ∘

Stealing, by customers or by staff, is the great unspoken in this business. Even though it's all around us, the paranoia runs so deep that it's as though giving voice to it would bring down scrutiny on yourself. It's considered you simply do it and everyone does or has, and no one asks and no one tells. It's odd how, in contrast, sex is always bandied about on the floor. I knew some of the most astoundingly intimate details of the sex lives of the people I worked with, both at the Odeon and at Kin Khao. But try to start a discussion about stealing in a restaurant and you'll feel the cold silence of the tomb. It's the only truly dirty topic. If people are willing to talk about it, it's always in the past—what I did at this place I worked at in the 1980s—and they always try to justify it, as I have, as though they were in fact due this money because of mistreatment or fiscal meanness on the part of the owner or manager. Therefore, instead of quitting and looking for a better-paying job with a restaurant that treats its staff squarely, they were entitled to pocket what they did.

The single thing owners of bars and restaurants fear the most is their employees stealing from them. Staff pilfering, unchecked, can wipe a place out without the owner ever knowing why. It's a maddeningly tough problem to deal with because it goes on virtually everywhere. I sincerely doubt there is a single restaurant or bar in New York, or anywhere else, that doesn't deal with it, knowingly or not. It can be impossible to stop and, in certain circumstances, inadvisable to stop, as strange as that may sound. In my case, as I've mentioned, I hire mostly only friends of mine or people I know fairly well through friends. Since I've worked for so many years in restaurants in this city, I still draw from a stable of people I know and have worked with for years, people I've observed working before I was the boss, and, in many cases, people I recruited and trained in those other restaurants. That is, admittedly, an unheard-of luxury for most managers. In my case, then, even if I suspect one of my employees of snaking cash somehow, I rely on the basic tenet of our co-employment and our friendship to keep it in check. I know my guys take good care of the place when I'm not around. In turn, my policy about comps—that is, the offering of a free round to a customer whom one feels merits it—is open-ended. Every bartender knows he may comp whomever he likes, with the understanding that he uses his judgment and writes down every comp meticulously, so that I can factor it into my liquor cost. Normally a customer will then tip on the free round, often generously, and the bartender thus makes out a bit better at the house's expense. Comping sets up a perilous gray area for both the house and the bartenders, distinguishing what is stealing from what is a thoughtful and perhaps far-reaching nod to the type of customer you both would like to return. It becomes a big problem in many bars that try to forbid it, resulting in headaches for the managers and unnecessary firing of otherwise solid employees. Every bartender is going to comp a few people, you just can't expect otherwise. A friend comes in, or you begin talking to a couple who seems cool, there's a cute girl or guy, whatever the case, in the normal course of the night it's going to come up. Allowing the bartenders to comp is my way of acknowledging the realities of the job, while showing them I have confidence in their judgment and their honesty. That kind of thing, I know from experience, goes further toward safeguarding the till than all the expensive, laborious high-tech measures you can come up with.

The buyback is also a complex tango between bartender and patron. Many people are under the impression that the buyback, or what we call a comp, is something the house is obligated to offer every third round. Irritated louts numbering in the dozens have told me as much. There must be a certain kind of bar, of the fraternity pub ilk, where this is an ironclad rule. There is no such transparency in New York. The comp is a bestowing of approval on the part of the bar-keep, a beneficent nod. As such, it's a strangely powerful tool to have at your disposal. Such a trivial thing, but people positively glow when you comp them a drink. Even I love being comped when I go out, the more so because I understand what it means and never push for it. People often ask about my criteria for comping a customer, and I can't really nail it down exactly. The only hard-and-fast rule I have is that I will never, ever comp anyone who asks in any way for a free drink. People somehow think that behaving in a manner that broadly illustrates their parasitical shamelessness is going to get them the float, in that squeaky wheel manner by which New Yorkers are constantly rewarded. I refuse to buy into it. If you're demanding free drinks, you can order twenty rounds and you're paying every penny. Whom I do end up comping is another matter. I like to comp people a round when they are pleasant and don't expect it. If you seem like someone I'd like to have back in the bar, and you're drinking several rounds, it might happen. I feel like, if it isn't a pleasant surprise to the people being offered the round, it's not worth the gesture. (Strangely enough, the Giuliani administration outlawed buybacks in New York, for reasons I never could quite get clear, putting yet another laugh-ably unenforceable law on the books.)

Outlawing comps is the kind of thing management widgets with their eye only on the bottom line think is being "proactive." We've all dealt with the specimen, wet still from Cornell's Hotel and Restaurant Management Program, no doubt, or some similarly weighty, costly, and ultimately worthless mill of hospitality industry know-how. I feel far worse for these suckers than I do the hundreds of hopefuls who leave off résumés attesting to having passed through an "accredited" bartending school. You can't convince me that spending your parents' money to attend an Ivy League college for four years is well rewarded by your exiting with a degree in how to work in a restaurant. Still worse, once inserted in your chosen profession, ready to kick ass and take names, you will find yourself the laughingstock of the house. I've seen them come, I've seen them cry, I've watched them go, one after the next.

An old boss of mine at Kin Khao, a Machiavellian Chinese woman whose mother ran a Chinese restaurant in Tokyo, once told me her mother's aphorism regarding employees stealing: "Sometime the cat have to close one eye to the mouse." To this day I have no clear idea what she meant. She said this while winking at me after a surprise raid on my till in the middle of the shift to see if I was stealing. Having found everything on the up-and-up, she was delighted and lauded my honesty and hard work. She was right to laud my hard work, which over the several years she paid me next to nothing helped make her a millionaire, but she clearly also knew I was poaching occasionally, even though she never caught me at it.

There are dozens of ways to steal, from the elementary to the Byzantine, and one can switch in midstream to outfox pretty much anything the management can throw at you in the way of barriers. Some bars go with video cameras, some try to monitor the pours through computerized portioners, others saddle the managers with counting empties and taking note of every level on every bottle and jibing that with the night's till and then jibing that with the weekly inventories to determine cost-to-profit ratios. Another common method in New York is to pay professional spotters, who come in and pretend to be normal customers while clocking every transaction and later providing a detailed written report of everything they saw.

Enormous headaches, all of which cost a ton and can be slipped around neatly by anyone adroit enough to understand what it is they're doing every night.

If someone has a mind to steal, they're going to do it, even if they're making amazing tips already. I've talked to bartenders who've told me of ruses that border on the slapstick. One guy said in his place the house made them save all empties in a box behind the bar and matched those to its inventory sheet. To skirt this, the bartenders used to bring in their own bottles of vodka, which they would pour and charge for, pocketing both the profit and the empty bottles so that the house missed nothing. There are so many ways to steal, and, like magic tricks, when you know them each one seems obvious, detectable and preventable in and of itself, but damming up all the conceivable leaks at once becomes nearly impossible. The bigger the enterprise, the greater the risk.

To that end, I've often thought the only way you could have a bar that's completely free of pilfering is to have a tiny place, open maybe three or four nights a week, and be the only bartender. It's not the worst idea in the world. If you made all the tips and all the profits, you could do as well as you might in any number of other professions. It would be a hell of a lot of work, though, and you'd have to be an unusually staminal type to endure it week in and week out. Still, I've seen people work a lot harder for far less. In Soho there's a matchbox of a shop on Sullivan Street called Melampo, run by an engaging Florentine named Allessandro. He was for many years a cook and then chef at a number of high-end Italian restaurants uptown, knows the business from the ground up. Then a decade or more ago he decided to dump it all and go back to the ground. He makes only panini, Italian sandwiches, in his vest-pocket-size shop. The sandwiches are supernal, using top ingredients, many of his own fabrication, like mozzarella and focaccia he makes every morning, and piled so generously that one can easily feed two people. They are expensive and to get one you stand patiently on line. If you step out of place, try to jump the line, or modify the sandwiches as he has listed them, he will bark at you, for now he is in his own little domain and, after a lifetime of doing what others demanded of him, he now does, impeccably, only what he wants. He never stints and never hurries, and he seems very content to be who he is and where he is. A couple of times a year he closes the shop for a week or three and takes a nice vacation.

Perhaps when I've made my way around the world and worn myself out, I'll come back to New York and open the bar equivalent of Melampo, just six seats, and the music every night will be someone quietly playing an instrument in a corner, one night the French horn or bagpipes, the next night the cello or harpsichord. Only a select few drinks will be served, and they will take damnably long to prepare, but each one will be made with the freshest ingredients and the utmost care, and served in Austrian crystal glasses. They will, of course, be insultingly expensive, but you'll be free to smash the glass in the fireplace when you've finished. The door policy will be so exclusive that if you want to come in, you absolutely cannot. Only people wandering in by accident, or those with no wish to be there whatsoever, will be allowed to sit and drink. Payment will be accepted, I'm afraid, in euros only.

CHAPTER IV

Distant Thunder

It's half-past five in the morning. In my room the pearlescent blue-gray peering in through the withered ivy covering the window makes their shoots and tendrils seem like gnarled fingers. The murmur of the past night still rings in my ears, and I'm agitated, racing. Lying down on the floor to pull my boots off, I close my eyes momentarily and feel the room spin about me, not from drink, but from the unfamiliarity of being sessile after so many hours in motion. That ephemeral predawn light still rivets me with its spooky neitherness, and I lie and watch the rain fall in the backyards and over the steeple of St. Peter's Episcopal, unable to pull the blinds yet. The pale-orange glow of that church's clock face nudgingly reminds me of the strange hour, just as its clamorously reproachful bells will, should I be caught dozing still by noon, sound me awake by tolling somewhere between three and twenty-five times, as is their wont.

Morning comes in a very different way for bartenders. Most nights I find myself shambling home in that steely prematinal light, completely wrung out from the night's labors, but still wired from the shift. Though my apartment has only one window, it's huge, and my bed is right up against it. I've had to install two different shades, an opaque blind behind a canvas sailcloth curtain, to contain the ebullience of the light come midmorning, when I'm deep into my best slumber. It's still not enough. I awaken several times during the morning, and finally get up out of guilt after something between five to seven hours of sleep. Even after more than a decade of tending bar, and countless efforts at justifying to myself that my nocturnal work habits demand that I sleep in the daytime, I still have a terrible time in the mornings. Subconsciously, while I'm trying to sleep, I'm gauging how late it's getting. Sleeping until eleven or so, when I've had, say, six hours of sleep, seems bad enough. The world has been up for hours, I'm the last one to be able to have breakfast. At eight hours of sleep, though, it's one in the afternoon. Breakfast is long gone and most people are more than halfway through their workday. I realize intellectually that a nine-to-five schedule has nothing to do with me, but for some reason it has always affected me adversely to live counter to the normal clock of society. Some bartenders I know have no problem with this and sleep happily until two or three. Others have it worse than I do. Typically it has a lot to do with whether you're just tending bar or are trying to do something besides, like acting or going to school.

My feet hit the floor, throbbing still from standing for so long last night, and nerve spasms jangle through them and up my calves. The ball joints at my hips feel as though they've been forced out of their sockets in my pelvis. My mouth is dry, my lower back aches, and I can't see straight. Trying to walk to the bathroom, I veer sideways and clip my hip on the edge of my desk. Muttering curses, I lurch on and, overcompensating, veer flat into the hallway wall. I'm suffering what I call my nonalcoholic hangover: fuzzy and blasted without having had anything to drink, just from the sheer brutality of the shifts, the smoke, and the lack of sleep.

It's only nine, and I need more sleep, so I gobble a glass of water and let the blinds down again to drift off fitfully, my slumber fraught with roiling dreams where I'm stuck alone in the weeds, ashtrays brimming, customers demanding fictional drinks I've never heard of. The Stranglers' "Nice and Sleazy Does It," stuck in my head from my prior night's shift, is churning over and over through the dream until I'm nauseous with it. Finally at eleven-thirty, after six hours of sleep, I can't take it anymore and open the blinds again to let in some of the world. It's raining still, so I prop myself on the pillows and watch the freezing rain pelting the rooftops. It calms me far more than my crowded slumber was doing. I get up and take a broiling shower. As the water hits my head I smell an intense surge of cigarette smoke streaming out of my hair.

Because of my diurnal paranoia about being left behind by society, I have to get out into the day as quickly as possible. I have, over the years, culled a network of restaurants and cafés that serve breakfast, or breakfastlike fare, late into the afternoon. For me, the farther these places are from my apartment the better. I like to walk, to shake off the stiffness in my calves and hamstrings from standing all the night before, and to feel like I'm taking in the air, the day, the sunlight, everything I'm missing in my vampiric work mode. Often I've quite a lot to do from the moment I get up; I'm behind, so to speak, before I'm even awake. Kegs and cases are arriving at work, waiting to be sorted and put away, suppliers and salespeople have to be called. The answering machine is filling up with people wanting to have parties, people who left their credit cards last night while looped.

I don't care, or I can't care yet. I've got to go somewhere, flakes of sleep still in my eyes, to shake off the night before. I feel like I keep my sanity in this job for a few simple reasons, even while I routinely see other people lose theirs and implode after just a few months. One is that I don't drink very much, and specifically don't drink very much behind the bar. Another is that I take a certain amount of pride in what I do. A very important third is that, even if I'm working four or five days straight, a normal workweek for most people but an unreasonably intense one for a bartender, I break up that hamster-on-a-treadmill feeling by insisting on doing one indulgent thing for myself every day. I realize that reeks of some kind of daily affirmation from the *Ladies' Home Journal*, but there it is. Even if I've only one hour, I'll walk down to the Village or Soho to have coffee specifically at the café where they have the currant buttermilk scones that I crave and that I've been thinking about for two days straight. Just that can be enough to stave off the encroachment of the bar. Given two or three hours, I love to ride my bike across town, up through Central Park and over to 91st and York, where there's another café, frequented only by the Upper East Side ladies who lunch or, in their absence, the black or Hispanic nannies who push their power offspring around in prams during the day. I always get funny looks in those parts, scowls of disapproval and suspicion for the guy with the long hair and five-day stubble who appears to have no particular midday engagement. It's all right, I'm used to it, and I'm only there for the banana chocolate chip muffins and the sticky buns. In the better weather I'll get them in a sack and zig over to Carl Schurz Park on the East River to flop on a bench overlooking the bucolic view across the tip of Roosevelt Island, where the tiny figures fishing make it look like the prow of the Île de la Cité, only without the willows grazing the water. Sipping coffee and pulling pieces of pastry apart with my fingers, the brittleness of my aching joints makes me feel perfectly in step with the old men and women perched resignedly about me like ailing birds. With the sun on my face and the salt air blowing up the East River, I'll feel my morning fog slowly clearing in succinct stages, like a glacial melt, until the day is fully upon me.

°   °   °

Once when I went to see a doctor seeking a nostrum for a flu I couldn't seem to shake, he looked me over and then began asking the usual questions. When he got to what I do for a living, I told him and he looked up again quickly, his interest piqued for some reason. His gaze lingered on me for a moment and he wrote something down. "You don't drink much, I'm guessing," he tossed off, still writing.

Perplexed, I cocked my head, trying to figure out what he was after. "I do drink, actually, yeah. I mean, I'm very into wine, I collect it and whatnot."

He smiled and put down his pad. "But I mean, you don't *drink*. I've noticed there seem to be only two kinds of bartenders, you know what I'm saying?" I did, and we took it no further. I've known and worked with a lot of bartenders, quite a few of whom have been through AA, and I've seen plenty of examples of how people get caught up in the worst way in the Lush Life. Although I may witness more than most people do the beneficial aspects of having a drink— unwinding at day's end with your lover over a glass or two, leaving the scrum behind and communing with friends while putting an edge on your appetite—I also see the walking wounded that alcohol produces. I openly acknowledge my role in what I consider nothing less than legalized drug dealing, in that alcohol is a drug and I make my living selling it. I had to long ago separate myself from making judgment calls on people's proclivities in the bar, in all except the most openly inebriated customers. Obviously, if someone is clearly drunk or is acting like an ass and annoying people, they get cut off and sent out. That's the law and it's also just common business sense. But there's an enormous gray area between that couple flirting over a glass or two of wine and the guy hanging around the lamp pole on the corner. Many people who have a drinking problem hold their liquor like camels; they have acclimated their bodies to taking in so much—what amounts to poison, really, in the way the liver processes it—that they can drink shocking amounts of alcohol without even slurring. I've served dozens and dozens of functioning alcoholics, many of whom seem to literally come into their own—sharpen up, become funnier, livelier, and more focused—only after imbibing enough vodka to send me to the emergency room. I say vodka because I've noticed with the lifers it's almost invariably vodka in some form. They've reduced the work part of it, the ingestion, to its essential elements, the path of greatest efficiency. But with these people, unless you've been watching their patterns for a long while, you may have little idea there's a problem. It's like that old commercial for hair color: Only your hairdresser knows for sure. Only your bartender knows that after five double vodkas, even though you're holding forth animatedly without missing a beat—in fact, *because* you're holding forth animatedly and not thrashing about on the floor like any normal human would be—you've got a problem.

I long ago, however, made up my mind about this: your problem is not my problem. No one is going to tell someone to stop and not offend them. I get cursed out nearly every time I cut someone off who's lurching about drunk. Embarrassing someone who is a functioning alcoholic is going to be ineffectual and lead to nasty scenes. People will stop, as with anything, only when they're motivated to stop of their own accord. Until then, it's their call. This may be tricky plumbing, ethically, but I have no way to gauge everyone's story, nor do I wish to. You ask for a drink, you pay for a drink, you get a drink.

A few weeks ago I went out for a friend's birthday and, over the course of the evening, ended up drinking a lot. Champagne for starters, then a few magnums of red wine with steaks, a blast of Underberg and then a couple of Ardbeg Scotches with cigars. So seldom do I drink this way anymore that I was actually surprised by the end of the night to find myself undeniably drunk. It's been a long time since I've felt the full press of the stupefaction I dole out every night. I forget how powerful alcohol is, and how far-reaching its effect. The entire next day my whole body felt poisoned. I couldn't get enough water, but also couldn't quite pee fully. I had been smart enough to gobble three aspirin and drain several pints of water before turning in for five hours, so my head, although compromised, was relatively intact. But my stomach was churning and fragile and my mouth was an evil vale, even after brushing my teeth twice. To do this more than once a year, I cannot fathom. That I see people in my bar nightly who must wake up like this five days a week leaves me in awe of the human capacity for endurance and stupidity combined.

Inasmuch as my job is basically twofold, to sell liquor and, largely through that, to facilitate the kind of camaraderie and openness between patrons that gives the bar its energy and personality, it could be argued that I am indirectly both a drug dealer and a pimp, though I don't suppose that analogy would make my mother happy to consider. It's a bizarre thing, I reflect routinely, to have as your work something that consumes you with busyness while everyone around you is, to a greater or lesser degree, getting shitfaced. But I have always found it important to acknowledge the duality of what I do; amid the highbrow pomp and storied history of bartending, the culinary aspect of mixology, the salubriousness of social exchange that goes on in the bar, there is always a dark flip side to the commerce of what is the most common and effective tool for people to alter their consciousness, to good or bad purpose. In truth, I go further than simply acknowledging this binary phenomenon of my job; in a type of cruel curiosity afforded me by my open concealment behind the bar, I enjoy the seedy display in front of it every bit as much as the friendliness and hail-fellow-well-met aspect of it. When bad behavior rears its ugly head, it can sometimes be far more interesting than the twelve conversations about rents in Manhattan you've had that night.

It's tremendously tempting, at times, to join in the party. After watching enough other people getting hammered and leaving their inhibitions behind, it can start to seem pretty normal. What begins with doing shots bought for you by "admiring" customers spirals quickly into coke in the bathrooms, blowjobs in the liquor room, and so on. I've seen many bartenders implode from becoming star players in the game they were meant to be refereeing. My friend René is an extremely successful sommelier in town, a brilliant, hysterically funny tornado of a man. I first met him when he was working at a small, precious restaurant noted for the beautiful bar he ran there. His irrepressible charisma, opinionated mastery of wine, and wild enthusiasm drove his tiny bar to secret cult status, and doting customers would leave him tips so outrageous I'll not bother to numerate them, so as to not be accused of fabrication. He could be a difficult character, thorny and bombastic, but I latched onto him as a friend in part because I'd never met anyone whose fervor for food and wine so neatly matched my own. We had head-to-head, finger-jabbing, spit-flying debates over the minutest bits of wine and food lore. I still recall bitterly the time I misspoke and referred to a Pomerol as a Pommard; he gloated about it for two years afterward. He loved to go out, and his appetites in all directions were near mythical. He wanted to taste everything on a menu and wouldn't flinch at a three-hundred-dollar wine, nor at the second or third bottle, nor a dessert bottle before cigars, nor the two vintage Calvados or grappas to follow. Invariably, on these blurry bacchanalian nights out, by the time I was near to throwing up or passing out, he was just primed to begin his rounds of gay bars on the Lower East Side, to scare up some coke and hook whatever rough trade happened to be swimming by. His stamina was astounding, though his mood swings were wild. When he was sober he became bitter and ornery, lashing out at friends over perceived slights. When lit, though, he literally roared with a canny, burning wit that was one of the most magnificent, horrific displays of humanity I've ever beheld. Sadly for René, the trade got a little too rough one night. With no idea where he'd been or what had happened, he was found by the police off F.D.R. Drive by the East River one morning, naked, bound, and beaten to a pulp, with a mélange of drugs and alcohol kicking through him that were probably the only thing tethering him to life. It could never be said that René did anything halfway, even bottoming out.

René is only one of the many examples I've seen of people getting bitten by this line of work. It's too breezy, the money's all cash, the people who work it are typically young and unfettered, there's booze for the taking at the end of every grueling shift and routinely drugs within asking distance. Unless you've got some kind of phenomenal personal discipline, especially when you're young and first step on, the temptations are Faustian. Of course, the job is so good in its way that even those laid low by it often return. René was in AA for years and now is contentedly back humiliating wine salesmen and oiling up diners at one of the city's most buzzing eateries. My bartender George hasn't touched an intoxicant in well over a decade, long enough that he loves to recount stories like how, after torching with a lit cigarette the sofa he had fallen asleep on while nodding on heroin, he was extraordinarily put out at his friend, whose apartment he was in, for having roused him during an excellent high by pounding on him to put out the fire.

o   o   o

Early on tonight I received a lovely compliment. A taciturn, bookwormy fellow who comes in every other week or so but has never engaged me other than to icily order a Manhattan, up, was one of the first customers through the door. With his unwavering brittleness he ordered his usual round. Though he's not in the least a likable guy, I have an automatically prejudiced respect for people who order certain drinks. The Manhattan and the Negroni are two of my favorites and, because on the rare occasion I myself imbibe a mixed drink it's always one or the other of these, I'm very particular in my attention to each. The Manhattan I prefer to make only up, in a cocktail or Martini glass, adding a couple of cubes later if it gets too warm. It works beautifully with any number of bourbons, but I love George Dickel No. 12 Reserve Tennessee Whisky better than almost any of the lot. I've taken to using a number of different vermouths, as well as substituting different Italian amari for deeper, stronger versions of the drink, but the quintessential vermouth for this drink is the Antica Formula from Carpano, a rare bird not easy to find but worth seeking out. Its strong aromatics almost negate the need for the bitters. For the cherries, which many Manhattanphiles wave off because of the specter of the formaldehyde-preserved, red-dye jobs most bars go with, I take preserved black cherries from the Union Square green market and soak them in a bottle of Maker's Mark in a big plastic Tupperware container I keep in the fridge. Two of these, along with two teaspoons of the nectar in which they bathe, go into each glass. They aren't terribly pretty after maceration, but they add rather than detract from the drink. Finally, I like to give the finished drink what I call an in-and-out twist of lemon, where I twist the zest above the drink to slick its surface with citrus oil, dip it, and then throw the twist away, imparting just an added whiff of depth to the nose. All of the preparation and frou-frou are as nothing to the proper proportions of bourbon to vermouth, of course, but that is a question of taste and practice. On his way out, after a second one, the curmudgeon filed by the bar and, with begrudging embarrassment, uttered, "You make the best Manhattan . . . well, in Manhattan!" and quickly swept out the door.

Though I love the occasional acknowledgment of my competence and take a great deal of pride in my skills behind the bar, I also realize that bartending prowess, like any other kind, exists on many levels. Those skills, moreover, taken in sum, are made up of so many intangibles that it would be nearly impossible to say whether I'm a better or worse bartender than I was ten years ago. Part of what contributes to a great bartender is simply the sound judgment that comes of experience. Arguably I have more of that now, but what of humor, patience, humility, and kindliness? Those certainly all play their part in the makeup of an excellent barkeep, and it would be my informed guess that, through nightly taxation, I draw from a lower reserve of those qualities than I did a decade ago. If I'm in a surly mood, or am being pushed too hard by the crowd, or just plain don't like someone, I can fall prey to indifference. I'm aware that there are plenty of bartenders out there who make my vision of professionalism look like chump change.

I've been reading quite a bit lately about these new and very hyped "bar chefs," as they prefer to be called. Resplendent in full suits and bow ties and cuff links, they fashion themselves not as lowly drink-slingers but as artists, deeply intuitive interpreters of the liquid medium. Most are located in the newer hotel bars, the current locus of those on the prowl. Their drinks are extraordinarily complex and bruisingly expensive, but that only makes sense given that their bars are often busy hybrids of a laboratory and a professional kitchen. Decanters of every size and color embellish their back bars, full of beguiling potions they've rigged up in conjunction with the kitchen of whatever restaurant they're serving: fresh pomegranate juice, passion fruit nectar, uglifruit and star anise–soaked grappas, infusions of every stripe. One guy begins an intriguing-sounding rum drink by sending fresh-cut sugarcane back to the kitchen to be ground through a special machine to juice it. That's pretty impressive, I have to say. It's the kind of thing that makes me jealous of those with access to a kitchen, much less a sugarcane juicer.

I can acknowledge the lift one gets when whim takes you down a path that leads to something delicious and strangers confer upon you the status of the omniscient lord and creator of all things bibulous. I love the attention I get when I pick up some rosemary or blood oranges at the market and subject my early customers to a self-indulgent free-for-all using them as primary ingredients and building outward. Occasionally I'll concoct something really great, too, though on the off-chance that happens I'll seldom be able to remember it accurately the next time those same customers come in, and certainly won't have the blood oranges or cilantro or candied lemons again. The bigger problem is that more frequently these whims just clank off the rim. I remember when we opened Kin Khao, my boss wanted us to come up with some kind of signature Thai cocktail that would become our staple. No problem. Along with the willing kitchen staff we went through every kind of seasoning used in Thai cooking, infusing vodka with galangal ginger, lemon grass, bird-of-paradise peppers, kaffir lime leaves, lychee nuts, mangoes, papayas, the list went on. Each infusion seemed to open up thrilling vistas of the exotic drinks we would be fashioning from them. The sadly unforeseen reality was the uniform yuckiness of those craftily conceived elixirs. What we got in exchange for our envelope-shredding experimentation was many, many gallons of wasted vodka. Nothing seemed to work out very well. At best they were inexplicably bland.

For flavors as intense as the peppers, galangal, and kaffir lime leaves, we were flummoxed that they gave up nothing, not even an aroma, to the vodka. Others were outright unpalatable. The mango and papaya both got mushy and tasted faintly rotten, the lemon grass tasted exactly the way Lemon Pledge furniture polish smells. In time the chef had the keen idea to use regular ginger and roast it before infusing. This made all the difference and led to a pungent brew that became, along with the pineapple that worked out estimably, the linchpin of the bar.

So I certainly understand how gratifying it must be for the bow tie–sporting maestro when the world swoons over his "Martini" of fresh starfruit purée and cachacas with a pastis and fresh vanilla bean foam daubed over the top. The problem arrives, of course, when you actually have to drink the result of all this frippery. When it comes right down to it, who really wants a basil-cumin Mojito rimmed with powdered rose petals and flecked with 18-karat gold flakes at the end of a long, tough day? Who is going to find it more satisfying to fork fifteen or twenty dollars over to some imperious fop to watch him cobble together a crème-brûlée and burnt almond "Gimlet" drizzled with lingonberry essence than to sidle up to the faithfully smoky succor of a bourbon on the rocks or the clean sear of a Martini? Well, some people, certainly; I'll admit it's attractive on a certain level, like watching that TV show where the retiree shows you how to paint charming landscapes in three simple steps, fascinatingly grotesque. But as a subjective drinker, I know the more you mess with it, the less anyone's going to want to drink it.

It's interesting that these showmen, cockteliers, bibularians, whatever they prefer, have their antecedents in hotel bars, also. Generations before Tom Cruise was ever induced to "flair," as the dubious practice of tossing bottles around like a Benihana chef has come to be termed, there was an entire circuit of entertainer/bartenders who traveled around the most famous hotels both here and in Europe through the latter half of the nineteenth century. Inventing drinks that allowed them to stage acrobatic displays whose pedigrees lay more in sleight-of-hand than mixology, some of these bar troubadours made enormous wages in tips and traveled from coast to coast in style and renown. One who gathered a rage following was the purveyor of the Blue Blazer, a flaming concoction he would dramatically mix by tossing it horizontally from cup to cup held at arm's length, directly before the face of the awed customer.

For me, the most accurate gauge of a bartender's competence is how he or she fields what one would consider the simplest of drinks, the Martini. The Martini is to bartenders what the omelette is to chefs: the starting point, as it were, the deceptively simple blank slate on which one simultaneously silences and dazzles all comers with originality, deftness, perfection. How can anyone who works as a barkeep not be able to make a great Martini? This is a drink that, for all practical considerations, consists of one ingredient. It's like pouring a bad glass of tap water. Despite that, I've found—and I'm not alone in this, if the grousing of my routinely grateful clientele is to be believed—that getting a decent version of the drink in this town can be a 50/50 proposition at best. In New York City, for heaven's sake, where you would assume that out of simple urban pride a bartender could no sooner turn out a limp Martini than a Philadelphian grill man would make a lame cheese steak or a Seattlite barista would front you a bitter latté. What's the problem here?

(As an aside I'll clarify that it's not even worth considering for the parameters of this discussion any of the recent upstart pretenses of Martinis, inane candy-flavored concoctions catering to the post-teen drinker looking to hone her dangerously adult edge by imbibing some fortified Kool-Aid out of a stemmed glass. These abominations, encompassing every fruit and spice and sweetened goo on five continents, are eagerly pushed by the places that serve them because their economics are not to be argued with. A Martini glass holds roughly half what a highball or rocks glass does, in normal circumstances. If you have drinkers seeking the affectation of sanguine urbanity they have been conditioned to believe a cocktail glass bestows on whatever it holds, and are willing to shell out ten or twelve bucks for a little vodka mixed with a lot of fruit juice, in seven-ounce portions, well, that's a win-win scenario for the bar, to be certain. The only loss is that of the establishment's pride, and that doesn't show up on the ledger sheet. I've noticed that the spate of apple Martinis, chocolate Martinis, passionfruit and vanilla Martinis has so broadened the spectrum that even chefs have jumped on the perilously overloaded Martini bandwagon. In the current wave, guacamole, ceviches of various types, mousses heaped with caviar, shrimp cocktail, and steak tartare all lay tenuous claim to the suffix "Martini" by virtue of being shoehorned into a stemmed cocktail glass. I suspect it won't be long before one can hopscotch through an entire seven-course Martini meal, from apéritif to dessert. A Martini, I feel sadly compelled to disambiguate, consists of either gin or, begrudgingly, vodka, with its accompanying dance partner, vermouth, set on their way with ice.)

There are several right ways to make a Martini, and many more wrong ways. Among the complications to be considered are the various camps debating the definition of how the drink is "properly" prepared, each as vociferous and assured of its own irreproachable correctness as the next. I understand that not everyone is in harmonic accord on what exactly constitutes the perfect Martini. That's not at all my grudge. There's a lot of wiggle room for subjective preference here, as with many drinks. Whether you shake or stir is certainly a big issue with both the fabricators and the imbibers of this cocktail. How much vermouth to add and how properly to do it are still topics of endless colloquia. Whether gin or vodka, twist or olive, or, with a slight renaming, an onion creates the purest expression, the Platonic ideal of the form is open to valid debate. I have no problem with any of that. I personally favor gin, slightly less dry than is the norm these days, shaken industriously as a matter of course, poured straight up in a chilled glass and garnished with a twist. The proverbial caveat about "bruising" gin or vodka is absolute nonsense. Liquor doesn't bruise with the application of ice, it becomes palatable. A Martini is not a complete and transformed entity in my eye until shards of ice are basking invitingly atop it. Up to that point it is gin or vodka, dreaming still of when it will grow up to be made into a Martini. Still, if you're the type who buys that ersatz insider savvy, or who just needs your alcohol with as little adulteration as possible, I'll grant you your stirred Martini. My problem is not with any of this hotly contested protocol. My problem is with slapdash bartending. Whether you like your Martini shaken or stirred, gin or vodka, twist or olive, the one bedrock absolute is that you want it numbingly, blindingly cold. That first limpid sip should make you feel as though you're standing night watch on the deck of a cutter angling through the Larsen Ice Shelf. It's the simplest thing in the world, and one that so many bartenders mess up that I rarely order the drink out anymore. Many missteps on the barkeep's part can be forgiven if the drink is just cold, but lo, this is simply asking too much of many of my brethren.

People not only get away with a great deal here in New York City that would never fly in other parts of the country, but they also reap an unconscionable amount of cash while turning in that mediocre performance, being thereby munificently rewarded for their slack behavior, lack of verve, and near-complete inattention to their job. I know firsthand: some of them have worked for me over the years. Even in my own bar, I can't make someone be good at what they are supposed to be doing, I can only take somebody who seems like they might be honest, bright, and driven enough to make a good bartender, train them as much as I can, and see what develops. Through the years I've had some funny, funny people working for me, and each has had to come to his or her own conclusions about how to best accomplish the job. Not all of those have been satisfactory, in many different ways. There was a petite Australian girl at Kin Khao who did the job fine, kept up with the pace and pressure, but who would strangely pick fights with the least likely customers, taking extreme offense at imaginary insults, and then dramatically demand that I remove the offender and his party. She would do this to regulars, couples who had come in for a quiet dinner. It got to be weird and was always embarrassing. The first couple of times I believed her and asked people to leave, though they remonstrated that it wasn't anything they had done. It took me a bit to uncover her pattern, and I never did figure out what was in it for her, to just pop off like that and start trouble.

Part of what I look for in a bartender is simply someone who will do the job and not rob me blind when I'm not there, since I simply cannot always be there. That's why over the years I've hired a lot of my friends. If they don't always make for the absolute greatest bartenders, I figure at least they're not stealing from me, or at least I hope they're not. My friend Burk is one of my favorite people in the world, an engaging lightning rod of creativity and humor. As a painter and writer, however, his drive left little room for worries about perfection—or often even adequacy—in his bartending. I frequently found myself gulping as an outraged customer complained about the arrogance and laziness of "that dick who was working Tuesday night," referring to one of my best friends. Yes, I would nod with resignation, that sounds about right. But they weren't saying anything I didn't already know. Burk didn't have any will to extend himself to people when they came in. If it wasn't busy he wanted to sit and read a book, and if it was he just wanted to grind through it and get his money and get out. He was saving his attention for parts of his life he felt merited it. All of this changed immediately if you were an attractive girl, but that only exacerbated the problem; nothing is more annoying than the neglectful bartender who's greasing up some ass while you're trying to get a drink from him.

Sadly, a number of my guys have been like Burk. I say guys because since I started Passerby I haven't hired any women to work behind the bar. This unspeakably sexist illegality is due to a couple of mitigating factors. The heavy lifting demanded on occasion isn't really an issue so much, being that I've worked with women bartenders who wrestle the hundred-pound beer kegs into place without a whimper. Well, really only one, to be honest. I've worked with many, though, who were very good at charming the guys into doing it, and, in the end, that works fine, as long as it gets done. The main reason is that Passerby is located on a fairly empty, semi-industrial block of West 15th Street, almost on the West Side Highway. Many nights the bartender is working solo and has to close up at four in the morning or later. At that time of night even I sometimes get creeped out closing up and making my way out of there. I simply don't think it prudent to put a woman alone in that scenario. There can be flash fights, lecherous guys, all types of unsavories lurking at that hour for a female bartender that, for example, in a restaurant setting, with an entire staff around for aid, qualify as nasty but wouldn't be cause for alarm. It hasn't been easy or pleasant for my guys to be back there when things go wrong, certainly, but I feel there's a far different level of danger possible for a woman. I've often been chewed out about my policy of refusing to hire women at Passerby, by both women customers who'd like to work there and male customers who want something more toothsome to ogle than our motley crew. My defense always starts out with me citing how many women I've trained and worked with at other places and then invariably degenerates to me concluding, yeah, sexist, illegal, whatever. There it is, deal with it.

CHAPTER V

Dirty Submarine Ballet

Thursday is when the week starts to tip toward the weekend, the night when New Yorkers go out before their town is overrun with Visigoths. Now you get the help and camaraderie of another bartender working with you later in the shift. Depending on who's slogging alongside you, this may be only a partial blessing, but at least someone else to talk trash with back there is a great relief. Tonight Eric is on, whom I call M.Q., which stands for Miserable Queen, a moniker he earned through years of his bitching and doomsaying, and one he answers to proudly. We worked together for years at Kin Khao, and I happened to be getting a haircut down in Soho on the day he was fired from there and ran into him as he was leaving the place. I scooped him up before he could even start contemplating what to do next for employment. As a result, he has never been quite sure he actually wants to be here. Freighted with an almost palpable existential squeamishness, he moans about growing old doing service work, waiting on vile people. There is almost daily rending of garments and gnashing of teeth when he comes on, although subsequently he digs in and works as hard as anyone. His ambivalence about this job tickles me, while making me feel somewhat culpable, in that I employ him. Both of us sour pickles in the same pot, I play the quasi-evil editor Shrike to his virtuous but floundering Miss Lonelyhearts.

Part of what I love about Eric is his innate pessimism, a trait I share with him, and that binds us together like two bitter old men laughing at the apocalypse. Another part is his nearly unbelievably trashy childhood. He comes by his reluctance to reenter the bar business honestly. He and his brothers quite literally grew up in a seedy bar and motel his dad owned on the edge of a trailer park outside of Washington, D.C. He tells astonishing stories about the place and his father's sad attempts to make a go of it. How, in the 1970s, attempting somehow to attract a younger and flusher clientele from farther afield than the trailer park, his dad made over the back room of the bar, from an unused storage area, into "The Psychedelic Room," trading on what he slightly belatedly figured those crazy kids were into. When that failed to gel, he began running strippers out of there. These girls, blowsy tech school dropouts and desperate young mothers, were veritable Amazons to Eric and his brothers, the most exotically concupiscent creatures imaginable. He tells of watching them breathlessly through a hole in the bathroom wall as they struggled into their pasties and g-strings, galvanized by their enormity.

My favorite scenario, though, which I've made him repeat to me over and over, was their version of a trip to Disneyland. His brother and he would fall asleep in the booths of the bar, their cherubic faces pasted to the linoleum banquettes, waiting for their dad to finish up playing cards and close the joint. Having disposed of his side work and seen the stragglers out the door, he would rouse the boys and say, "C'mon, let's go into town," eliciting delighted shrieks from the six- and seven-year-olds. Post-bartime, in the middle of the night, he would rev up his Pontiac and head across the Potomac to the city.

They all knew the drill: as he neared 14th Street, the strip where the prostitutes plied their trade, he would slow down and tell the boys ominously, "Fellas, you'd better roll up those windows and lock the doors." Eric and his brother would lie down on the wide backseat, their heads touching and their feet kicking wildly at the doors, bouncing like springs and trembling with anticipatory terror as their dad prowled slowly up and down the strip, allowing the hookers to amble up and try the door handles. Their dad would goose their terror by providing a rolling commentary: "Uh-oh, look at this one coming . . . whoo-ee! Heads down, boys!" With the monsters in lurid makeup outside pawing at the windows while Dad chuckled to himself in the front seat, they would buck and scream until they were beside themselves. Afterward they'd pass around to get an ice cream before heading back across to the Maryland/Virginia side, pulling back into the motel just around dawn.

We have various dumb games we employ to kill time when it's quiet early in the night or in a later lull. You can't really read or write letters, because even when there are only a few people in the bar, they need things with a frequency that quickly becomes irksome when you're trying to concentrate. It's better not to try to focus on something, to stay on some kind of alert. I lean against the back bar and survey things. Naturally, the customers start coming under scrutiny. I try to guess where people shopped for the clothes they're wearing. I try to determine their relationships based on the way they're talking or gesturing to one another. I try to guess their weight.

One game of chance we trot out infrequently as a tonic to the spirit is called Ten Seconds. It's very complex and very highbrow. What happens is that during the height of commotion, when you're both slashing frantically through the weeds—with the machetes that are your ability to cope dulling by the minute—and the bar is packed with toads dotting the stools, one bartender will tap the other and say in a bright, jingly voice, "Ten seconds!" The heat is on. You have ten seconds to case the room and determine one customer with whom you must have sex (theoretically, of course), or you die. The point is to call Ten Seconds when the timing is terribly inappropriate, causing the other bartender maximum vexation. Opting out of play is, naturally, unthinkable. Typical play goes like this:

"Ten seconds!"

"What?"

"TEN SECONDS!"

"What are you, fucking crazy?! Grab me two Red Stripes and a Negra Modelo while you're down there. That canister of tonic is out, I'm gonna change it. Also the Sierra Nevada's about to blow, so be careful."

"You've got eight seconds and counting. . . ."

"Oh no, for God's sake" (looking about frantically). "Ach, uhm, maybe . . . yikes, Jesus, no. I don't know, shit, maybe that older woman in the striped thingy . . ."

"Gun's to your head, four seconds."

"Um, the fattish girl with the red bangs at three o'clock?"

"Is that a question or an answer?"

Sometimes you just have to choose death. Disgustingly puerile? Believe me, Ten Seconds is like high culture for us, given the drivel that normally gets bantered about behind the bar. It's seldom about current events, occasionally about movies, and much more frequently about you, the customer. And it's not usually kind. Stuck for hours on end in a tiny little enclosed space with just one desperately bitter ally, how can one resist comment on the passing fauna?

As juvenile as all this might seem, in our defense I'll add that our trash talk, though acerbic, is fundamentally good-natured; basically we're just killing time. Ten- to twelve-hour shifts on your feet without breaks ride you hard, in a way you can't understand if you've only ever been a desk jockey. While observation, and drawing obvious connections, is instinctive in humans, the pace of the job makes an instant casualty of nuanced, serious conversation. Venting the steam that builds up from running like a slave all night is only to be expected.

Long ago at the Odeon I contrived a phrase to describe the peculiar dance we perform behind the bar in our moments of alarm, when everything hits at once and you're buried in the weeds: the dirty submarine ballet. The analogy is not terribly far-off, I realize still.

The dirty part is a snap; with the confluence of water, juices, different kinds of syrups—from soda concentrates to grenadine—alcohols, many of them sticky, sugar, salt, fruit, wine, cleaners and detergents of various types, a bar becomes, over time, and despite whatever Herculean effort the bartenders and porter heave at it in the way of scrubbing, an unholy mess. The cleanest bars I've been behind are some of the rankest corners I hope to ever find myself in. It doesn't matter where or how lovely the bar, in back there, they are all disgustingly filthy. The grime just becomes, after a bit, another part of the job, of the whole situation. You learn not to wear good clothes while tending, because varicolored liquids fly in all directions when you shake or spill. Most back bars are painted black, simply to incorporate the grime into the general miasma. In theory you float above it on the rubber hexagonal mats, but in reality, like the smoke, it seeps into you from everywhere, osmotically. At the end of the night it is actually fascinating to see what washes from my hands, despite them being constantly plunged in water. The nightly shower feels like a baptism.

Restaurant bars are far worse in this respect, typically speaking, but even bars that don't serve food can't escape the principal elements that combine to make for some unpleasant realities. Consider how hard it is just keeping your living space clean. Hair and dust build up, things go bad quickly. Now multiply that by a few thousand, add a lot of water to the scenario, people spilling stuff everywhere, smoke, which all settles somewhere when it's done being smoke, liquids of varying viscosity and sugar content being splashed about, and you're looking at some grim buildup. Granted, the bar, unlike your apartment, gets cleaned every night. Also, once a month all the bartenders are pried grouchily from their beds in the daytime, bribed with breakfast, and then made to storm the place with rubber gloves and rags. We remove everything from the shelves, scrub the room from stem to stern. It tends to make only the minutest difference. Two days later the ashen dust from cigarette smoke has built up to the point where, when you pull a bottle from the shelf, you can see the clean spot where it lay. The combination of water and all the varieties of alcohol and juice that end up spilled or splashed about the space is an intertwining nightmare of effluvia. The drains, flowing constantly with every kind of flora, develop malodorous molds; the beer drain on the taps feeds its own particular bacteria, while the drains on the ice bins harbor low-temperature molds that bloom like jellyfish when they are rinsed down at the end of the night. It's a constant battle, albeit one no one in the industry is very keen to discuss. Landlords are loath to rent intact retail space to people who want to open up what is termed a "wet wall," an area where water is brought in for sinks and bins, unless that space has already been a restaurant and thus is more or less ruined for anyone who wants a space that won't take a major overhaul to get back to normal.

The second part of my moniker has to do with the actual physical space we inhabit and how we move around it. A bar—I'm speaking here about back behind the bar, where we work—is like a boat belowdecks, a claustrophobically tight, purely functional space where human comfort is a secondary concern at best. Every inch is employed and every item back there has a specific purpose and a specific niche. Most bars have something between two and three feet of space behind them for the bartender to move. In reality, you don't actually want any more than that, as the constant process of reaching back and forth to grab bottles, pour them, and return them becomes prolonged the more distance you have to cover to do so. Airplane cockpits and stations in professional kitchens employ the same principle of proximity; when things get hot, you've got to be able to reach it all quickly, without thinking, often without even looking.

In this tiny dog run, then, it goes without saying that when you add a second bartender, and then often a busboy on top of that, you have a scenario where tangled frustration, drawn out over ten-plus hours, multiplies wildly unless the parties in question find some kind of synergy in their movement. We speak of one another's "ballet," as in "What's up with your ballet tonight? You've friggin' cross-checked me like ten times already and it's only nine! Have a coffee, willya?" Great ballet requires being thin, to start with, and peripherally aware. Like jockeys and coxswains, bartenders have one of the few jobs where it becomes something of a challenge if you're not on the svelte side. It is a kind of dance, too. There is a constant Morse code–like system of touching, nearly imperceptible taps on the arm or back that let the other bartender know where you are, or longer rests to let him know not to move for a second while you pull a bottle past him or whip down a handful of Martini glasses. Bad ballet is, obviously enough, being unaware of where your body is, flailing about, stepping on feet, hitting into the other guy like a side of tuna, knocking things out of hands, jarring drinks being poured because you failed to telegraph where you were. The difference between good and bad ballet can virtually transform your working life. Although Jerry complains about having to work around Joe, who is a large fellow, it's not so neatly put that one either has good ballet or bad. It's a lot like, I suppose, real ballet, where you're all seasoned professionals, but where on any given night you step on the floor and, depending on a lot of factors, you're either Balanchine or elephantine. The great motivator, however, is the weeds. When you're the busiest is always when you're the most fluid, in that way that all the synapses are firing at once and you've no choice but to streamline everything.

In addition to your coworkers there are plenty of other hazards amidships: sharp angles from the counters, the ice bins, the refrigerators. Everything back there becomes a potential punji stick when you're throwing yourself wantonly about. It takes, I've found, roughly six months to completely familiarize your muscle memory with a new space, but those can be six painful, oath-filled months of jamming your hips into stainless steel corners and your shins into the lowboy, the anvil-like condensing unit for the soda system. There is also the exasperating phenomenon of working solo one night, wherein you become acclimated to covering large swaths of the bar in two uninterrupted swoops, and the next night pairing up, when those same pirouettes are abruptly halted in a midair collision that leaves you hastily apologizing to the other bartender, who is now wearing the drink you were conveying. It happens infrequently. You both look dumb, and looking dumb is the antithesis of what we desire behind the bar. Hence, the better your ballet, the better you're liked back there.

Another inflated-value result of this Lilliputian 'environment is the importance of location. In a macro sense, of course, the bar's design—how it is set up for flow—is hugely influential, akin to the obsessive and secretive manipulations of shipbuilders searching for the infinitesimal hydrodynamic edge that shaving three centimeters off a specific part of a hull will confer on their America's Cup contender. Having to turn a corner or work around a supporting beam, schlepp up and down a hidden trapdoor in the floor, or simply take five steps to reach the Dewar's, rather than two, multiplied by the umpteen million times you will be performing that same movement, all can make enormous differences in the ease or annoyance of doing your job. But I mean location also in the micro sense. Early on I learned how the wine key has to be, every single time you use it, exactly occupying those thirteen square centimeters that have been delineated for all as "where the wine key is." Maddeningly, it is easier to lose things in a small, crowded space where everything is visible than in your entire house. It's bad enough, even when I'm opening leisurely, that I can be found cursing and searching for seven minutes for the clam knife, which has been moved exactly twenty-seven inches from where it properly nests, to the other side of the cash register. The frustration level approaches meltdown when you're on skates, of course, and a ten-second delay to search for the cocktail spoon produces internal temperatures in the average barkeep that threaten spontaneous combustion. The dictum about location being everything is truer than ever behind the bar.

o   o   o

Around ten Mark shows up with some of his cronies in tow and is hanging out with Jesse at the turntables. Mark used to spin a night here that he put together called Booty Bar. His girlfriend, Lizzie, is one of the singers in the satire/pop outfit Fisherspooner, and Mark is a very affable fellow who, as a DJ, became overwhelmingly enamored of a particular offshoot of house music known as Ghetto Tech, which sprang unbidden from the bowels of Detroit's inner-city strip clubs. It started out being just a funny idea when he proposed it. We had no notion what Ghetto Tech was, but we decided to let him stage the night anyway, because he was so gung ho about how cool it could be. His enthusiasm was fetching.

In brief, Ghetto Tech is breathtakingly obscene and profane lyrics, repeated ad insanitum and set against any number of stock house beats, those seldom dropping below 240 beats per minute. Exemplary perpetrators of the form are artists like DJ Assault, whose CDs can contain eighty-three tracks, with titles like "Shake That Ass, Bitch and Let Me See What You've Got" or the perennial favorite, "Big Booty Ho." It's mind-numbing stuff to take in, even in small amounts. Stretched out over six hours, ground into you at 180 or 200 decibels, with a powered subwoofer thrown in to churn your intestines with the bass, it becomes a sort of extended exercise in humor versus patience. At first it's hilarious, then it quickly becomes tiresome. Remarkably shortly following that you find you want to cut your ears off your head.

I'll grant you that nothing to me merits being blasted into my skull at such, literally, painful volume. But even when I was a young punk and liked to listen to what I then considered loud and raucous music, there were, I can now see, limits, both moral and physical, on my transgression. Richard Hell and the Voidoids' "Blank Generation" sounds toy and cute, like the Carpenters, against what passes muster in peripheral pop and rap today. Were I to find myself surrounded for weeks by the BATF, with their tactic of driving aggressors from hostage situations by pounding them with atrocious music nonstop until they cry uncle, I feel certain I'm now inured enough to hole up cozily for several months, or possibly even years, under a constant barrage of, say, Tony Orlando and Dawn doing "Tie a Yellow Ribbon Around That Old Oak Tree."

I'm forced to admit, however, that Booty Bar worked at first on a certain level in the bar, as a sort of social oddity. The first time Mark and his crew played, the unwinning lyrics and banging tempo literally made my head spin. But the reaction in the bar was a perplexed galvanization, I couldn't help but notice. In this rarefied environment of postcollegiate arty-pants, predominantly white kids from upper-middle-class backgrounds working in creative fields, who clearly pride themselves on their open-minded urbanity, no one was quite sure how to react. It seems heretical to find yourself tapping your foot to medleys that blend power ditties like "Ass-'n-Titties" with speed ballads like "Say My Name," whose lyrics are an unending call-and-response between a woman and a man singing, "Nigga, say my name/BITCH, say my name/Nigga, SAY my name/Bitch, say my NAME." It's so transgressive, so blatantly stupid and uncool, people don't know quite what to do with themselves. That off-kilterism, tossing an element of uncertainty into a crowd whose sense of place and entitlement renders it nearly unshockable, seemed worth the endeavor in a way for which I have no true justification. It simply seemed funny to me.

As much of an intriguing social experiment as it was initially, however, Booty Bar quickly became functioning proof of the old adage that if you play atrocious music, they will come. Atrocious people, that is. Though it was only once a month, the party tarnished quickly, one-line joke that it was. The music ran anyone sane off like a sharp pitchfork, which my partner Gavin found hilarious, but then Gavin didn't have to stand behind the bar and put up with the throngs of slack-jawed, grunting, postteen white boys from Brooklyn and Queens who, it turned out, are the genre's true arbiters. My bartender George and I worked those Thursdays together, and we learned to gird ourselves days in advance for the coming onslaught: standing for hours with nothing to do but watch various waves of kids filter in who seemed to all be in on the same bad joke. The ringing absurdity of this whole bar full of these bogus white kids all ghettoed out—white DJ and his white posse, playing to a bunch of white guys—you can rest assured there wasn't a girl left in the place—all decked out identically in Triple 5 Soul and Fubu hooded sweatsuits, trying to look "down" as hell, with big Gucci 1970s-style sunglasses on, even though the bar is cavelike to begin with, talking black, walking black, lurching up to greet one another with soul hugs, calling each other "nigga." So goddamn stupid, I'm thinking, watching it all transpire. Was there ever an age as stupid as we are? Or is my revulsion watching these kids exactly that of gimlet-eyed bartending brethren who beheld the flappers in the '20s, the "longhairs" of the '60s?

When we had to tell Mark Booty Bar was not working out for us he was crestfallen, and I actually felt terrible about it. As loathsome as I found it, it was touching how much he loved the music. He begged to do one more, and against my instincts it was somehow agreed. The last Booty Bar was such an abomination, it was as though God himself had sent down a sign—several actually—that He disapproved. I got the message.

Mark showed up around eleven, chipper as ever, looking like a puffy Beaver Cleaver in his plaid short-sleeved shirt. The demanding velocity of the music's beat is such that Mark would always arrive early to alter the speed of the turntables in order to faithfully customize it. As he began taking apart the platters, he told me excitedly that he'd done a mass e-mailing to promote the night and that the bar could well be packed with Internet disciples of Ghetto Tech. Marvelous, I thought. Soon enough his crew drifted in as well, bumping fists and running through intricate greeting rituals carefully practiced in private, no doubt, for maximum blackness.

At first I thought it could be an exceptional night. There was a decent mix of people in the bar when they began playing, and as they started in a bit mellower, no one seemed to be running out screaming. It was filling up quickly, and the fact that at least the women in the bar were staying put seemed a good sign. It was so crowded an hour into it that I was slogging hard to keep up when George approached me, saying, "There's like a hundred seventeen-year-olds out on the sidewalk and in the entrance hallway, and some of them have slipped in and are in the bathroom hallway." I went out into the hallway and it looked just like the corner of 8th Avenue and 18th Street when all three high schools in the area let out after three, just a tidal pool of these pimply little striplings with baggy galligaskins falling off their asses, flailing about epileptically, trying to throw gang signs. "Good Christ," I told George, "some of these kids probably haven't been weaned yet." We fanned out and began carding and ejecting as many as we could corral at once, while others dispersed like minnows and realighted in another part of the bar. Eventually we got them all out, but they kept trying to sneak back in.

No sooner had I returned to the bar than the room flooded once again with the noxious spawn. This time I sent George out to hold the line on these puppies, and he was still in the middle of the fray, over near the bathrooms carding outraged children who were twenty-one years and three hours old, according to their fake IDs, when the door to the street opened and in filed a line of unlikely, middle-age outer-borough types. Looking up, I knew something very strange was going on, but I wasn't sure what exactly. As fourteen of them eventually piled in looking nearly identical in matching navy windbreakers, acid wash jeans, and white leather New Balance strolling shoes, I remember thinking, What's this now, did all of New Jersey just decide to come in for a drink? They looked like a gaggle of camp counselors. Several of them were sporting full mullets. When the head guy flashed his badge and said, "New York City Police, Vice Squad," it all made perfect sense. I told Mark to chill the music and led them poker-faced into the gallery office to work out whatever was up.

They turned out to be quite genial. They were investigating a complaint that we had no liquor license. "Probably someone pissed off that you threw them out of the place," the main interrogator told me. "We get it all the time. But we've got to follow up every complaint."

While I went to get the license and chatted with the head officer, the rest of them, bored, began milling about the office and nosing into the gallery, laughing at the art and calling out to each other. One of the guys started complaining about his back to one of the women. From the side gallery one crew-cutted officer erupted, "Get the fuck outta heah!" laughing openly. "Ray, d'jou see dis? Hey, how much is this thing, this paintin', whatevah?" He was pointing to a video still by John Waters, the director, that consisted simply of large yellow letters on a black background reading "Shut Up and Blow Me!"

"Um, I don't know, actually," I told him. "A lot, though. A lot more than you'd guess. Probably more than any of us make in a year."

"Nah!" he said, screwing up his eyes in disbelief. I nodded my head, to imply I was afraid so. "Christ, I say that to my wife all the time," he brayed. "I never thought to make me some money by writin' it down on a paintin'." The main interrogator gave him a look, and one of the lady cops punched him in the arm.

His superior informed me, regretfully, that he'd have to write me a citation for having candles on the bar without an Open Flame Permit. "A what?" I cried, laughing. We went through months of applying for permits of every description when we opened. I've worked in restaurants for how many years? I've never in my life heard of an Open Flame Permit. "Did you just make that up?" I asked him. "That's good, actually. An Open Flame Permit, so that you can, you know, have an open flame. You just made that up, didn't you?"

He smiled and said, "You get 'em, like, when you're installing your grill and salamander and all that in your kitchen."

"Yes, but see I don't have a kitchen. I have five candles on the bar. What say I blow out the candles and we call it even?" He wouldn't budge, but all the same he was being very generous about it. He said he'd have to give me the several-hundred-dollar citation, but that all

I would have to do to get out of it would be to show up in court and the judge would dismiss it. I countered that if the judge were just going to dismiss it, why write it to begin with? He said he's gotta do his job, but they all looked apologetic about it and seemed genuinely sorry. I liked the vice squad. I'd invite them back.

I was still joshing him about having made up the Open Flame Permit as we all made our way back to the bar. Upon entering I found Jesse at the turntables blasting NWH's "Fuck Tha Police," presumably in my defense. I gave him a strangled look and tried to shake my head without the lead officer noticing. He turned and asked, "Uh, I hate to bring this up, but you got a cabaret license for all these people dancing here, right?"

Casting a glance across the sprinkling of skinny, tent-wearing kids bobbing in place like sullen birds, I frowned. "These *people*, officer? These are not people, I assure you. These are dopes. And that could hardly be called dancing, now could it? Look, their feet aren't even moving. These kids are clearly just writhing in existential agony, as would you if you had to live their lives." He sighed, but took pity on me, and told me how to apply for the cabaret license if I wanted to have dancing in the bar. I told him we actually don't want dancing in the bar, and we let it go at that. As they left they were tossing around names of other bars nearby, debating where they should go next like any other bar crawlers, only rather than getting loose and hooking up, this group was dedicated to lining the municipal war chest. Why it took fourteen of them I couldn't quite figure, but I didn't really want to ask, either. I felt I'd gotten off pretty clean, for what it could have been.

Two months later found me and my friend Timmy, who's an attorney, up very early of a morning, fresh-scrubbed and turned out in suits for the court date to fight *Passerby v. The State of New York*. Heading up to the Midtown Community Court where the arraignment was, we were concocting fallback strategies in the cab. Once inside the shockingly rundown courtroom, we picked our way past rank homeless men sleeping across the benches, transvestite prostitutes looking grim in their morning shadow, and junkies rocking manically, all waiting for their names to show up on the electronic docket, a smeared TV wedged into a corner of the room. The judge was almost half an hour late. When she finally showed up, zipping up her black robe over a pale-green business ensemble and a cream-colored scarf, she looked harried and permanently disgruntled, like someone's mom whose favorite Hummel figurine you just broke. By definition if you are in this room, she hates you. This woman went through a lot of schooling and professional hurdles to become a judge, I was thinking, watching her snap at the court officers, and for that she got to sit in sagacity on this cesspool. Life certainly has some dirty tricks up its sleeves.

Mercifully, we were the first case called. She told us to approach the bench, then immediately shouted at Timmy as he began to do so, pointing out a white line past which we were not to go. He apologized, addressing her as "Your Honor," and we both jumped back, standing at full attention to await her swift and furious judgment. I was having trouble keeping a straight face after hearing Timmy address Justice Someone's Angry Mom as "Your Honor." I know that's what you have to say, and being a litigation attorney who must use the phrase two hundred times a day, it didn't even register on him. To me, though, particularly given our surroundings, it was a crack-up. I was itching to add "Yes, your highness. I beg your pardon, my liege, we saw not thy white line of demarcation." Frowning through reading glasses at a sheaf of papers, she croaked, "You have an 'Open Flame Permit Violation,' is that correct?" I allowed that it was, noting that her wavering uncertainty and further eyebrow wrinkling when reading this out made clear that she, like me, had never heard of such a thing in all her many days of jurisprudence. She looked up at us fully for the first time and you could literally see her almost smirk: Who are the clowns in the suits? She shook her head tiredly and tossed the file on the desk, pronouncing the case dismissed in a quietly sour manner that, though it signaled our glorious ten-second victory, and righteous vindication for me, made me feel sorry for the judge. And this, I thought, is only the beginning of her day.

o   o   o

From far-off you can hear the thunder of Friday and Saturday nights gearing up. In Chelsea, where Passerby is, during the art season, meaning all autumn, winter, and spring, the difference between the weekdays and the weekends is jarringly clear, particularly when there are multiple art openings in the neighborhood. Though any night has the potential to blow up in your face, weekend nights are as a rule the most intense. Bridge-and-tunnelers and nine-to-fivers are let loose in the city to pack in on top of the full-time scenesters and art world sycophants normally sleazing about, to make weekend nights cataclysmic, even frightening, at their high-water marks, when holding the helm can seem akin to manning the Alamo. People are hanging from the ceiling fans, squeezing between the cracks in the walls. I've had certain bartenders—and in fact still have two—who unconditionally refuse to work weekends.

We're hustling already, Eric and I. Jokes and chitchat have been dispensed with for hours already and he's looking red-faced and a little pinched. Roberto, the busboy, has pulled in and Scottie, our provisional and entirely too congenial door guy, is sitting out in the hallway on his stool, regulating the flow. I glance up at some movement out of the corner of my eye to see twelve more people pushing in, then another group right behind them. Straightening up for a moment to stretch and twist my back, I look over all the heads facing me and murmur to myself, "All right, game time." Here's where it clicks in. The bar is lined with anxious faces, all bent semihostilely in my direction. People want their things to drink. You are only cursorily "out at a bar" until you have a drink in your hand. It doesn't matter that the place is a mob scene and that everyone lined up can see you zipping in tightly choreographed lunges out and back, up and down. It doesn't even matter anymore that I take note of who appears in what order and hold my finger up to acknowledge them and point out others there before them. At a certain juncture it becomes a mobocracy, and that juncture is known in the business as being "in the weeds," that is, lost in very tall grasses. I have no idea of the origin of the term, I only became aware of it in New York. But it is an elegantly accurate depiction of the wash of utter helplessness that overtakes you behind the bar when you see twenty more people wedging themselves into the crush when you are three sets of orders behind already.

As dire as it is in the weeds, and as much as one arranges and plans out scheduling and staff to avoid this misery, there is something morbidly fascinating about hitting that tipping point and seeing what happens to everyone in the place. This is, perhaps not surprisingly, when we work best, with all cylinders clicking. Stripped down to the barest, most mercenary use of our time and actions, Eric and I slip into a robotic trance. The blare of music and shouts fades away. I stop even looking up at people. I can see waving hands in the periphery of my vision, but I'm locked in, ripping now, and there's no more room for politesse. Wordlessly Eric and I maneuver about one another, our ballet seamless and mechanical. In the midst of the bedlam, it feels as though we are the only two people in the place, with Roberto punctuating the flow like a speed bump. Eric's got five different glasses set up at once up at the second station and shots lining part of the bar waiting to be filled. People are buttonholing Robertino in rickety Spanish, trying to wrest drinks from the busboy. I note it, smiling grimly and shaking my head, as I pour from two bottles at once down the bar at the main station. The glassware is low, all of it out on the floor now, which is so crowded Roberto can't make it through the bodies to retrieve any. Every few minutes I hear something else break, from deep within the throng. There's nothing to do, no way to tell what's spilled, what's broken.

There's a kind of sickly beauty to these screeching, urgent moments for me, if only because they strip away all the niceties and solicitation of careful bartending and pare what I do down to a simple, brute contest of endurance and production. Locked in that little dugout, when all becomes speed and reflex, I can feel the eyes of all the day-jobbers on me, staring hard even if they don't mean to. Propped cooling your heels in front of a cross between a donut machine and a carnival sideshow, it's hard not to watch the crazy, tight spasms of this trained animal churning out refreshments at a hundred miles an hour. In the way that athletes speak of being in "the zone," I can now feel my muscle memory take over and, as though a spectator myself of my own actions, even I am fascinated. There's no thought exactly anymore. My hands and feet are simply dispatched in blips to where they know the shaker is, icing it down, snatching three stem glasses off the shelf above my head with one hand while the other anoints the ice with a drop of vermouth. I feel like an octopus, turning, grabbing, depositing everything back exactly right. The gin gets counted automatically and the bottle turned up to arrest the pour at 28, for three Martinis, accounting mentally for the space the olive juice will take up, as they were requested dirty. In the midst of the grinding I feel a strange, throbbing felicity, as though part of me is levitating above all of this mayhem, smiling.

At a certain moment, as if a small silver bell sounded, we both suddenly become aware that everyone has a drink. Prowling hungrily, scanning the faces that only minutes before were imploring, all are strangely content, there is no one looking back, no hands shooting out, gesturing agitatedly. What seemed like some very tense minutes turns out to have covered three hours neatly. When you're in the weeds time morphs in and out deceptively. It seems to go on endlessly when you're being pounded—you feel like a child laborer chained to a boot-blacking assembly line, you feel like crying—but when it's finished you always have the impression it might have been twenty rough minutes, where in fact it transpired over three or four hours.

It strikes me as a bit sad to consider that there may be nothing I can do better than this. This one niche thing I can do so well it's actually inconscient, so fast and precise and economical that it takes on its own brilliance. But it's not a brilliance worth crowing about. Despite the raised eyebrows of people lining the bar watching, and the occasional comment, it's nothing that anyone values enough to be worth noting. I wish I could be this good, this masterful and assured, at something other than bartending, but there it is, that's how it worked out. If this insignificant talent could be commanding a sailboat, painting frescoes, or performing surgery, I might be lauded by peers and public. If it were tennis or chess, defending divorcées or trading stocks, my competence could have made me a millionaire. Such as it is, I get the occasional inquiry wondering how long I've been tending bar. There are no trophies, no rings. Only we know and celebrate, the locusts having passed, our tepid glory.

I am pacing back and forth, still on hyperglide from the rush, snatching up ashtrays to clean and whisking away every empty glass almost before it touches the bartop. There is no need for this level of vigilance now that everyone is served and people are just milling and drinking, but it's hard to slow down when you've been railing at top speed for several hours. Finally I force myself just to step back and lean against the dishwasher and let others clear the tables while I unwind a moment.

Sometimes this comes along and I've no idea why. I love being behind the bar, and for the most part I understand the extent to which I feed off of the energy of the room and what goes on in it. Being in the Position of Authority has actually helped me learn to be more tolerant of people, in fact, with whom I have very little in common and would otherwise perhaps snub and ridicule. But sometimes comes La Grande Tristesse from watching the proceedings.

Maybe it's the process of gearing down after working at light speed for so long—I've noticed it before—but suddenly, as I look about me, the entire room strikes me as a terribly sad and pitiable collection of grisly human appetites on display and I'm filled momentarily with a mixture of melancholy and revulsion. Men and women chortling, pounding the bartop, their viscera and questionable designs on unseemly display. What are all these people doing here, I wonder, shaking my head, and what am I doing here serving them? Surely this is not what my parents envisioned for me as I sat playing in my crib, filling my diapers. Why would people go through these contortions to wedge themselves sideways, literally, into this infernal shoebox of a place? It's 211 degrees in here; to cool it down you'd have to turn the heat on. The smoke is so thick you can wad it like tissue. No one can move, except us. We have the only space in the entire place, our little fifteen-foot veal pen, and I don't even want to be here, though I'm paid to do so. You can't possibly speak to anyone, even screaming at the top of your lungs, because the music is damning, all-annulling, twelve hundred million decibels. It hurts my ears and I have ear plugs in.

These hideous girls, shrieking harpies in their perfectly assembled outfits: how much collective time, money, human energy, and thought went into making them all look the same, with their screechingly straightened hair, their stretch tube tops with spaghetti straps and seventies-retro skirts all falling just perfectly below the knee? How carefully they toe the line, some tacit, mutable code of how exactly they should appear. What are they looking for here, all hobbling around on their Sigerson Morrison pumps, clutching Balenciaga handbags? They're looking for love, what the fuck else? Who isn't looking for love, at bottom, in their twenties and thirties? But it's horrible to contemplate, it makes me stare sadly, how they all dress up so carefully and they come here, and then they go elsewhere, and they're prowling these filthy environs panning for gold, scratching around for diamonds of some sort. It's likely they have no clear idea themselves what they're doing here. They only know, by the end of the night, that whatever it is they're looking for, it's not here.

And the guys, are they looking for love? These drooling idiots in their buttoned-down Banana Republic best, with the slightly tight—but not *gay* tight—dress pants and chunky black footwear they bought after reading in *GQ* or *Esquire* that this is the way they should go if they don't want to appear—and who does, God forbid?—as though they just came from the office. Scanning the room hungrily, huddling to consult like runners on the trading floor, are they, too, courting fickle Eros? They are not. They are passing blunt phrases and priapic grunts about the size of tits and weighing the odds against their success in bedding one of the inane girls who is carefully groomed to meet her glowing future. It's simple, ugly commerce out there on the floor on a busy weekend night. They drink the lovely drinks required to loosen them up enough to confront one another, they smoke because they are immortal, of course, and they shop for their fate in ways they cannot fathom and over which they have, in reality, no more control than a mollusk has over the waves that pin it to the shore. And people have done this forever, in bars not unlike this the world over, with different music but with the same smoke, the same blowsy, shouted humor.

Why should this common human ritual, as old as civilization itself, strike me now as so snub-nosed and obscene? Maybe I'm just tired, I reason. Or is it the coffee? Caffeine can get me looping in huge, misanthropic ovals around perfectly benign subjects in that way. But I haven't had any joe since this morning. There's nothing inherently wrong with what these people are doing; it's my bar, in fact, that allows them to do it. But my bar is just a tiny little cog in this whole objectionable wheel. All these people, they won't be here in another few years. They meet one another, or someone like one another, here and get together. Here is where they prove themselves knowing and hip—enough so to find this place, in the know enough to make it to the selective spawning grounds. But this piece of gravel is just a way station. In time they will move from the city, when they can't take the inconvenience any longer and they are done with proving how hip and plugged in they are. In time, too, my bar will have to close to make way for another not too unlike it. One generation's proving ground must needs be trashed by the next.

All of this, or something like it, I see and acknowledge in the ten seconds of leaning against the dishwasher, staring blankly across the room at the blue power light of the speaker in the corner, seeing it all while seeing nothing.

My moment of exhausted biliousness triggers a combat flashback, dragging me back to the debacle, the Waterloo, that was New Year's Eve before last. Just before I took off for Christmas to go back to Wisconsin for a visit, the bar was seeming great. New York felt as though it was pulling itself slowly out of the lethargy created by the attacks on September 11. Some of the same film companies and fashion people who had rented out the bar in years prior were giving smaller, private parties for their employees for Christmas. The customers seemed happy in December, everyone jazzed by all the spending and consumption going around. Despite all the dire economic talk, we were pulling gigantoid tips from these parties, as though New Yorkers were flaunting their refusal to be moved by the terrorism.

We've never been open on New Year's Eve in the past, feeling, rightly I knew, that trying to control the marauding hordes pushing through the streets on that night, foraging for alcohol and any of myriad varieties of trouble, would simply be too much for our tiny bar. We have a permanent loathing of the velvet rope and bouncers-with-lists piffle. Passerby has always gotten by on the benevolent vibe it puts out. For the most part, the few people who have known about the bar have always guarded the secret proprietarily, like a hot stock tip, and have treated it with the kind of affectionate respect due the raffish clubhouse it is. We don't have fights in the bar, to any appreciable degree, or thievery. We've rarely needed to call the cops on anyone. It's a genteel space (as far as bars go, that is), mostly due to its sub rosa identity outside of the art world.

Still, I've been loath to push our luck by opening up to the public on the mother of all amateur nights. I've always hated New Year's Eve, with its overblown expectations, and particularly in New York City, when morons by the busload are foisted on the hapless populace, spilling out of Times Square vomiting and punching at shadows as though it's V-J Day every January first. I'd really rather be ice fishing.

Each year in the past, however, when Gavin and I would agree to be closed from Christmas through New Year's, I would think about the money we were passing up by not having planned some kind of private party on that night. Obviously our bar has its little following, and regulars have whinged about our being closed on New Year's Eve, citing how difficult it is to find anywhere decent to be. I, of course, couldn't care less that people have nowhere they like to be on some fractious, idiotic excuse of a night to go out and get plowed. I wasn't going to risk my bar on it. But if it was a controlled sort of thing, I began thinking, it could be a plump night, cashwise.

This was my undoing, the indecisive moment of greed that softened my underbelly sufficiently that I didn't openly balk when Gavin told me Seth and Ben, two very young DJs who spin under the moniker Neon Kobra, approached him about having a party on New Year's Eve, open only to people on their list. I had misgivings galore. Gavin claimed it would be fun and that we'd all be here for control, he and I and all of the bartenders, no doubt among them Joe, who at six three and just over two hundred pounds is more than capable of squelching any Passerby-size problems. True, I agreed, but shouldn't we rather host some kind of party at fifty or a hundred dollars a head with an open bar and all the Champagne you like? We could send out a mailing to his collectors and the bar regulars and have a list set in advance. The true regulars spend that routinely in a night of heavy drinking, and all we'd need is thirty takers to fill the place and make for a twisted, select celebration of the occasion. The rabble, the flotsam that drifts in occasionally with foul winds from the East Village, traveling always with Sharpie markers in hand and complaining vociferously about the price of a pint of beer, would be left wilted at the door. But Gavin found that too elitist, and so gave Seth and Ben the go-ahead.

I scheduled my trip to Wisconsin to return just before New Year's Eve, so I could be on hand to make certain the bar wasn't torn to shreds. Jerry, the somewhat itinerant Chinese American actor prone to wandering into, and slithering quickly out of, trouble behind the bar was lobbying me to let him work the shift, saying he had nothing else to do. I thought better of it. Jerry and Joe are friends, and I knew they would both be in attendance most of the night anyway, whether or not they were working, as they are the only bartenders who come by the bar on their nights off. Better, I thought, that I work alongside the steadfast John, the painter and carpenter and arrow-straight southern boy I hired specifically for his uprightness, while Jerry and Joe relax in the wings in case they're needed.

Early that evening Seth and Ben show up with two other DJs, Amy and Meredith, who play with a contingent on Monday nights. As they begin setting up for the night, I can tell they haven't thought anything out and didn't have a concrete plan with Gavin. When I notice this I query them on when Gavin is to show up. They tell me he's in Long Island with his family and won't make it. Now I foresee problems. Gavin has his DJs and I have mine, more or less. Although we all get along fine, some of his crew tend to answer only to him, and these kids are decidedly his protégés. They tell me Gavin has okayed the opening of the door from the bar to the gallery, so that they can set up another DJ to turn his office into a makeshift "chillout lounge." They register my instant mistrust of this idea. "Do you realize that would be exposing all the displayed art, all the stored art, the computers and everything in the office to the prying malevolence of drunken kids?" I ask.

"W-well," Meredith stammers, "it's just going to be people we know, right? It's all people who know Passerby. I don't think any harm's going to come to anything."

I regard her perhaps a touch too derisively. I try Gavin on his cell and can't get through. Anton, the ever-thinking gallery assistant, hatches and executes a plan to board off the parts of the gallery into which we don't want interlopers wandering. He forms a Pamplona-style bull run leading directly into the propped-open frosted glass doors of Gavin's office. I still don't like the looks of it, so I gather all the DJs and tell them I want one of them patrolling this back room at all times, as well as the hallway between the bar and the room, for any signs of trouble. They argue that there will be one of them spinning in that room at all times and that that will be a deterrent presence. "A DJ, lost in beats per minute, with his head down trying to cue shit up? What exactly is that supposed to be deterring when two guys are in the hallway jimmying open the door of the liquor room?" I ask. They roll their eyes and look from one to the other nervously, clearly worried that I'm about to rain on their party. I feel, as I frequently do, like Dad to a bunch of idiots. I'm hyped up and clearly being overly protective of the bar, but watching them act out their annoyance with my caution I can barely contain my urge to smack their heads together. I'm pissed with Gavin for not being there and pissed with myself for being there.

John and I set up the bar, stocking extra glassware and Champagne, cutting tons of fruit. I call Polo to confirm that he'll be there at nine to bus. Polo is the Mexican porter who cleans the bar each morning. His brother Roberto, our normal busboy, is hosting a New Year's Eve party and has asked if Polo could step in for him. I consented, even though Polo tips in at something close to three hundred pounds and is a terrible busboy. Maneuvering around him in the tight space behind the bar is aggravating as hell, and he hates going out on the floor to retrieve the glassware because he tires of burrowing through the packed crowd. I think of Roberto's party, where they're undoubtedly pounding down the empyreal tamales his wife makes for all festive occasions. For neither the first nor the last time that night I wonder why I decided to allow this.

John and I have to eat before opening at nine. He cuts out for Brooklyn, to join his girlfriend, and I decide I need the tempering fortification of Grand Sichuan International's searing Beef with Wild Sichuan Peppercorn and Sichuan Wontons in Red Oil. If I'm to undergo trial by fire, I'd at least like to make it voluntary. By the time we return from dinner, there are already artists and some of their hangers-on milling in and out from the gallery to the bar, beers in hand, setting me into an immediate fit of pique. They all scramble like frightened birds when I start ranting, demanding to know who said they could walk into my bar and open up the refrigerator and help themselves to beer. I'm clanging around angrily then, opening up. The only person who will approach me is John. Polo wanders in a half hour late, smiling and ready for action.

By ten, when we're fully ready to go, I'm in the blackest of moods, so much so that I force myself to halt for a moment back near the cash register, watching people push through the doors, and try to pull myself out of my grinding anger, knowing well how this can spiral throughout the night into something not simply much more unpleasant but actually dangerous. People pick up very quickly on whatever mood is coming at them from others. I can often tell in seconds, frequently before they reach me at the bar, what kind of temperament someone is in, and how that might color my interaction with them. If *I* start out in a foul mood, that impairs my ability to defuse any potentially awkward situations with guys who may be spoiling for trouble, a not-uncommon scenario under normal working nights, a near guarantee on New Year's Eve. Buoyancy, and the ability to laugh off people's inanities and drunken foibles, will stand me in much better stead tonight, I realize, than my current smoldering. My self-induced anger-management lecture becomes moot, however, as there are suddenly too many people pouring through the door at once. Meredith and Amy have started to spin and crank it right off the bat, dispensing with the buffer of quieter grooves we would have on a normal night. John and I are still trying to set fruit and napkins out, Polo has disappeared somewhere. The crowd is being impossibly rude from the start, shouting out their orders on top of one another, waving twenties in the air, leaving no tips. It's a lot of dumb-ass kids in their early twenties, not particularly our normal clientele. After serving pints to an egregiously odious bunch of frat hounds I wave down Ben at his station at the door. "Who's supposed to be controlling the door?" I scream across the numbing clamor of the music. "Who is this bunch of assholes in here?"

He regards me quizzically for a second before shouting back, grinning, "These are our friends!" I nod, then stalk off down the bar and try to once again regauge myself for what I know is going to be a grim night. Seth and Ben, both very amiable guys from the school of sweet and dopey, have been entrusted by Gavin to control the door, so my hands are somewhat tied. I also don't want to be Mr. Harsh, inflicting my misgivings and terrible mood on everyone else, so I swallow again and set to work.

The hours between opening and midnight pass in a blur. John and I are so swamped that when he calls to my attention that it's ten to midnight I'm shocked. All the Champagne glasses have long since vanished, and everyone wants Champagne now for a toast. I send Polo out to the gallery to collect up what he can and I case the bar for the few there. People are queued three deep, cranky already by the time John or I can reach them, tossing us enormous orders for entire groups or doubling up because they don't want to come back and do it again. At four minutes to midnight I simply stop taking orders and scare up four flutes for John and myself and our girlfriends, who have both shown up looking bewildered, just to have a toast with us. Lacking for flutes, I grab as many wineglasses as I have and, eventually, just begin pouring Prosecco into highballs to get them into all the demanding hands before midnight. We clink glasses and kiss at midnight, amid the hoopla, but our brief respite is immediately broken by carousers angrily demanding more drinks.

If by midnight I've already had it, then by two, then three, then four long hours later I feel exponentially more like a zombie. John and I are slogging back and forth like marionettes in Punch and Judy, but we simply cannot keep up with all the orders. From back where we stand, the crowd has become just an amorphous, demanding blob, one enormous liver with hundreds of imploring eyes locked on us and countless arms and mouths, into which we pour an unending river of vodka, beer, and Champagne, plucking twenties from its waving pincers and stuffing singles back into the incorporeal mass, where they disappear with only the occasional belch floating one back. After several hours of being perpetually behind, with everyone surly by the time we finally reach them, our eyes begin to glaze with fatigue.

Sometime after one o'clock I spot the telltale round purses worn by a bunch of poseur douchebags who have formed a supposed design collective they call Plus-four. I simply think of it as the Collective of Snotty Ponces Who Wear Round Purses and Need a Collective Kick in the Slats. One night last year they came to a party Bjork's record label was throwing in the bar for her last album release. They were in the dubious company of a Turkish swine who owns a bar in Soho called Sweet and Vicious. This Turkish putz got drunk and started picking Champagne bottles out of the trash can and throwing them around. He hit the DJ with one and, when John ejected him, threw another one through the window from outside, bringing the party literally to a crashing halt. The following day I found out who he was from someone at the party who knew him. I called him and told him he'd better come down and talk to me before I contacted the 10th Precinct and let them take care of it. He arrived posthaste and faux-conciliatory amid this crowd of creeps with beards and shaved heads, all wearing tight, sheer women's blouses and big spangly bell bottoms and with big round purses slung around their arms.

I see people in all manners of dress and undress, and not much fazes me in New York anymore in terms of people's lame attempts to buy attention. There was, however, a profound ickiness to these guys I just couldn't come to terms with. I told them they were never to come back and they exploded with wounded, Euro-accented flounce so absurd I thought I was being put on. They filibustered that they were longtime customers, that they were friends with one of our DJ's, that whatever that Turkish pig had done he acted alone and they did their best to stop him and remove him from the bar, etc. In the end the Turkish guy paid for the window and promised never to come back to my bar. He told me I could go trash his bar if I liked. I declined the offer, neglecting to mention that I'd been in his bar only once, years prior, and found it, now understandably, loathsome.

On noticing them again now, I thought it might make me feel good to go over and give them the heave, but eyeing the crowd I realized I literally couldn't even see through the tiny, packed room to where they were sitting, much less maneuver my way there. Polo wasn't doing much of a job as stand-in for the more svelte Roberto, so I squeezed through the throng infrequently to view the carnage. Loopy revelers swooped about in mindless imitation of dance, clutching endless bottles of cheap sparkling wine and "forties," 40-ounce bottles of malt liquor they had sneaked in. The floor was covered with our broken glassware, which crunched tauntingly under my boots. I plowed through the densely swaying bodies like a diver threading my way through an enormous kelp bed, snatching the contraband out of astonished hands. In truth, by this point I was actually looking to start something, I'm not quite sure what. But simply tearing beers and bottles of Cold Duck out of some idiot's grip is, one must concede, not the most diplomatic solution to the problem of people thoughtlessly bringing their own coals to Newcastle. I was casing the place agitatedly and basking stoically in the wails of outrage from the quavering lips out of which I had just plucked a warm Korbel brut or an Olde English 1800. I stopped even trying to admonish people that they couldn't bring their own liquor into a bar and thereafter would just snatch the bottle or can, turn on my heel and retreat wordlessly, leaving furious invective piling up behind me. Both trash cans were filled several times over through the night with these nonindigenous containers, and Polo and I made slapstick figures heaving them through the wall of terpsichore to the hallway and out to the street to be collected.

True to form with kids in New York these days—that is, white kids all trying their hardest to be "street"—the hallways and bathrooms got tagged up, down, and center with moronic graffiti. The bathrooms had just been repainted a week before, so I was further disheartened and enraged to register the stark, hideous swaths of black these little vermin make with liquid shoe polish applicators. The newest twist on this monumental urban annoyance is a type of hydrochloric acid, which, when sprayed onto glass, etches into it permanently. Our twelve-foot front door now bore some wigga's scrawl, a $1,500 pane of glass to replace. Paper towels and toilet paper had been thrown wildly around both bathrooms, and shattered glass filled the tub sinks and littered the floors. Someone had torn the toilet seat from the rear bathroom and both toilet paper holders had been ripped from the wall. My blood pressure was reaching the exploding point when, on another sweep to the back room, where seeming children lay sprawled out on the carpet in fuzzy indolence, I noticed someone had kicked in the frosted glass on the doors to Gavin's office. Directly facing them Seth stood nodding sedately, spinning records behind the little table he had set up there.

I didn't explode—I didn't have it in me to by that point. The entire night's constant lapidation of insult and imbecility just seemed to rise up and suffocate me. I juked through the thronged bodies back to the bar, where I found both Jerry and Joe making drinks for friends of theirs, and grabbed John by the shirt. "I want it shut down now!" I growled at him. "I mean *now*! Not one more drink goes out—I want this shit swept, man, bulldozed!" I had never seen John so weathered;

though I could tell he agreed heartily, his usual bounce had atrophied to a curt nod of relieved approval.

I told Meredith, who was spinning just then, to yank the music. She nodded incredulously, trying to gauge what exactly that meant in terms of how much longer she could spin. I hollered that I meant now. "It's four o'clock and I fucking hate everyone in this entire place!" I spluttered. "Pull the plug on that shit right now!" She complied doubtfully, and when the wall of din ceased there was a mumbled outcry of befuddled protest. I hopped around the bar and yanked open the door, kicking down the wedge to let the chill air rush in, and then turned off the heat, leaving the HVAC fans blasting still. Finally I cranked the lights up. People shielded their eyes and squawked their resentment more loudly, true music to my enflamed ears. I began screaming for everyone to get out. "Thank you for coming, thank you for leaving—GET THE FUCK OUT!" I heard my own voice cracked and weak from the night's strain. No one was moving.

I sailed into the back "lounge" and flicked the harsh fluorescent lights on there. Writhing couples disentwined blinking and squalling, and I told Seth to kill the music. The carpet was soaked with wine and beer stains and glass was smashed everywhere there, too. I was sifting about for what glassware still lay unbroken and hustling people on their way when I heard the music go on again in the bar. Now like an enraged mother animal I flew into the hallway. As I entered the bar I found the lights had been turned back down, the door closed, Meredith at the DJ station spinning again, and Jerry behind the bar pouring shots for himself and all the DJs.

The ruckus I set up shames me somewhat to describe now. I've never felt more at odds with so many people, but I've never cared less. Joe actually came back behind the bar to help restrain me in my lambasting of Jerry and Meredith, claiming it was his fault, as well, that he put Jerry up to it, which only started me venting invective at him. I snatched the needle from the record Meredith was playing and snapped the power to the turntables off at the surge strip. I had some outer awareness of how out of control I must have seemed to everyone around me, how uncool, but I was like a top gyrating in rage at that point. I sprinted around the bar and once again cranked the house lights up and opened the door. The sidewalk outside, and as far up the street as I could see, glittered with our broken glassware. Gangs of kids were drifting about the door, others lay sprawled across the hoods of cars parked along the block. "Fucking Christ," I muttered, thinking of the police making their rounds tonight to give out summonses.

Reentering the bar with my hands full of glasses, I began literally herding groups of people toward the tendrils of cold air licking from the door. I could hear people grumbling about me as they donned their coats and scarves, "God, what a dick, that guy!" I redoubled my volume as I swept through the room, shouting "Get out, get the fuck out! Get out, get the fuck out!" An ugly Hispanic kid in baggy pants and a headband I had noticed earlier involved in some scuffle staggered up to me and slurred that he didn't like me, standing with his hands clenched. I looked over at Joe, who was sitting at the bar with his eyebrows raised and a grin on his face, waiting to see me explode. I growled at him, "Get this mutt out of my face, please." Courteous as ever, Joe gently led the kid, whose eyes couldn't even focus, out to the street as though he were a kindly but infirm old gentleman who had lost his way.

As there had not been a single person in the bar all night I wished ever to return, I was relieved of the obligation of politesse of any kind. In fact, just the opposite was called for; one of my main worries was that this night opened the bar up to a passel of vile punks who now knew where to find us. You have to figure you're in the business: a bar is often a repository of bad behavior. But there is a big difference between adult bad behavior and kids, even kids who are of legal drinking age. Kids, when drunk, mark up the walls with their inane scribblings and start fights. They bring in their own alcohol because they're unscrupulous dipshits. Adults do coke in the bathrooms and grope one another. The former behavior is objectionable because it annoys and harms others. The latter, I couldn't care less what you do to yourself in the bathroom. Only adults are allowed in bars for a reason. It turns out to be a very good reason.

In hindsight it's easy to spot errors in my thinking. Clearly I should have taken Jerry and Joe both up on their willingness to work, Jerry behind the bar and Joe on the door with me. With two on the bar, Joe screening the door and me free to roam and keep an eye on everything, we would have had security covered. Joe and Jerry wouldn't have been schlitzed when I most needed them, and the night's outcome, I suspect, would have been far different. But at the time, who's thinking apocalypse? Sadly, I have to more or less admit that, in fact, I was, but I took things too much into my own hands, counting on my normal ability to steer the right course when I'm at the helm, rather than bringing in manpower and delegating strategically. Deluged, I ended up going down with the ship.

By the end of the night I was speechless, literally. I had lost my voice from screaming. Taking in the bedlam that was formerly the bar and gallery after everyone was out would have left me in tears, had I not been too exhausted to register emotion. I silently nodded good night to each of the DJs and bartenders in turn, still smoldering at the senselessness of the night's debauchery. In the ensuing days I would have to deal with the smashed and etched doors in the gallery, the torn up and tagged bathrooms and the entire inventory of glassware, over seven hundred dollars' worth, that was now vanished. The floor blinked on and off now on a slurry of detritus that included several cell phones, sunglasses, coats, sweaters, scarves, shoes, and even panties left behind by the bacchanalians. I trod through the piles unthinkingly as I wandered back and forth turning off switches, counting out the till, locking doors, and running down shades.

At five forty-three, when finally I slipped outside into the thin morning frost, the cabbies at the garage next door were just finishing the changeover of their shifts, washing up in the open spigot and joshing each other loudly in African-tinged French. I noticed an incongruously pristine clear plastic container set on the sidewalk under the pay phone near the taxi garage. It held the funny apparition of four chocolate cupcakes with pink frosting and red sprinkles. I smiled and shook my head at the wonder, then turned and began locking up. As I reached up to pull down the heavy steel shutters to padlock, I heard a thump and felt something softly thud against my leg. I looked down to find my pant leg smeared with the pink frosting and the cupcakes, their dark crumbs now desecrated among the cigarette butts and broken glass, heaped at my feet. I turned in shock to see one of the garage managers, a squat Indian, striding angrily back toward the garage entrance. He had, inexplicably, kicked the cupcakes at me.

As I stalked up behind him in blasted disbelief, spluttering indignation for the umpteenth time that night, the two Senegalese drivers readying their cabs at the curb in front of us began taunting him, "Mmmmmm, oh no, now look what you do! You in beeg trouble now. Dees man going to keel you, an am goin' to watch! Ha!" He tried to duck into the garage, but I grabbed him by the shoulder and spun him around, hissing my rage in a stream of imperceptible accusation. Eight solid hours of screaming over the noise had rendered my throat preadolescent, and now, facing this glib bastard, all I could do was pipe reedily "Did, did you hear me?!" He smirked, clearly in no danger from this spent, bedraggled creature, and replied that, yes, he had in fact heard me. "Well, all right, then!" I heard myself chirp angrily, turning to stomp past the two Africans, now nearly falling out of their cabs in hysterics. "Yah," one of them hooted, "juz look what you done to dees man's pants!" I shuffled back to finish locking up, shaking my head wearily. This fucking town, I thought . . . This is what I do for a living? Down the block and up Ninth Avenue, familiar shards of my broken glassware along the route carried on mocking me halfway home. Never again.

CHAPTER VI

Sweet Release

I see myself dying behind my bar. One night I'll be cutting limes or marrying bottles up and three seventeen-year-olds with panty hose over their faces will breeze in, demand the till, and then, getting jumpy and impatient, just go ahead and pop me three times anyway, launching over the bar to grab the twenties out of the register I'd just rung open with shaky hands. I'll be down on the rubber hex mats, my legs buckled under me, looking up past the speed racks hanging askew from the ice bins to the smoke eater on the ceiling, now gulping in the sulphurous wisps from the 9mm that smote me. As my blood mixes with the gruel of water, alcohol, and assorted filth that nightly coats the floor I'll notice how dirty the speed racks are underneath. Customers will bob above me, asking if I'm okay. I'll move my jaw to speak but nothing will come. Some well-meaning sot will be hovering over me, yelling that I'll be all right as I feel myself dropping, as if on a very fast elevator. I roll my head to the side and my last vision of this life is the tattered Old Mr. Boston gin box that holds what constitutes the backup stock.

Grim, I know. I have long toyed with this persistent vision, the sort of daydream you replay constantly to torture yourself, like when a girlfriend dumps you for another guy and you construct in your mind a spot-on scenario of the two of them rutting gleefully. Nothing, my subconscious must have reasoned at some point, could be more ignoble.

Sometimes I'll make little changes to it. Whenever I had a brief crush on a new waitress she would generally make some sort of gripping cameo, but it all comes out the same anyway. I always die in the utmost ignominy and waste on the floor of my bar. For added measure of outrage I like to envision the guys who shot me getting away clean. I think about this so frequently the sting of it has become almost like a comforting touchstone, the way one pokes a sore tooth with one's tongue, or picks at a scab.

Still, I have my own addiction to this bedlam. The bar itself has become my drug. It's true; I fear leaving the warm, dark cocoon of noise, speed, sex, smoke, ashes, fuzziness. You know the outside world, what it's like out there; it's cold and bright, all harsh right angles and pressing obligations, decisions to be made, each with its own permanent consequence. While outside my life may be raining shite, and frequently is, inside these dingy confines it's all roughly the same as it's ever been, *gemütlich.* The bar is mopped clean, or covered with glasses and ashtrays and bags. The candles are lighted and the music's quiet, or it's blasting. The floor's going strong, people come in and drink, smoke, leave, and are replaced by others. Some want to talk. It's always been like this, it feels like. And to me it's automatic, mindless, lovely, like floating in the womb again. As a friend's mother once told me, "It's easier to grapple with a devil you know than a devil you don't." There is a covert exhibitionistic thrill to tending bar that makes me understand, on a tiny scale, the kind of junkie wallop that keeps driving performers back to the stage. For, whether or not you think it, you've but to stand behind a busy bar on a weekend night to understand that it *is* a stage, and if you don't want to perform back there the customers can and will punish you. But I find even when it's making me nuts, this gig, I'll take a break for a bit, go away and see some pine cones or ocean somewhere, and, though I'm loath to admit it, in the back of my mind I miss it. By the time I return I'm invariably champing to get back to it.

Long before I was twenty, I remember having this terrible fear of becoming entrenched in this profession. It's nothing unique or original to me, either. I recall clearly one time at the Ovens of Brittany in Madison, where I began working on the floor at the age of seventeen with my friend Monty, who is ten years my senior and now owns eight restaurants in Madison. I knew at the time that he, like me, yearned to be clear of the grease and stress and bickering of restaurants, though perhaps he hid it better than I. We played a lot of basketball together, but were more competitive with our mouths than our jump shots, both on and off the court. One day I asked him tauntingly how old he was and when he told me twenty-eight I sniffed that by that age I was going to at least have a real profession. I was just trying to land one, and he was so sharp—older and cleverer than I—that I was being extra pointed in my cruelty. But I'll never forget the look of frozen horror in his face as my snide remark found its target. I don't suppose I'd ever seen Monty at a loss for words, but he looked as though I'd actually slapped him. After a moment he roused himself and forced a curdled grin, replying ominously "Yeah, well, we'll see about that, won't we?"

I couldn't immediately understand what I'd done to so shock and, I imagine, hurt the seemingly indomitable Monty until much later, when I began to fully grasp the generally unacknowledged taint of shame that runs just beneath the surface of any service job. Moving from the floor to tending bar was certainly an improvement, but the second-class status of the work will always cling to it. People are fond of pointing out that this is only so in America, where people are valued for their net worth and status more than for their hard work, and that in Europe and elsewhere one often finds older bartenders and waiters who are accomplished and proud in their profession. I haven't found that to be true in the least. There are many Americans in the service industry who take pride in their work and Europeans don't seem at all immune from the bitterness produced by one's labors being quietly maligned or taken as less than significant. Even people who make out well in the industry acknowledge a faint stink associated with it, as though it is somehow beneath one's dignity. Amusing evidence of this is the lemming effect that ripples through the staff whenever someone is sprung, off presumably to a better life. I always marveled to register the panic that took hold at the Odeon whenever a staffer took off on a Fulbright or landed what seemed a plum job in film production; it almost invariably precipitated a rash of jumping overboard. People would quit without having anything else lined up. Contemplating someone else moving on to better things, getting ahead of them, the indignities of the job, already tenuously fought down from day to day, seemed to double, threatening to enslave them dolorously for the rest of their lives unless they acted *now*.

I've certainly dogpaddled along in the same dirty bathwater as everyone with whom I've worked and was immune to none of these fears. For me it somehow became crystallized as one dread prospect, that of discovering myself still in the business when I am forty. That, I reasoned early on, would be the outside limit of pathetic indolence, a clear sign that I had let go my hold on life's promise and had slid indifferently into the mire of myopia that would allow one to mistake this temporary holdover for a "real job." Mind you, I didn't have any actual misgiving that I could possibly find myself in that situation when my fifth decade came up; it was a theoretical shudder, the way one considers what it would be like to be attacked by a shark. I just enjoyed teasing myself with the monstrousness of the scenario, like replaying a horror movie's premise in my mind and inserting myself as a character to imagine what I'd do. Certainly all of this was simply playing around, making "easy" money at a job that, though both mentally demanding and physically punishing, was a trifle, a juvenile phase that, like delivering newspapers or mowing lawns, is moved through naturally by anyone bent on cutting an actual trajectory in the world. I could no more see myself lingering on in it than I could imagine attending high school at that age. When people asked what I do I would preface my response with a kind of apology or justification, embarrassed to be seen as doing nothing more than tending bar, an unfit calling for a grown man, anyone with aspirations. "You do have to know when to leave it, you know," I would acknowledge to other bartenders I knew. "You don't wanna be forty and still tending bar, for God's sake." All would nod hauntedly, as if on cue. What I was embarrassed to tell anyone, especially myself, is how much fun I was having in the job, how much I loved the grinding pace and pressure, the intense friendships on the floor, and how terrified I was of quitting what had become the only life I know and one through which I move quite comfortably. You're not supposed to want to stay in this kind of job if you've got a brain, if you've gone to college. You're not really, I guess, supposed to like what you do, if society determines it's an inferior position for you to hold.

This year my earliest professional nightmare becomes real. For a long time leading up to that benchmark, I couldn't figure out what to do about it. I've become so skilled a bartender that I've remained one long past the age when most of my peers consider it a seemly profession. My friends and girlfriends have all, in their turn, tenuously brought up the subject, as though I were still living with my mother or whizzing around town on one of those kick scooters.

"Uh, dude, don't you think it's time you, like, got a real career, maybe?"

Nearly everyone I spoke to for years corroborated my denigration of the job, until one summer I took off from the Odeon to spend in Italy. In Florence, where my father was raised, we still have relations, and I've visited them a number of times. My uncle Giuliano is the unacknowledged patriarch of the clan there. He's a self-made man; his father died when Giuliano was a very small boy. He was reared working as a porter in the train station, and eventually worked his way up to the top of the management of the union. Upon retiring, he ran through the usual time-fillers, played tennis, sailed a boat he keeps on the Mediterranean, fixed up an old Moto Guzzi he found in a field and putted around on for a bit, before he realized he was bored and still in need of challenges. He took another job running the public transportation system in Bologna. When I arrived that summer, Giuliano asked me what I was doing with myself. I told him sheepishly I was still working as a barman, but that I had more ambitious plans for the near future. A storm seemed to cross his considerable brow and he pulled me aside. "Why are you talking that way?" he asked sternly. "You should never disparage your job, regardless what it is. The kind of people who do that are doomed to languish in the misery they have made for themselves. The job will always change, you see. What you must do is make certain that whatever it is you're doing, if you are spending your time on it, it is worth doing it absolutely as well as you can. You must try to be the best bartender, because only in doing something truly well is there nobility in working. Then you will move forward, because when people notice you bring something special to a job that seems nothing special, they take notice of you and your attitude. Others get left behind." He was deadly serious, angry, even, with my flip dismissal of my work, which, he said, living through the war and its aftermath there, he never had the luxury to take for granted.

Though I initially found Giuliano's depression-era lecture hokey, it had a profound long-term effect on me. It wasn't exactly that I dug right in and dedicated myself to becoming the best-damn-bartender-in-the-world, but slowly I began changing my concept of and approach to the job. Where formerly I would stand about bored and calculate how many more hours I had until dinner, and would roll my eyes at people's founderings or requests for silly drinks, I began to step forward and try to be of help. Simply because—it occurred to me as though a complicated theorem had just unknotted itself for me alone—simply because I realized I could. What had before seemed beneath me, and had made me surly and unwilling to extend myself in any direction, became just another part of the job, seen through Giuliano's definition. This was the beginning of what I came to call for myself my zen bartender act. If I could be polite to the most impossible customers, mop up spills with a tolerant smile, wipe out ashtrays, and remove chewing gum from under tables with the humility of an Indian untouchable, I figured, at some point the door to The Other Life would open and I would step serenely through it. With forty approaching fast apace, I can't exactly say that happened, but something else did. Banishing from my thinking the shame and desperation I had always felt about the job, and the resultant chip on my shoulder about people in other, more lucrative and socially alluring professions, made me acknowledge that there are aspects of this job at which I excel, which I love, and about which I feel proud, and I don't need to feel embarrassed over any of that anymore. Moreover, it freed me up to actually look closely at what I do behind the bar and try to improve on it, which sounds obvious, but really is not. In going nowhere, I had taken a huge leap.

o   o   o

Sundays are the bar's hangover. Throughout the city, the second-tier staff gets put on to clean up after the bedlam of Saturday night. Many of the more cutting edge places have their gay night on Sunday, figuring, pretty much correctly, that only the professional thrill-seekers will go out and spend money when everyone else is in watching *The Sopranos*.

We used to be open on Sunday nights, but we never made any money on them. For a while we maintained a conceit that despite the fact that Sundays were dead, and we actually ended up losing money by being open, we were going to stay open, simply to say we are open seven days a week, an inchoate idea of nouveau entrepreneur cool. Soon enough, however, the sophomoric stance of not making a profit on a given night wore through. Since I guarantee my bartenders $150 per night—meaning if they don't make that in tips, the house ponies up the remainder to that sum—it peeved me to pay my Sunday bartender, Jerry, to sit in an empty bar and dole out free drinks to three or four of his acting class buddies, plowing their way steadily through the entire top shelf.

Then my partner Gavin scheduled a Sunday night stag party for one of the painters who showed in his gallery. Because I like Robert, the groom-to-be, and he requested I work his bachelor party, I reluctantly took the shift myself. Robert also hired Spencer as his DJ, for which I was grateful. Spencer's not really a DJ, he's more simply a roving personality in the art scene, a rakish cross between Jean Cocteau and a used-car salesman who lives and dies by 1980s C-list pop. I've only been to five or six bachelor parties, but it seems the meter goes from embarrassingly boring to excruciating, with really no other stops on the dial. Guys stand around a bar somewhere half-heartedly razzing the victim, whose trepidation about the upcoming event is always palpable enough you swear you taste salt in the air from the hot tears about to spring forth above his terrified grin. Having grown up in a small liberal enclave in the frozen north, where men are sometimes permitted to be men, provided they behave, and women are respected, or else, I've only been to the kind of tepid bachelor parties where nothing goes on that would even rumple the brow of the bride, were she sitting in the room hoisting an expensive single malt and puffing away on a Dunhill's blue label like the rest of us. I'd never seen a stripper do her thing in my life. Robert is from Texas, though, and I figured he'd have some old shit-kicking buddies blowing in like twisters from the other side of the Rio Grande. In the back of my mind I thought maybe I'd get a nice voyeuristic jolt from a real stag party. Even if it was grim, I reasoned, it could be grim in a funny way. Or lurid in an educational way. I wasn't sure what exactly, but at least I'd be working and so could watch the squalor without being directly involved, the bartender's blessed remove.

Somehow the day got beyond me. I went bicycling out to Brooklyn with my girlfriend, really just to cross the Brooklyn Bridge in the sun, with the tart salt breeze ripping up the East River, and figured I had just enough time afterward to throw together dinner before having to head out. It didn't work quite that way, however, as eight-twenty found me gulping down hot cheekfuls of linguine with pesto, trying to make the eight-thirty starting time.

As I pedaled up to the bar, the whole bachelor party was standing there, stuffed with steak from dinner at the Old Homestead and looking at their shoes before the closed-up facade. I tried to be as nonchalant as I could while prying the locks from the pins holding down the steel shutters over the window. The main door was opened, however, which I found odd. Just as I was leading the party into the hallway, Jerry, the actor-cum-bartender, came steaming up from inside, shushing us furiously. I had forgotten Jerry's little theater troupe was to be rehearsing this week for a showcase performance they were going to be putting on in the gallery. Jerry emerged feigning officiousness at all the noise going on. Behind him, two very thin, pretty girls and a skinny bald guy were looking thespianly upset. I looked at him skeptically and told him this was Robert's bachelor party, and if he thought our morose arrival was noisy, just wait a bit. He stormed back into the gallery and I unlocked the bar and began flipping on switches like mad. Everyone was, I think, trying to figure out if this was how it was supposed to happen, but no one was complaining outright. Still, I felt lame that the bar hadn't been open and set up upon their arrival. I began pouring beers and what few drinks I could without anything set up, some shots, mustering up what false joviality I could to pep things up a bit. Spencer shuffled in looking exactly like what I supposed DJs look like on Sundays, if one had ever been spotted up and about.

The party was the antithesis of what I had hoped, consisting of maybe fifteen guys, some of them artists I recognized, others just mild-looking Wall Street types in their Sunday Dockers. As I sliced limes one of Robert's friends, the best man, came over to give me the scoop. There would be, he told me, three strippers performing. The first girl was to go it alone, in about a half hour, he said. Following her would be two others who performed together. I was already deeply embarrassed. I was having trouble envisioning how this unlikely assemblage of uncomfortable guys who seemed to want nothing to do with one another was going to be able to breathe with the further vacuum effect a naked woman in the room would bring the enterprise.

Happily, Spencer started the music and the guys all got down to drinking hard, there being virtually nothing else to do. They were tipping hugely, almost obscenely. Men are, I've noticed, very pleased to part with money at such times. It gives them something to do and takes away their awkwardness, confirming their place in the universe as one who wins his own bread. Though they still didn't seem any happier, they began vying to see who got to pick up the round or who got to buy Robert another shot. Robert, for his part, was wandering about a little dazed looking but not in the least pickled. When we first opened the bar four years ago, Robert was the somewhat too-boisterous kid whom we had to boot a couple of times before he got the message to calm down. Still, before he met Jennifer he could knock back three or four of our 15-ounce Margaritas and seven beers and still be getting going. Now he took me aside and told me to make his drinks out of soda and sour mix only. A fat guy with a bushy mustache and three gold chains to match his gold watch had been milling incongruously about the edge of the room looking angrily glum for some time. Suddenly he called for Spencer to stop the music. He announced in a thick Brooklyn accent that Sondra, a very talented lady, was about to start her show. He enjoined us all to behave like "gentlemen and professionals," which gave me pause. Professionals? How does a professional stripper ogler behave? I had been talking to a very sweet fellow named John who was, it turned out, the bride's brother, and who was blind. I tapped my index finger lightly on his chest, "That's right, keep yer bloody hands to yerself, lad!"

I didn't even notice the arrival of the first stripper, I was so busy with drinks. I just looked up at one point and there was this tragically fake-looking girl. She was a walking porn cliché, with ferociously straightened, dyed blond hair, giganto breast implants that looked blocky and uncomfortable, an orangey tan that functioned as clothing, so completely and opaquely did it cover her, and a homely, sallow face devoid of any expression whatever. What fascinated me about her was her pubic hair, or what was left of it; she had dyed it blond and trimmed it into one of those little Hitler mustache-style bikini trims you see if you open up a *Playboy* or *Penthouse* these days. I'd never seen a girl in real life with that going on.

Her stupendous unsexiness was actually a point of interest to me. She was tottering about on a pair of horrid, clunky high-heeled pumps, bright red, as ungainly as they clearly were uncomfortable. She didn't seem as though she particularly minded either her task or her environs, rubbing herself up and down various members of the party, as pointed out by the best man. On the other hand, she looked no happier or occupied than the toll booth clerks in the subway. I stared at her from behind the bar as she went about her rounds, wondering who determined that this sort of look on a woman should somehow be considered sexy. The generic banker guys were laughing uncomfortably, giving her the requisite, polite attention one would, say, a waiter clearing your table. The artists in the room, however, being way too cool actually to notice a naked girl among them, were bunched up at the end of the bar, chattering away about their prospects for a show with this or that gallery, or how Williamsburg is definitely *over*. No one seemed to be tipping the poor girl. It was like watching a car crash.

True to form, when Sondra's *maquereau* gave the signal, she dropped whatever blushing fool she'd been frotting and stomped over to a pile of clothes arranged on one of the bar stools. I watched her donning her thong and tights, brassière and spandex dress like an exhausted gravedigger. She was the antistripper, I reflected, in that she came out nude, did her bit, for better or worse, and then got dressed. I wondered if somehow we could intervene, implore the beefy Italian chaperon to call off the next girls. He, the whole time, had been collecting what few tips his girl could shake out of these tightwad sophisto-artiste dweebs and kept coming up to me to change them in for bigger bills, which was depressing me all the more, as I clocked the hard proof that this poor girl was showing off her slice for less than the price of a pie.

I was again caught with my nose to the grindstone when the second act made its grande entrée. I became aware at some point of a shift in the room's center of gravity. Still acting like none of them could be bothered to take notice, the boys were all being magnetically drawn across the floor. Even John, the shy blind man who had been holding court with me and several others at the end of the bar all night, picked up his red-tipped cane and timidly shuffled his way forth to get into the action. These two girls were cut of a very different cloth from Sondra. They arrived with skimpy clothing intact and were, perhaps because they had one another as backup, full of piss and vinegar. Where Sondra had been more or less what I expected a stripper to look like, both of these girls were shockingly pretty. One was a petite English girl with dark blond hair that seemed reasonably to be her own color, and the second was a fantastically muscular black girl with long hennaed braids. They both had, once the skimpy outfits became an afterthought, their own breasts and pubic hair, the normality of which made their sexuality now reverberate through the bar like a slap; these girls were suddenly so much more naked, somehow, than Sondra had been. Spencer, ever the opportunist, was spinning a 2LiveCrew anthem with the delicate refrain, "Yo, we want some pusssss-sy!" Even the faux-jaded artisti were standing up on the bench to get an eyeful. Roberto, my busboy, was hopelessly AWOL, having burrowed nimbly into the crowd to get a choice spot.

Sadly for me, the girls spread a big, white tablecloth over the lighted floor in front of the bar to do their act on, and once they got down to it, with all the guys huddled on stools in front of me, I couldn't see a bit of it, save for an occasional foot thrust into the air or the flip of a braid through the tangle of onlookers. Eventually I gave up trying to see the show and contented myself watching the guys standing on the bench on the other side of the narrow room. It was like watching sixth graders viewing some grisly educational film on the miracle of birth. It made me laugh to see these grown men grimacing, literally covering their faces with their hands, tittering nervously, and bellowing in disbelief at whatever tricky plumbing the girls had gotten up to.

Nobody was ordering anything while the wonder twins were at it, so I wandered down the bar to where their pimp daddy was hanging out counting singles. Just before I reached him, the door to the gallery opened and Jerry emerged with his acting troupe in tow. Jerry's mouth gaped and the two actresses following him went white at the spectacle. I stepped up on the ice bin and up onto the bartop to look over the heads of the amassed voyeurs. The girls had placed the best man on his back in the middle of their tablecloth and had clamped their legs together around his head in a very asphyxiating sort of Roman knuckle lock. Jerry pushed his horrified troupe quickly through the door to the exit hallway as I stood on the bar laughing. The spindly Michael Stipe–looking actor lingered for a moment on the other side of the glass door, his eyebrows raised in fascination, before disappearing.

Jerry, being the only person I know who frequents strip clubs, promptly reappeared, his anger replaced, now that his colleagues were safely seen to cabs, with a suddenly keen thirst. I was actually relieved to have the company behind the bar, since I now had nothing to do. I figured with all his experience in the field he could give me some color commentary on the action. Roberto emerged from the fray tousled and grinning. "What'd you learn in there, Robertino?" I asked him. He just shook his head in wonder, giggling in the funny, girlish laugh he has when he's embarrassed. This gave me a sort of epiphany: the squirrelly guys on the bench, the artists distractedly feigning indifference, the beet-red actors filing to the door with their eyes locked on the lurid display: it's not meant to be sexy, these girls taking their clothes off. It's meant to be exactly what it is, embarrassing. The same way people shell out money to be frightened out of their wits by horror flicks, another entertainment that has always seemed indecipherable to me, these guys are actually paying these girls hundreds of dollars to embarrass the shite out of them.

I looked up to see some kind of stirring in the crowd. Someone had called for John, the blind fellow, to be sent to the lions. Whistles and catcalls rang through the room, but I felt my heart sink as I watched him tapping his way gamely to the front of the mass, handed from one person to the next. "Oh, God," I said aloud, "please don't do this to this poor man." The girls got up from whomever they'd been ravishing and fell upon John, who stood grinning good-naturedly and shaking slightly. But where before they had been whipping off belts and roughing up their prey, they immediately geared down for John, God bless them. The blond girl whispered something in his ear as the other girl gently took his cane from his grip. They licked his ears and neck and removed his tie. Everyone in the place was hooting deliriously. Spencer had put on some old vaudevillian trombone-and-drum striptease saw. The girls took John's hands and placed them squarely on their breasts, rubbing their torsos up and down him. I was in agony. I can't even say why. John seemed fine with it all, and the girls were being very sweet to him. I got squeezed between their tawdriness and their tenderness. So did John. By the end of it he was laughing it up, openly pawing the both of them. I looked over to their business manager to see if he was up to enforcing his no-touching policy, but he was just looking on stupidly, his eyes as alert and shallow as a rooster's.

After they loosed John the girls strolled over and began dressing again nonchalantly, all pretense of sexiness dropped now as they foraged for their wadded-up thongs and hose. Some of the guys began calling for them to come back, whereupon they fell into a huddle with their chaperon. He again had Spencer stop the music to announce that if we could amass $160 more, the girls would perform another fifteen minutes. I was amused by his math. How did he happen to pull out that peculiar sum? Why not simply $200? One of the wedding party fellows borrowed a pint glass to collect up funds. Several difficult minutes later they announced they had just over $100 after everyone had been hit up, and the endeavor was looking doubtful. Just when the girls seemed on the verge of packing it in, Jerry, of all people, jumped up and said he would pony up the remaining $60 if the girls would perform on the bar where the bartenders could see what was going on.

In a blink the game lasses were nude again and up on the walnut bar. Jerry was ecstatic, bopping to the music and egging them on. I recalled the red spotlight that one of the DJ's had installed last year for a drag show, still affixed to the ceiling across the room and pointed at the bar. I went back to the liquor room and got an extension cord, wriggled under the bench to the socket, and hooked it up to a round of applause from the room. Now the girls were bathed in a seedy red glow, dancing on top of the bar, nine feet in the air. I came back around behind the bar and hopped up to sit on the back counter and take in the show. Jerry had taken out two more twenties and was waving them about the girls' knees, imploring them to do to him whatever they'd been doing to the partygoers. The black girl snatched the bills from his paw and then shoved him away, to cheers and laughs from the assembly. They both then turned and beckoned to me. I shook my head firmly and tried to wave them off, but the room was having none of it. Cheers erupted and the girls jumped down to my side of the bar and pulled me from where I was sitting. I figured at this point I might as well just be a sport and not spoil the situation. Even their manager was laughing as I looked around the room. The girls placed me flat on my back on top of the bar and stood over me gyrating, in a display that, from my vantage point, looked less sexy than simply gynecological. The English girl suddenly dropped down painfully onto my crotch like a wrestler straddling an opponent. She began cantering up and down on me, crushing my balls. I tried not to grimace, wondering when she would let up and allow me a breath. She was then up in a trice and snatched me up by the ankles. The black girl joined in from above my head, helping to hoist me up onto my neck and shoulders, yogalike. Her white pumps ground into the bartop perilously close to my cheek. I was having serious misgivings about the adroitness of their improvisation when the English girl let go of my ankles to attack my belt buckle. She got it loose just as my legs began to topple her way, and she grabbed my ankles again to prop me back up. With my chin cranked into my chest, darts of pain shot up my neck. The English rose then again let go of my ankles and began tugging at my pants to pull them down, or rather up, being that I was upside down. The whole place was going bonkers now. Guys were howling through cupped hands, pounding the bar next to my head. For some reason they were incredibly stimulated by the sacrifice of the bartender.

I scarcely had time to reflect on the unsavory specter of myself upended on the bar with my dick flopping in the breeze when I felt, as in slow motion, the whole of the machinery going awry. My legs began swaying too far to starboard and the English girl was still ill-advisedly yanking at my pants. The black girl wasn't able to hold me from the other side, and suddenly we all three fell from the bar to the grimy rubber hex mats in a tangled, swearing heap. It was a comic-nightmarish version of every man's fantasy, being intertwined with two beautiful girls at once, but sadly not in any way I might have wished.

The English girl had rapped her head soundly against the tap stem on her descent and was holding the back of her skull. I checked to make sure she was all right, then the other girl, before pulling them both up and dusting myself off. The guys were all, predictably, cheering, and I shot another look quickly over to the brooding Italian manager to see if he was irate, but he sat unconcerned on the bench as though he'd seen it a hundred times.

Our tumble signaled the unspoken end of the night, quenching the fires of lust and spectacle that burned in the room just moments prior. The girls got dressed again, grousing a bit, and the guys began breaking up and setting off in small groups, wishing Robert the best of luck. Spencer finished up and packed his records away and the beefy chaperon traded in his twenties and few remaining singles for larger bills. Jerry made the girls Cosmopolitans and tried to talk them into coming to see his play, pushing the flyer on them as their retainer looked on now suspiciously from across the room. Well-honed instincts, I suspect.

Trudging back to my girlfriend's place late I passed through the gauntlet of transvestite hookers who ghoulishly prowl the loveliest West Village blocks now, having been recently deposed from the meatpacking district. Normally I keep my eyes averted as I pass them to avoid the come-ons, but tonight I was curious about them. A couple of them seemed more attractive, clothed at any rate, than Sondra, the first stripper. It's all part of some grimy circle of use and consumption, I thought, that I'd rather not contemplate too deeply, though as of tonight I'm certainly part of it, too. As the vendor of the mind lubricant as well as the voyeur and accessory tonight, I helped make the grist wheel gyrate. Turning onto the cobblestones of Jane Street, dappled with orange from the streetlights filtering through the arch of plane tree branches overhead, I considered that, in some vacuum of suspended morals and commerce, that may not necessarily be a bad thing.

o   o   o

It is important to realize that everyone entering a bar is there for something, and seldom is that just a drink. I don't mean for that to sound as sinister as it might, but a bar is a place for human exchange—of every variety—and a drink, if that's all you want, is invariably cheaper at home. One thing I feel fairly certain of, having observed for so long this admixture of appetites, is that most people who enter the bar don't themselves have a clear idea what they want there. Our generation doesn't seem terribly comfortable simply going out to a bar, meeting friends, and hanging with them to chat. Raised on passive viewing, groups large and small—what a friend of mine calls "single-sex packs"—rake through different bars on the familiar pub crawl, waiting expectantly for something interesting to happen to them, around them, in their presence—they're not quite sure. I am constantly asked by people who have made the trek over to my bar, which, perched on a forlorn industrial block is clearly a destination-only trip, where they should go next. I'll ask them what they're looking for and they can never define it. "I don't know, something happening, someplace where something's going on." I politely abstain from pointing out that, for self-sufficiently interesting people, *something's* going on literally everywhere, and, conversely, that spoiled, unthinking, and drifting amoebalike in perpetually jaded urban malcontent, they wouldn't really consider there to be something "going on" if Queen Elizabeth's jubilee were slated in the bar that night. Instead I tell them, almost truthfully, that I don't really go out to other bars that terribly much. Busman's holiday and all.

Years ago, at the tail end of a summer I spent flitting about Europe, I washed up broke and brokenhearted in the vaulted, Speeresque marble palladium that is the central train station in Milan. I needed to kill another week or so before my flight back to America, but I was burned out and bitter and wished no part in any more adventures. I took a room in a fleabag *pensione* near the station, where I figured I could stay out of trouble and sleep the week away. On my first night there I headed out to find a trattoria of some sort, or even just a *tavola calda* counter where I might grab a slice of pizza or a single hot dish, the type of thing they have all over the larger cities there. Meandering down a side street, I passed a small, cozy-looking bar, of the variety you see everywhere in Italy, normally packed with old men standing around gabbing, ogling women, and shooting down *espressi* in that way they do, in one quick toss. This bar caught my eye, however, in that something seemed different or out of place in it. It lacked the dourness many of the small places there embody, that ground-in sense of going nowhere giving onto silent hostility that rises out of neighborhood bars along with the drift of smoke. The clientele was a bunch of kids my age, all laughing and cavorting in a breezy way that arrested me for a moment in that gray city and in my gray mood. There was only a scattering of customers in the place, and no one seemed to be over twenty-five. I figured I could use an apéritif and so strolled in.

My entrance signaled a halt in the merriment, though not the usual, mistrustful one. The handful of kids there all looked up, like a knot of curious cats, exchanging knowing smirks. I stood, a bit self-consciously, before the marble bar for a moment waiting for the bar-keep to show up. There was continued tittering from the group over on the tables. Gelato gleamed in steel boxes behind glass at the bar and the taps featured Nastro Azzurro and Peroni. A redoubtably technical-looking espresso machine perched on the back bar, its immaculate chrome and lipstick-red panels gleaming like a Ducati. A minute or two passed during which I still couldn't detect anyone working there. Finally I ventured to ask the kids at the nearest table if there was someone on duty. This somehow caused the assembly to break into mischievous peals. A pixieish girl with a short blond bob hopped up from one of the rear tables at the same time as a shorter fellow with dark hair and drawn eyes like a basset hound's stood to his feet. They elbowed one another playfully in heading behind the bar, and then several others leapt up and did the same, all apparently part of some ruse on the barkeep, who was evidently absent for the moment. Nudging one another, they faced me puckishly, each inquiring solicitously over the others what I would like. Smiling, but not wanting to get involved in any wrongdoing, I said as diplomatically as possible that I might wait for the return of the bartender. This caused, of course, more hilarity and I sighed with puzzlement, having somehow become the butt of some type of prank.

The elfin blonde finally took over and shooed the others out from behind the bar. She told me playfully it might be quite a while before the bartender returned, so I would do well to simply tell her what I'd like. This she delivered in a deferentially slowed-up Italian that redoubled her cohorts' amusement, though I could tell from her quick eyes that she wasn't being cruel, just waggish. I gave in and ordered a Montenegro with ice. Protocol in Italian bars is to pay a cashier for your drink beforehand, whereupon you are presented a chit to give the bartender. There was no cashier and the pixie girl asked for no money upon delivering my drink. She nodded her head, smiled at me, and bounded out from behind the bar like a doe, to rejoin the table in back holding her friends. Now I stood more confused than ever. To avoid any future fray with the barkeep, I left a pile of lire on the bartop and took a table in the front window.

I cracked open a copy of *The Crying of Lot 49* I had gotten in a swap on the train down from Amsterdam and, while rereading the same paragraph ten or eleven times, I spied on a scenario that grew progressively more perplexing and, as a bartender, more fascinating to me. Each time one of the kids wanted something, they would get up and go behind the bar, sometimes fetching multiple orders for their friends. I couldn't figure out who possibly could have left the bar unattended for so long, or why these kids could be so brazen in their poaching. Clearly they had some kind of rapport with the owner. Still, it was like watching a very mannered version of a high school house party, with all the teenagers ransacking the liquor cabinet when the parents are off in Cancún. There wasn't a kid in the whole place who wasn't back behind that bar at some point, pouring drinks and making coffees nonchalantly, as though they were in their basement den. I watched in continued puzzlement while pretending to read, but I just couldn't get a handle on it. The street outside was busy with strollers heading out for a *passegiatta*, the evening constitutional before dinner, but no one else came into the bar.

Half an hour passed and I felt like another drink. When I got up and approached the bar again, the sad-eyed fellow was holding forth animatedly at the closest table. One of his friends nudged him and pointed me out. Barely interrupting his story, the sad-eyed fellow made a casual whisking motion to me and called out that I should just go back and serve myself. I backed away shaking my head and the laughter once again broke out. The pixie girl got up dutifully from the back table and came about to serve me, offering coquettishly, "Another, my love?"

I had to put the scene into some kind of order for myself, so I asked: "Who is the proprietor of this place?" The conversation at the tables ceased instantly and I felt all eyes on the back of my neck. Pixie girl smiled demurely and motioned about the room: *"Noi, all'ora!"* (Well, us!) The kids behind her burst out with loud hurrahs and more jokes flew about, too rapid-fire for me to grasp. She presented herself as Sara, pumping my hand like a candidate, and, motioning to the sad-eyed fellow, who tipped his head respectfully, said that was her brother Emilio. I was taken to the tables and introduced around to each of their friends in turn. When I told them I had been wondering what the hell was going on, watching them all pouring drinks, Sara said normally they just ignore *sconosciutti*—unknowns—until they clear off, but that they could see I was either lonely or stupid, so they let me stay and drink. When I asked how they make any money, they again smirked patiently, as though dealing with a favored but daft child. "We don't need to make money," Sara explained. "This is for us to play in, essentially a gift from our parents." I looked about and got several affirmative nods. I couldn't tell if anything they were saying was the truth, but I liked them all just the same. They were clearly having fun and they seemed supremely at ease in one another's company.

"Really?" I said. "Yours? Your parents must have a pile of money if they gave you this to play in."

Emilio just raised his eyebrows and nodded slowly, pursing his lips in that noncommittal Latin way of intoning "Well . . ."

"They own several cinemas in the city," Sara chimed in. "They let us open this to keep us out of trouble."

"Yes, but we manage to get into plenty anyway," another boy offered.

"So when do your parents come and close up?" I asked.

"No, *stronzo*, you don't understand, silly! They never come here, this is ours. We open when we want, we close when we want. We all know each other"—she gestured across the fifteen or so genial faces—"from the time we were born, practically. This is our meeting place, in the afternoon or evening, before we go out. Tonight we're going outside of town, to a pig roast and then dancing. Do you want to come with us?"

"That's very kind of you, but I'm a bit tapped out of cash, actually. You see, I've been traveling all summer and I'm just in town waiting for a plane—"

"Amore!" she thundered. "Don't be an ass! We are inviting you; you don't need to be fidgeting about money . . . Emilio, tell him!"

Emilio shrugged his shoulders and made a gesture with his hands as if to brush aside any such trivialities. The plan was thus laid, and with another round of drinks called for, I was scooped up by this merry band and deposited a week later at the gate of my flight. In between I was chauffeured about to other bars that met with their narrow approval, restaurants of every sort, from humble, hidden *trattorie* to lavish places on large squares, where plates just kept emerging unbidden. Though there was drinking, it was relaxed and sporadic, mostly low-alcohol aperitifs and wine with dinner, and I never saw any of them drunk. Late into every night, streaking about in four or five cars, they would head to clubs to dance and chat more. I had no idea where I was on any given night until we arrived back at the bar for a nightcap. The bar was the beginning and the end of all their excursions, the hub of their lives, seemingly, and as such—proximity being the great fertilizer of friendship—the facilitator of their continuing closeness with one another. Asked if they ever got sick of just hanging out in their bar every night with each other, they looked at me as if I were sick before starting in razzing me. "You've got some better ideas, maybe?" Behind the joshing it was clear they loved the little scene they had created, and, for them, there was no better way of passing their free time than playing in one another's trusted company. It struck me then, and has many times since, how different their socializing would be in America, where adulthood is now measured from the moment you run shrieking not only from your family home but often from your hometown and the people you knew growing up. The obvious rootlessness that has resulted in our society is difficult to measure, even as social scientists bend themselves to develop meaningful models and gauges for the concept of "social capital." But it's easy to see from where I stand. People just aren't as comfortable around one another anymore. Raised in an individualist society where the emphasis is on a popular culture centered around television and computers, people no longer know how to go out and enjoy themselves and each other. For a majority of young adults, going out in America is now synonymous with getting smashed. Watching Emilio and Sara and their friends' easygoing connection reminded me bittersweetly that it was not always so. Standing behind the bar on any given night, I frequently find myself shrugging away the thought that we're watching something important slipping away here, without even the means to measure the loss.

As the week progressed I fell naturally in step with their routine; I would wake in the mornings with a diabolical hangover in my room at the *pensione*. After coffee and a stroll around town to clear my head, I would alight at their bar in the early afternoon, now just one of the gang. We would drink a little and discuss plans for the night, to which discussions I contributed mostly fodder for ridicule with my halting Italian, and it would just go from there. It was an intoxicating, magical, almost unbelievable week, the more so for its unexpectedness. The moment I least wanted any kind of excitement or complication, I ended up in the most engaging company of complete strangers, whose open charm and generosity begged nothing in return.

At the close of that whirlwind week we met on a scant few hours of sleep in the morning for a final coffee in the bar and they drove me to the airport. Things had been very loose and knockabout, and I thought I might be falling for Sara, but pondering the situation as we blazed out past the grim suburbs, I realized I actually was just in love with their lifestyle and their situation. I never saw or heard from them again. I still think fondly and often about their bar, though, and their inexplicably inclusive friendliness. I love the concept of their bar as just a private place for them, unless you happen to walk through the door by accident in search of something that might only incidentally be a drink. That became another guiding principle for me in opening my bar. The private clubhouse anyone might come to, respectfully.

○   ○   ○

The part of the job I've always loved the most, in truth, is the going-home part. I'm sure that's true for many people about their jobs, but going home as a bartender is singular. Other people relish the closing whistle for the lure of camaraderie, the opportunity to reunite with their spouse or friends, have a drink, break bread. There is nothing to do and nowhere to go after I leave work. My girlfriend, like the rest of the populace, has been asleep for hours. Restaurants are all closed. You feel like the last human being alive, but after a while that becomes a solace rather than a drawback. There is never any hurry for me to leave work. I finish up my till and side work leisurely, the first breath of repose after running frantically all night. The quiet of the empty bar, the empty streets, the empty apartment, is a balm after the affront of the pounding music and urgent orders all night.

By the week's end the shifts become intense—blurry-busy—and I finish punch drunk. Friends who work in the daylight love to give me grief about my easy schedule, working three nights a week. I'm past trying to make them understand that twelve-hour shifts, with no breaks, on my feet, assaulted by noise and asphyxiated by smoke, hardly constitute a holiday. The corporeal toll of this job can be frightening. Your hands are papery dry from the slurry of water, alcohol, and citrus, which makes them crack and slice easily, which then stings horribly when exposed to more of those same solvents. Your legs and feet howl with a leaden ache and your lower back cinches from the hours of bending over involved in a night of steppin-fetchit.

When at last the crowd subsides after two-thirty, I'll duck outside to pull down the heavy steel shutters on the window and fire door. The chilly winter rain spitting fitfully out of the orangey overcast sky glazes the street, speckles my face and hands like a benediction at Christmas mass. The freshness of the air outside the bar is shocking, bracing. It makes me frightened once again for my pulmonary health to consider that, if the air on a particularly industrial block of the meatpacking district in New York City seems utopian in comparison to what I've been breathing all night, then what the hell have I been breathing all night? I hate to think about the cigarette smoke we deal with. I frequently wonder what my lungs must look like after so many years of sucking it up. It's like having a death sentence hanging over my head, like being fully apprised of the dangers of asbestosis but clocking in every day to a job removing old insulation, without the benefit of the OSHA-certified filter mask. My friend Reid, who makes his living as a builder in California, once offered, only half facetiously, to construct for me in the bar a system of suspended tubing that slides back and forth on separate rails, one for each bartender. Like Victorian diving costumes, the tubes would connect to brass helmets with glass portals. Fresh air would be pumped into them and orders would be taken through a system of walkie-talkies. After a while all you can do is stop thinking about it. There's really no other way to deal with it, aside from quitting my job and changing to forestry management. I hate the cigarette smoke from the bottom of my heart, and I loathe the smokers whose deathsticks

I light all night so that they can blow it in my face. It's no exaggeration to state that I'm perfectly aware these people are killing me. I feel it, we all do, the difference in how hard it is to wake up the morning after working. I have a persistent little smoker's hack, unpronounced but always there, every time I take a deep breath. I have never, I might add, been a smoker. We've done what we can in terms of ventilation, having last year installed a $35,000 system that controls heat and air-conditioning and puts the entire air supply for the bar through two different filters, one a special carbon filter designed to extract smoke before mixing it with 75 percent fresh air. Still, the facts are simple: the bar is a tiny box, in which there are often fifty to seventy-five people sandwiched, most of them chain smoking. Secondary smoke isn't even an apt term for what we undergo nightly; I simply take it on my own faith that I smoke two packs a night behind my bar. Studies released by the American Lung Association show that employees in bars and restaurants where smoking is permitted receive four to six times the exposure to secondhand smoke as the general public and have a 50 percent higher risk of lung cancer and heart disease as a result. Secondhand smoke kills approximately one thousand New York City residents every year.

Mayor Bloomberg has recently gotten a stronger measure to pass, banning smoking in all bars and restaurants, with very few exceptions. I followed closely as the bill was proposed and gained momentum in the city council, and gave a silent cheer when it was passed. Maybe in a while it will work. But being realistic, it's going to take a lot to get young New Yorkers to stop smoking in bars. Spitting on the street and jaywalking and riding bicycles on the sidewalk and prostitution are all illegal here, as well, for all the good that does the city. If there aren't enough cops to keep the tranny hookers and their malevolent pimps off of the bucolic, cobblestoned West Village streets, then who exactly is going to respond to some stubborn

Eurotrash inflicting their smoke on a bar? Me? It's a delicious thought, really, having a new legal basis to back my indignation, but in reality all it would mean is several fights a night between me and some pig-headed creep who's going to just keep smoking anyway when he sees I'm too busy and outnumbered to take it any further than getting angry. I hope coming years will prove me wrong, but I don't envision New Yorkers permanently repairing out-of-doors to smoke as a result of this law. It's pipe dreaming to think that just because Californians did it, New Yorkers will. I'm told that in Los Angeles, no one will step off a curb until they have the walk light, in part because it will bring every car on both sides of the street to a screeching halt. Here people sort of lace themselves in and out of traffic, hitting out at taxis that veer too close to them. *Autre peuple, autres moeurs.*

Outside, I breathe deeply for the first time in many hours. I haven't peed in five hours, partly because I've been so busy I forgot to drink anything. This happens routinely, and sort of makes me laugh at the irony; I wash up on the other side of an insanely busy night having poured maybe four hundred drinks but completely dehydrated myself. I have nothing to do outside in particular, so I just stand about for a few moments, looking down the street past the taxi garage to Prince Lumber. Atop the old Nabisco factory that now houses the Chelsea Market there is always an American flag flying, heroically lighted. I read recently that if you keep Old Glory aloft past dusk, you're required to illuminate it appropriately. I hadn't known that before, and take notice now of the rain slanting through the parabola of the lights perched on rooftops across the street.

Even in my most exhausted moments, and sometimes specifically in them, I find there can be a certain beauty in all of this raucousness. There can be this place, this feeling one sometimes gets, of all the wrongness somehow creating something inexplicably right, this inkling that there may be a disguised perfection in what seems a small world gone akimbo. Gavin gave voice to it one night when Oliver Payne and Nick Relph were doing their drag/pop cabaret, and I've felt it on nights like the one when the Beta Band played and then DJed a set that evolved quite naturally into all Beatles' songs, that this exact scenario could exist nowhere else. You're somehow standing in the unacknowledged center of the world. Nobody knows you have the coolest bar on the planet, for these three hours, say, except the forty people here right now. And maybe they don't even know.

I'm thinking of the night a few months back when the busload of English lesbians pulled in. From where, I have no idea. They found us somehow, maybe in one of those underground guides for hipster tourists, who knows? George and I were on together when they came barreling through the door on a quietish Thursday, whooping for blood. We exchanged the usual glance and shrug across the distance of the bar. Immediately a feisty, stockily constructed gal is on George, demanding something that is making him shake his head doubtfully. I drift over to see what is so urgent. In a nearly incomprehensible Cockney accent, she is insisting that she is a bartender back in England and could she please come back and serve her friends. I begin to snicker watching George pointedly explaining that simply because she tends bar somewhere doesn't mean she tends bar here. She is bright-eyed and undaunted, however, and, changing tack in a way neither of us were quite prepared for, suddenly chirps, "Woodjew allow it if I wuz naiy-kud, then?" Stumped, George turns wordlessly to me. "Uh, naked?" I stammer. Before I actually answer, she grabs the ankle-length black sheath she's wearing and whips it over her head, to the cheers of her girls, now standing on the bench and lining the walls. She unhooks her bra and drops her panties, kicking them aside with an unconcerned smile. She then skips past me behind the bar, clapping her hands in readiness, and calls above the screams of her cohorts, "Roight, then, who needs a drink?" George is clocking me, goggle-eyed, waiting for my response. I shrug to him, laughing, and say, "I don't know, man, I guess just let her pull beers and keep her away from the register." Soon she is joined by three of her Sapphic horde on the bartop and by many more standing on the bench facing them, peeling off their shirts and skirts. Other women in the bar are looking around in perplexed alarm. Guys are looking up with baby-like stupefaction, mouths agape, knowing they have reached the magic destination to which their entire life's travels have circuitously yet providently led: the place where all the women take their clothes off without anyone telling them to. Still, the night just kind of trickles on the way it was going, just with a few more dark looks or sidelong smirks for the fact that the bar is suddenly punctuated with naked women romping, courtesy of Jesse, to Joan Jett singing "I hate myself for loving you." In a moment that reminded me somehow of a haiku, I looked up at one point to see four of the girls oscillating about a table of two couples who seemed to take no notice of them. One of the men, smirking coyly, held a bottle of Champagne in one hand and his girlfriend's mule in the other, weighing the possibility.

There are a million bars across this country; how many in the world, fifty million? I wish I could be omniscient and see into every one of them on one single night. There, in that fetid hothouse environment, painted with the smear and stain of human interaction, you would see the most surprising orchids punching up out of the manure. People, when bereft of their sobriety, strut their monstrous appetites and spill their heartbreaking vulnerabilities like terrible children. See married women kissing strangers and grown men crying in the corners. But who am I to sit in sober judgment, who is anyone to say that these fevered appetites, unmasked by alcohol, are less squalid than our more cautiously pruned ones? Why is it assumed that this is the compromised world, where only the impaired and the desperate come to stay? There in the dark, with the idle chat of strangers, the magic of the inhibition-lifting potions, the broken are fixed, the hideous made beautiful. With all that befalls us in this life, perhaps this, inside the bar, is as close to heaven as we get, the way it will all be in the afterlife. Poor us, then.

There are moments when I have clearly seen an alternate validity of the strange universe here. Even acknowledging the weird, sometimes pathological inversion of reality, I still find that at times when all the mayhem crystallizes, it can seem just as valid in its unpredictable insanity and random pathos as the larger world outside. Inebriation—a malady, a clinically categorized disease—turns the wheels in this twisted world, and I don't at all mean to be flip about that. But it doesn't quite get to the whole of things to simply then conclude that reasoning people are obligated to reject it as false and imprisoning. Having been forced for years to stand and observe the nightly ramping up, the zombie figures impaired with drink and drug pushing back and forth, howling and testifying for all to hear, ecstatically lost in the mayhem, I sometimes find myself swayed by another argument. It's a silent one that no one is making: a nagging in the farthest reaches of my mind that says yes, maybe I'm watching the fall of Rome again, that's possible. But maybe also, simply because so many go to such lengths to impair themselves, to tear themselves open, pushing through the crust of correctness to the place beyond judgment, I wonder if there isn't a kind of predetermined correctness, a worth by which, in the convoluted math of late at night, many, many wrongs can somehow make a right. Considering even this possibility, I can survey all the lemmings-to-the-sea madness and waste with a calm acceptance, even a kind of diluted optimism, for this fractured, nocturnal populace. I realize I'm arguing for a certain indefensible beauty here, a beauty of the sad and the talentless. I may well be wrong, of course. But that's the thing with all of New York: you often can't tell whether you've been made privy to some esoteric kiss or whether you've been defiled in some irreversible manner not in your immediate capacity to comprehend.

o   o   o

The inevitable plea from a group of British late owls for "Just one more," well after last call at 3:30 A.M., has zero effect on me. Sure, I think, just one more hour I have to stand on throbbing feet waiting for your drunken asses to slurp another beer. Not likely. Roberto dozes in the corner, his arms folded and his head slumped over his chest. Eric stomps grimly back and forth to the tables, his eyes ringed with harried fatigue, clearing everything abruptly to the mild protests of the hangers-on. My throat is raw from smoke and from shouting out prices over the racket all night. Jesse threatens to spin all morning, but then DJs are a different type of fauna. I ask him to shut it down and he incorporates a nod into his head-bopping.

Although the temptation hovers constantly, I try to make a point of not drinking when I'm behind the bar, but after I've counted my till I usually have one. Back when I lived in Brooklyn it would be literally one for the road. I would take the glass with me and fold myself into the back of a cab. Watching the aura of a red light fill the rain-spattered windshield at Fourth Avenue and Union Street, with the meter at $10.75, I'd have one sip of cognac left before home. Now, however, I pour myself a glass of Champagne while stocking the bottled beer and mopping the tables and bartop, toasting the end of the evening's labors. With the first sip I feel the night's vigilance begin unknotting from my shoulders. I start in recording the charge tips into the terminal, correcting people's errant math as it veers from early nontippers to the illegible and misplaced slashes of the later ciphers. The last customers slink off, leaving a pair of ski gloves and a woman's sweater on the bench. Eric and I are joking about people's foibles during the night. Roberto chimes in that maybe he can have the gloves. "No," I begin, "they go in lost and found first, and if they're still there after two weeks . . . oh fuck, just take 'em." He snatches them up with a smile.

Putting up the barstools I ask Eric if he wants to go for a steak. He never does. He says he likes to finish quickly and get home to sleep. Tomorrow or next week he'll tell me where he really went, what he took or drank, whom he met in the shadows of which gay bar or club and where they ended up fucking, but for some reason we always go through this pantomime of correctness, where we both pretend he's tired and so can't join me for a late supper. For my part, there's no hurry, especially at this point. After running frantically all night I need to close up leisurely, regardless of the time. Roberto wants to go home, so I pay him out and he leaves Eric and me to finish up. I never have the heart to make him stay longer, even when I end up having to do some of his closing work. He's got another job prep cooking in a restaurant that begins in just a couple of hours.

Outside it's bracingly clear and I gulp in the freezing wind lacing along 15th Street from the Hudson like it's ambrosia. We lock the doors, pull the clanging metal shutters down, and exchange shivering good nights. Loping west on 15th, I spy the moon playing behind some ragged clouds, the starless night washed by the orange of the sodium vapor streetlamps. Someday there will be trees and fresh air in my life again, I consider. Someday, but not just now. Turning south past the gas station, I start passing the transvestite hookers down Tenth Avenue, catcalling and tottering around like out-of-work linebackers in stilettos.

The old saw about New York being the town that never sleeps is, I've found, patently untrue. A running gripe of mine has always been how you cannot scare up a decent meal after midnight in this great metropolis. I don't care that the rest of the country takes their dinner at six, nor even that by nine all the best restaurants in San Francisco are already folding up their service. This is supposed to be the center of the world. In Madrid, they sit down to eat at a civil hour, like eleven or twelve, and nosh serenely until two or three in the morning, whereupon they go dancing. Now, there's a town that doesn't even own pajamas. But New York, contrary to the adage, offers little of any worth past eleven. Some grotesque supper-club type places, too lugubrious even to contemplate, along with a few restaurants that keep their doors open to late birds, withdrawing their cadres of elite kitchen shock troops and replacing them with one or two clueless and sleep-sick illegal immigrants, left to dunk the fries and toss the steaks on the burner. There is often nothing for it of a night but to head over to Hector's. Hector's is an airy cinder-block café wedged into an oddly angled corner of the meatpacking district. To say it's an insider's secret would be giving it way too much credit, implying that "outsiders" would be queuing up on the grease- and offal-riddled pavement to get in, if they only knew. They would assuredly not. But Hector's, if it is only the humblest type of establishment, proffering the same workaday fare that diners everywhere dish up, has one distinct advantage over other nocturnal beaneries in this town: it has turned night into day, turned the clock on its ear for its patrons. Hector's caters primarily to the breadbaskets of the hardened men who work by night in the meatpacking trade here. These firms are at their peak working hours in the dead of night, like food markets the world over, and so then, too, is Hector's. Most anywhere else you are liable to turn up at 3:00 or 4:00 A.M., you will be given the inescapable impression you are imprisoning the staff with your damnable patronage and your ill-timed hunger. Your presence will be grudgingly acknowledged and, quite some time later, something like food may be hurled at you. Not chez Hector's. Hector's doesn't open until 2:00 A.M., and it closes at 2:00 in the afternoon. At 4:00 A.M. the counter is lively, crammed with men in layers of wool and white smocks bearing geographical splotches of sienna, snorting and ribbing each other and pounding down, curiously given their profession, huge plates of meatloaf and burgers and steaks. They sit in groups, elbow to elbow with the trannie hookers who have pushed into the West Village from the lower reaches of 10th Avenue where they used to prowl. The lighting is garish, unfairly harsh fluorescence that reveals far more than one might wish to scrutinize at this hour and in these environs. Still, regardless what time you stumble in, the place is disorientingly welcoming. The Dominicans behind the counter are fully awake and sharp, the coffee is fresh. You can have whatever you want at Hector's. There is a menu, one of those twenty-page tomes that lists things you would never imagine them making, or ever dare order. You ignore that and think instead about what you want to eat. You simply tell the pleasant men what it is and they nod and make it, quickly, and for next to nothing.

The food is fine, actually better than decent, but at that hour it's the cheery fulsomeness of the place that I love. Aside from the fact that the clientele is entirely either men in bloody smocks or men in pancake makeup and wigs and tremendously ill-conceived miniskirt/tights combinations, you could be sitting at any breakfast counter anywhere at nine in the morning. There is a certain comfort in that to me, knowing I'm not the only misfit skulking about who, at 4:27 in the morning, absolutely must have a grilled cheese with tomato and bacon.

There's never anyone sitting at the tables at Hector's. The meat cutters and the whores are not given to idling pensively. They squat at the counter, ignoring one another, for only so long as it takes to gobble a BLT and fries and then cut for their respective employments. Hector's homely tables are my solace, though, the place where I dump myself with audible abandon after standing for so long. Checking my watch, I calculate that I've been upright for fourteen hours and twenty-seven minutes straight. When I sit, it is an action rather than a rest, so completely do I collapse into the chair. I feel my pulse in my feet, the blood pounding in unison with my heart. I filch yesterday's newspaper from my pack, and the kind, older gray-haired man comes from behind the counter to take my order. I turn again to unzip my backpack and pull out a copy of Wallace Stevens's collected poems that a customer gave me, imploring me to give it a chance, despite my allergy to poetry. I crack it open and browse until I find a poem called "The Man Whose Pharynx Was Bad." I plod through it blankly, until the last line: "One might. One might. But time will not relent." Yikes. I close the book and fish the sports section out of the *Times* to go over the NFL matchups and predictions for the weekend.

Working my way back up Washington Street, the only matinal activity I pass is that of the meatpackers. One, decked in a bloody apron and chain mail gloves, heaves a huge box of tallow trimmings into a red Dumpster marked INEDIBLE. The flowers normally beckoning outside the Korean deli have been pulled in, away from the frost. A white garbage truck spews bilge on the corner of 15th Street and the Pakistani man setting up his coffee and donut cart in front of the Chelsea Market hollers at the driver to take it somewhere else. The wind is behind me, pushing me up the avenue, lifting the smell of the stale smoke from my hair. All the storefronts are shuttered. An idling green van outside the Port Authority Terminal Building sports a bumper sticker that reads: "Got Jesus?" which prompts me to say to myself, "Come to think of it, no, I'm fresh out." But taking in the deep cerulean sky that's creeping into dawn, against some old red brick tenement facades on 16th Street, I reconsider; maybe I've got some of that old, old-time religion, however you might define it.

At 6:13, it's beginning to be dawn, that peculiar lambency that makes you feel you shouldn't be seeing it somehow. In the same way that light makes the noble old brownstones on my block look even lovelier, it makes the prisonlike complex of the Robert Fulton Houses look twice as squalid, the fluorescent lights on each floor of the towers bathing them in a doubly perverted glow. But all the little homies, normally pushing about on the corner outside the magazine store trying to sell drugs, have slipped off to bed now.

Farther up Ninth Avenue there's a cabbie pulled up to the curb. He's in his socks, crouched on two pieces of cardboard next to a fireplug leaking water. His shoes, some terribly worn beige brogues, sit one on either side of him, looking like roasted flounders. I'm impressed that he has stopped in the middle of his shift, removed his shoes, and is facing Mecca to pray. Then I realize that he's facing west, and Mecca is routinely taken to be in the opposite direction. He's actually washing his feet, is what he's doing, in the freezing cold. I move on quickly, avoiding eye contact. This is the hour when the city belongs to the impaired and the desperate. Simply looking at someone can net you more attention, of several varieties, than you care to take on. I shoulder past two figures standing talking on the corner of 18th Street. A stout old man with a long white beard I recognize from the neighborhood for his resemblance to Santa Claus and his insistence on wearing shorts, held up by suspenders, year round, is chatting with a skinny black guy. As I pass them, the black guy is saying, "You see, in seafaring times they didn't need all that excess . . . they kept things in their trunks." That guy, I think, checking my watch, just used the term "seafaring times" at 6:15 in the morning. Impressive.

Three blocks up there's an empty bed awaiting my sweaty and smoky arrival. I palm the $318 in my left-hand pants pocket and finger the wad aside to find my keys. Tomorrow I'll sleep till two. Except tomorrow is now.

Appendix

ง

The Negroni

3 parts Campari

3 parts sweet vermouth, Carpano Antica Formula or
   Martini & Rossi

8 parts gin

In a shaker filled liberally with ice, combine all three ingredients. Stir until exterior of shaker beads with frost. Strain into chilled cocktail glass and garnish with orange slice, with bonus points for authenticity and panache if you can find a blood orange. Squeeze a lemon twist above it, rim the glass with the peel, and either dip it and throw it out, to leave just an extra slick of citrus, or drop it in, as well, as I like to do when making the drink for myself.

One of the most perfect drinks in existence, I think, and something of an acquired taste for some, it's a unjustly little-known import from Italy. I make several different versions of it, substituting other Italian bitters for the vermouth, but they are mere diversions; the straight ahead drink is the definition of a cocktail. Served up in a Martini glass, with a coil of fresh orange, it presents a gleaming red profile that catches the light like a polished ruby, and will have half the bar inquiring what you're drinking. The gin gives it a racy, astringent structure while the Campari imparts the play of sweetness and bitterness. The vermouth grounds these elements with a dense, smoky wineyness that triangulates with precision.

The traditional recipe has always been equal parts of all three liquors, but current palates often prefer lighter, drier versions of the drink. I make mine with roughly three parts gin to one each of Campari and vermouth, more like a dashing Martini in a fitted Italian suit. Some people prefer the drink on the rocks, an acceptable alternative, but recent vodka versions are to be taken no more seriously than freeze-dried espresso in Rome or ragú from a jar in Bologna. As with many of the classic older drinks, you will find two schools on the subject of shaking versus stirring in preparing this drink, each adamantly certain of its correctness. I bunk in the second camp. There are only two drinks I insist are not shaken, the Manhattan and the Negroni. The bubbles and ice shards that give zest to some cocktails would mar the Negroni's sanguine limpidity. That first sip should be like drinking from a cool brook that happened to perambulate past a spice bazaar on its route.

The Sidecar

8 parts brandy

3 parts triple sec or Cointreau

3 parts fresh lemon juice

In a shaker filled liberally with ice, combine all three ingredients. Shake vigorously for ten seconds and strain into chilled cocktail glasses rimmed with sugar.

I don't feel there are many things you can do to brandy without hobbling its ethereal voice. The Sidecar, with its utter reduction of elements to the most basic notes of sour and sweet, is perhaps the only adulteration of which I wholly approve. Another of the underappreciated drinks from the heyday of cocktail culture, this sleight-of-hand can be a cloying abomination unless made with fresh-squeezed lemon juice. Sour mix won't cut it here. You may wish to start with less lemon juice than prescribed and tart it up to taste. I like them with a bit more grab than some people do. A bartending rule of thumb is to always err on the underside of such mixers; you can always add more, but you can't remove it once it's in. Whether to sugar the rim is at the discretion of the drinker. As with salt on Margaritas, it's seen as frivolous these days if you don't take the minimalist route, which is all the more reason to embrace the irresistible silliness of the sugared rim.

The Margarita

7 parts tequila
5 parts triple sec or Cointreau
3 parts Rose's Lime Juice
6 parts fresh lime juice
dash of orange juice

In a shaker filled with cracked ice, combine and shake all ingredients. Strain into a large rocks glass with fresh ice. Salting the rim of the glass is optional, per taste.

Many and vocal are the Margarita's legions, and I can hear the shrieks of dismayed protest over this recipe even as I pen it. The war of purity with a Margarita, however, was lost before it ever began, as far as I'm concerned. Much of this drink's appeal, whether you concede the point or not, is its ability to render agave juice palatable, a considerably tougher task than high-end tequila producers would have you believe. Through years of making thousands of these, I've reversed my normal approach to cocktails—simpler is better—and padded my version for mass appreciation. The Rose's and OJ would earn a sneer from self-styled purists, but they gird the mix in a way people love. No one turns this drink down once they taste it.

The Manhattan

2–3 dashes of Angostura or Peychaud bitters

8 parts bourbon

3 parts sweet vermouth, preferably Carpano Antica Formula or
   Martini & Rossi

In a shaker filled with cracked ice combine all ingredients. Stir for two minutes with a bar spoon and strain into a chilled, stemmed cocktail glass. Garnish with cherry and give an in-and-out lemon twist to slick surface with lemon oil.

As, really, with all these drinks, the Manhattan can be made on the rocks, as well, and many people prefer it that way. You have to weigh the desirable convenience of dilution and chill against tradition and aesthetics. The Manhattan varies considerably depending on what bourbon and what vermouth you employ. The original recipes call for rye whiskey, which can be difficult to find nowadays and prove harsher than today's more popular bourbons, especially wheat-softened blends like Maker's Mark. Wild Turkey, for example, whose regular 80-proof bottling is still one of my favorite bourbons, produces an inexplicably jarring, angular rye that is just this side of unpleasant. I've never found the authenticity fetish worth the payoff here: any decent bourbon makes this drink a deep satisfaction, the natural sweetness of the corn blending seamlessly with that of the vermouth. Men, I've noticed, often prefer to skip the cherry and go with a twist instead. I suppose they fear it looks too girly, or makes it too sweet. I find something irritatingly spoilsport about that. Even if it is one of those mushy, cancer-inducing red-dye coughdrops now incorrectly known as "maraschino," stop being such a prig and just get the damn cherry in your drink; it's part of the deal, and by the time it's been steeped in this elixir for ten or fifteen minutes, you'll slurp it down greedily.

The Martini

Daunting, the thought of trying to define exactly how to make a Martini, like telling someone how to keep love alive: so simple a thing, yet there's so many right ways and so many wrong. The older books, which risibly refer to it as a Martini Cocktail, give proportions that would mortify modern cognoscenti, calling for far more vermouth than anyone dares. I'll break it down, then, the simplest way I do it. If it isn't the way everyone you know prefers, at least you'll never be wrong.

Chill as many stemmed cocktail, or Martini, glasses as you'll need beforehand. In a large shaker filled liberally with cracked ice, pour a bit of dry white French or Italian vermouth. How much exactly isn't important, since you then swirl it briefly about the ice and then strain it all off. This is called an in-and-out Martini, the simplest and most foolproof way to make certain the drink will be bone dry. Just a trace of vermouth will be left coating the ice before you add the gin or vodka.

For each drink, then, pour in eight parts (2 ounces) gin or vodka and seal the shaker tightly. Shake savagely for twelve seconds and then let rest for a moment while you arrange the glasses. This allows the drink to reclarify, permitting bubbles to dissipate before you strain it into the chilled glasses. Garnish with whole green olives of the best quality you can find, small pickled onions, for a "Gibson," or a twist of lemon, per preference. Dive in.

The Cosmopolitan

5 parts lemon vodka
5 parts triple sec or Cointreau
4 parts fresh lime juice
Dash or two of cranberry juice

I conceived of the drink using Cointreau and Absolut Citron, because I am—or was—as absurdly susceptible as anyone to upscale marketing that would have me believe I'm just not taking things very seriously if I don't use the top-drawer products. In a mixed drink, a lot of those lines get blurred. Pundits will pretend you're not being scrupulous if you don't pour the obscenely expensive triple sec doppelgänger, Cointreau, into drinks like Margaritas and Cosmos. This is uninformed posturing. Obviously good ingredients are paramount, but there's no point in wasting your money. I find for mixing I actually prefer a good triple sec, like the one from the Italian cordials company Stock, which I've used for years now. It blends more smoothly than Cointreau, which is, not unimportantly, four times the cost. I defy you to tell me there's an appreciable difference in a mixed drink, all other ingredients being equal. Better that you spend all that extra coin on higher-quality vodka or, certainly, in the Margarita, a more reputable tequila.

Just slightly less fresh-squeezed lime juice than vodka and triple sec means a *lot* of lime juice. The main infraction I see lame bartenders making with this drink is stinting on lime juice. No one wants to stand there and squeeze twenty-seven lime wedges into a mixing cup to make a drink, so if you don't have fresh lime juice prepared before your shift or a juicer at your disposal and set up, you're simply not going to be making this drink correctly. Part of why the Cosmo is seen as a grotesque mockery of a decent drink is because lazy bartenders turn out lopsided, cloying versions of them, and that's what is then interpreted as the drink. A proper Cosmopolitan—which is not, by the way, an oxymoron—should be just that nudge over the balancing line into tart. I know the Catch-22 bartenders face here; made correctly, many people will complain it's too sour. It's essentially a girl's drink. They see the pink, they think it's candy, that's what they want. I get young women returning them all the time, scolding me, "You made this wrong, it's too sour!" Though I may raise a contemptuous eyebrow while refashioning their drink into the Slushee they actually wanted, I know enough not to voice what I'm invariably thinking: I made it wrong, or you like it wrong? Sticking to my principles in this kind of impasse—pausing to explain, for example, that since I made the drink up, when it comes from my hand it is by definition made correctly—is of no use to anyone. It becomes simply a question of taste—or, of course, lack thereof. If you want me to ruin a perfectly made drink by dumping another shot of sugar in it, I'll do it. It's your money, it's your drink.

The cranberry juice is just a stain, really, a dollop to make the thing fresh-looking and cheeky. Any more than a splash and it throws off the balance. I frequently see people in bars nursing what I take to be Negronis, dark red and transparent, which are then revealed to be supposed Cosmos. I shudder to think.

The other gaffe I witness lazy bartenders make in preparing this drink, and a passel of others, is not shaking it enough, and over insufficient ice. Like any shaken drink, the Cosmopolitan wants to be brutalized. There should be aeration, collision, and dilution galore going on in that shaker. I used to maintain it needs shaking until your hand freezes to the shaker and frost forms on the outside of it, but I've found that can depend overmuch on the temperature of your bar. Now I just say shake it like mad, in a full shaker of ice, for at least ten seconds. Strain it into a chilled cocktail (Martini) glass and garnish with a fat twist of lemon.

(A personal aside on twists: Every bar guide in the world will paint you a hopeless rube unless you preciously shave your twists only from the micron-thin, yellow outer rind of the fruit, avoiding at all costs the bitter white pith. Whoever made this doctrine took care to make it sound so official that every writer since has reiterated it as an unquestioned part of the canon. I say it's nonsense. The bitterness of the pith adds an extra element to a drink, a note every bit as interesting as the oil derived from the outer peel. In fact, I carve my twists so as to take a neat swath out of the pulp of the fruit, as well. This makes for a much more pyrotechnic visual garnish, releasing a spray of fresh juice onto the drink's surface along with the citrus oil, and introduces three different flavors—all the lemon has to offer— rather than just the one. I've been doing this for years, and have been corrected and branded a heretic so often I no longer even respond to the charges. So is change wrought; I defend my fat twists against any naysayers.)

About the Author

Toby Cecchini is part owner of the bar Passerby, located in New York's far west Chelsea neighborhood. He began his bartending career in the mid-1980s at New York's fabled bar/restaurant Odeon. Cosmopolitan *began as a series of diaries on* Slate. *Cecchini has also written for the* New York Times, *both the Style section and the magazine. He lives in New York City.*